NINTENDO® Wii™

FLASH®

GAME CREATOR'S GUIDE

DESIGN, DEVELOP, AND SHARE YOUR GAMES ONLINE

ABOUT THE AUTHOR...

Todd Perkins is an Adobe Certified Instructor who spends much of his time teaching people how to use Adobe's web development software. Todd has many years of experience teaching people of all ages and backgrounds, and he is an expert at teaching complex concepts in a way anyone can understand. Todd is half of the dynamic duo at the All Things Adobe Podcast (chadandtoddcast.com), and he has authored a vast array of video training titles. He is also the author of *Adobe Flash CS3 Professional Hands-On Training* and *ActionScript 3.0 for Adobe Flash CS3 Professional Hands-On Training*. Todd teaches in classrooms, consults for businesses, and trains people online, but what he loves most is playing video games with his amazing wife, Jessica.

ABOUT THE TECHNICAL EDITOR...

Raoul Rañoa is senior editorial artist at the Los Angeles Times, where he thoroughly enjoys illustrating and animating infographics accompanying everything from Pulitzer Prize–winning investigations to feature stories on new art museums. His work (www.raoulranoa.com) has received multiple awards by organizations such as the Society for News Design and Associated Press News Executives Council. Raoul loves teaching and holds regular Flash and infographics workshops at the University of California, Los Angeles.

NINTENDO® Wii™ FLASH®

GAME CREATOR'S GUIDE

DESIGN, DEVELOP, AND SHARE YOUR GAMES ONLINE

Todd Perkins

New York   Chicago   San Francisco   Lisbon   London   Madrid   Mexico City
Milan   New Delhi   San Juan   Seoul   Singapore   Sydney   Toronto

The **McGraw·Hill** Companies

Sponsoring Editor
Roger Stewart

Editorial Supervisor
Patty Mon

Project Editor
Laura Stone

Acquisitions Coordinator
Carly Stapleton

Technical Editor
Raoul Rañoa

Copy Editor
Robert Campbell

Proofreader
Paul Tyler

Indexer
Ted Laux

Production Supervisor
Jean Bodeaux

Composition
Apollo Publishing Services

Art Director, Cover
Jeff Weeks

Cover Designer
12edesign

Cataloging-in-Publication Data is on file with the Library of Congress

McGraw-Hill books are available at special quantity discounts to use as premiums and sales promotions, or for use in corporate training programs. To contact a special sales representative, please visit the Contact Us page at www.mhprofessional.com.

Nintendo® Wii™ Flash® Game Creator's Guide: Design, Develop, and Share Your Games Online

1234567890 FGR FGR 0198

ISBN 978-0-07-154525-9
MHID   0-07-154525-5

To my brother, Chad,
who introduced me to Flash,
and to my wife Jessica
for putting up with me
during the writing process
yet again.

Contents At A Glance

Contents

2 ActionScript 2.0 Essentials   43

Acknowledgments

Thanks to everyone who made it possible for me to write this book—Matt Wagner and Roger Stewart—and to those who helped me write and edit it—Carly Stapleton, Laura Stone, and Raoul Rañoa.

Introduction

This book is set up to teach you the basics of Flash and what you need to know to design Flash games that are playable on the Wii. The first two chapters teach the basic concepts of working with Flash and ActionScript (Flash's programming language). From there, you will learn to create a basic game and play it on your Wii. After that, each chapter teaches a new technique you can use in your Wii Flash games. The game-creating chapters build on each other, so if you're new to Flash and ActionScript, you can go through them in order. If you feel comfortable with Flash and ActionScript, you can skip around the book to any chapter you'd like.

The example files for this book can be downloaded from this book's page on the McGraw-Hill Professional web site (www.mhprofessional.com).

CHAPTER 1

Flash Fundamentals

BEFORE

you dive in to learning how to create games in Flash, it is important to know some Flash basics. In this chapter, you will learn essential Flash techniques, including drawing, animating, and adding simple interactivity. To keep this book focused on creating Flash games for the Nintendo Wii, this chapter will not show you everything there is to know about Flash. Rather, you will learn all the Flash you need to know to build the games in this book.

If you already know the basics of how to use Flash, this chapter will be a good refresher for you. If you don't need a refresher, feel free to skip to the next chapter.

FILE TYPES ASSOCIATED WITH FLASH

There are many different file types associated with Flash. To keep things simple, I will only discuss the two file types you will use most often.

.FLA File (aka Flash File or Flash Document)

The .FLA file is your Flash project file. When creating games for the Wii, you will create .FLA files to build your games. You will spend most of your time working with FLA files. When you are ready for your game to go on the Web, you will create a .SWF file (aka Flash movie) for the world to see. Throughout this book, I may refer to FLA files by their extension (FLA), or as Flash files, or as Flash documents.

.SWF File (aka Flash Movie)

The .SWF file is the actual Flash movie. .SWF files are embedded into HTML, so they can be viewed in a web browser and played on the Wii through the Internet Channel. For this book, no knowledge of HTML is required. You will let Flash create the HTML for you.

UNDERSTANDING THE FLASH INTERFACE

If you are new to Flash, it can be a very intimidating application. Figure 1-1 offers a look at some of the elements of the Flash interface. If you have a version of Flash other than Flash CS3, some things may look a little different. Don't worry, though; many of the features are the same.

The Stage

This is where you place all the graphical content of your Flash application, and the area of the application that people will see. The gray area outside of the Stage is called the Pasteboard. The Pasteboard is used for several different things, but you will use it most to deselect items on the Stage.

FIGURE 1-1

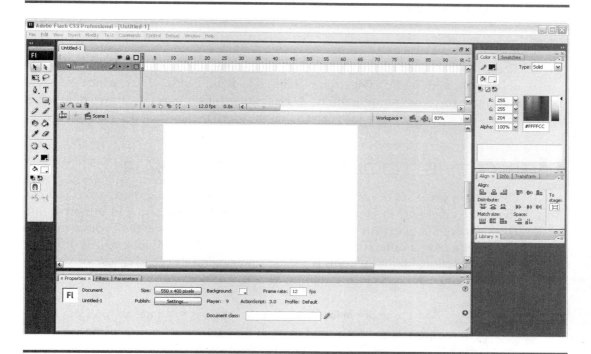

The Flash CS3 interface

The Toolbar

The Toolbar contains all of Flash's drawing and editing tools. You will learn about the Toolbar in detail later in this chapter.

The Property Inspector

The Property Inspector is used to edit settings for all kinds of elements in Flash. The important thing to note about the Property Inspector is that it changes depending on what element you have selected. If nothing is selected, you can modify properties of your Flash movie, like size, background color, and frame rate. You will learn more about the Property Inspector later in this chapter.

Panels

Panels contain different tools for editing elements of your Flash applications. You will use panels to align graphics, to store graphics, and to work with colors. They can be expanded or collapsed by clicking the name of the panel. If you ever have trouble finding a particular panel, all panels can be accessed through the Window menu at the top of the screen.

The Timeline

The Timeline is used to navigate through different points in time, and is used to build animations and simple navigation systems. It is divided into frames, which play consecutively to create an animation. A Flash application plays a certain number of frames per second (FPS), which determines the speed of playback of a Flash movie.

USING THE TOOLS IN THE TOOLBAR

Flash has a great set of tools to help you draw and manipulate artwork. You can choose to create art in Flash, or create art in another program and import it into Flash. Figure 1-2 offers you a general look at some of the tools in the Toolbar in Flash CS3. If you have a different version of Flash, the Toolbar will look a little different, but the functionality of the tools is the same in general. If you ever lose or close the Toolbar, you can access it by choosing Window | Tools.

NOTE Some tools are hidden beneath other tools as flyout items. Tools that have flyout items have a small arrow at the bottom-right corner of the tool's icon. In Flash CS3, the Free Transform tool, the Pen tool, and the Rectangle tool all have flyout items. Also note that the bottom area of the Toolbar changes depending on which tool you have selected. This area gives you extra options for working with that particular tool. Hover your mouse over any tool in the Toolbar to see its name and keyboard shortcut.

Introducing the Tools

Here's a brief look at the tools in Flash CS3.

The Selection Tool

Use the Selection tool to, well, select things. When drawing in Merge Drawing mode (Flash's default drawing mode), the Selection tool selects the fill (its inner color) of a shape when you click it, and selects a line segment of a shape's stroke (its outline) when you click it. To select the stroke and fill of a shape, double-click the shape's fill. To select the entire stroke of a shape, double-click its stroke. You can select all other elements with a single click. Once an element is selected, you can click and drag your selection to move it.

Flash Fundamentals

FIGURE 1-2

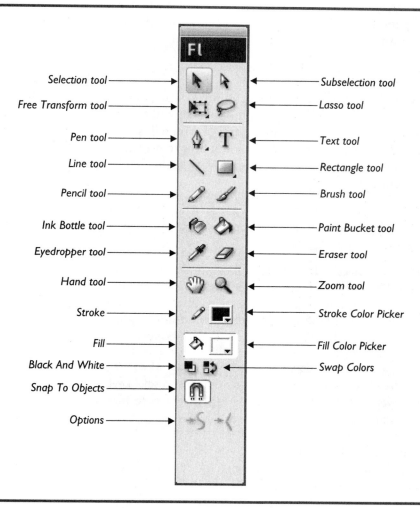

The Toolbar

NOTE When you select a merge drawing shape, you will see white dots in the selected area. With all other elements, such as text and grouped objects, you will see a blue bounding box. To create a copy of any selection, hold ALT (Windows) or OPTION (Mac) while dragging. When you release the mouse button, you will have created a copy. If you hold SHIFT while dragging a selection, Flash will constrain the movement of the selected object to the same horizontal or vertical plane that you dragged from.

The Subselection Tool

The Subselection tool is used to select individual anchor points in a shape. Anchor points and their curves are the elements that make up shapes in Flash.

The Free Transform Tool

The Free Transform tool is used to move, scale, skew, and rotate objects. Its flyout item is the Gradient Transform tool, which will be discussed next. When you select an object with the Free Transform tool, you will see eight black boxes surrounding your selection. What follows is a list of how to use the Free Transform tool to accomplish common tasks. If you are using Flash 8, the Free Transform tool is not nested in a flyout menu.

Moving an Object   To move an object, make sure the object you want to move is selected. Then, roll your mouse over the object until you see a four-directional arrow at the bottom right of your cursor. You can then click and drag to move the object.

Scaling an Object   To scale an object, make sure the object you want to scale is selected. Then, put your cursor over one of the black boxes on the outside of the selection and click and drag. To scale vertically, drag the top middle or bottom middle box. To scale horizontally, drag the left middle or right middle box. To scale horizontally and vertically, drag one of the corner boxes.

> **TIP** Hold CTRL (Windows) or COMMAND (Mac) when dragging a corner box to keep the same proportions. This is a ridiculously useful keyboard command. Hold ALT (Windows) or OPTION (Mac) when dragging any box to anchor the opposite edge or corner of the object. This is also ridiculously useful.

Rotating an Object   To rotate an object, make sure the object you want to rotate is selected. Next, roll your mouse outside of one of the corners of the selection until your cursor changes into a circular arrow. Then, click and drag to rotate.

> **TIP** Hold SHIFT on your keyboard while rotating to constrain the rotation to 45-degree angles. You can also adjust an object's rotation point by clicking and dragging the hollow circle in the center of the object when it's selected using the Free Transform tool.

Skewing an Object   To skew an object, make sure the object you want to skew is selected. Next, roll your mouse over one of the edges of the bounding box of your selection (make sure you're not rolling over any of the black boxes used for scaling—you want an edge) until you see the cursor change to skew arrows. Then, click and drag to skew your selection.

The Gradient Transform Tool

Use the Gradient Transform tool to change the position, rotation, scale, and size of a gradient on a shape. The term gradient refers to a color that fades to another color. When using the Gradient Transform tool, first select the tool, and then click a shape with a gradient on the Stage. Use the handles that appear to transform your gradient.

The Lasso Tool

The Lasso tool is used to make a non-rectangular selection. Using the Lasso tool, you can click and drag around the area you want to select to make the selection. You can also toggle to the Polygon Mode button at the bottom of the Toolbar in the Options area and click multiple times to draw a polygonal selection.

The Pen Tool

The Pen tool is used to create complex shapes.

The Text Tool

The Text tool is used to add text. There are three different types of text: static text, dynamic text, and input text. *Static* text is used to display and animate text. *Dynamic* text and *input* text are text fields that can be managed using ActionScript. Input text can also receive and respond to text typed by someone watching the Flash movie.

The Line Tool

The Line tool is used to draw lines. To draw a line, select the Line tool and click and drag on the Stage.

The Rectangle Tool

The Rectangle tool draws rectangles. To draw a rectangle, select the Rectangle tool and click and drag your mouse on the Stage. In Flash CS3, you can set the corner radius of a rectangle (the amount of roundness on the corners) in the Property Inspector before you draw it on the Stage.

The Oval Tool

The Oval tool draws ovals. To draw an oval, select the Oval tool and click and drag your mouse on the Stage. In Flash CS3, you can set the inner and outer radii of a circle in the Property Inspector before you draw it on the Stage.

The PolyStar Tool

The PolyStar tool is used to draw polygons or stars. To switch between the two and set the number of sides or points, select the PolyStar tool and click the Options button in the Property Inspector.

The Rectangle Primitive and Oval Primitive Tools (Flash CS3 only)

These tools work the same as the Rectangle and Oval tools, but using these tools allows you to modify the radii of your shape before or after you draw the shape on the Stage.

TIP When drawing a shape using the Rectangle, Oval, PolyStar, Rectangle Primitive, or Oval Primitive tool, after you start dragging your mouse, hold SHIFT to constrain the width and height of the shape, or hold ALT (Windows) or OPTION (Mac) to draw the shape from the center.

The Pencil Tool

The Pencil tool draws strokes. You can choose to have Flash straighten or smooth the strokes you draw in the Toolbar once you have the Pencil tool selected.

The Brush Tool

The Brush tool paints fills. You can modify brush settings in the bottom of the Toolbar after you select the Brush tool.

The Ink Bottle Tool

The Ink Bottle tool paints a stroke on a shape with no stroke.

The Paint Bucket Tool

The Paint Bucket tool adds a fill to or changes the fill color of a shape.

The Eyedropper Tool

The Eyedropper tool is used to sample a color from an object on the screen. When you have the Eyedropper tool selected and roll over the stroke of a shape, your cursor will show a pencil, indicating that if you click, you are going to sample the stroke color of that shape. When you roll over a fill, your cursor will show a paintbrush indicating that if you click, you will sample that shape's fill.

The Eraser Tool

The Eraser tool erases strokes and fills. You can customize settings for the Eraser tool at the bottom of the Toolbar.

The Hand Tool

The Hand tool allows you to pan around the artwork you have on the screen without affecting the positioning of that artwork.

 Press and hold SPACE on your keyboard to toggle the Hand tool no matter which tool you have selected.

The Zoom Tool

The Zoom tool allows you to zoom in or out of your work.

TIP To zoom in no matter which tool you have selected, hold CTRL (Windows) or COMMAND (Mac) and press +. To zoom out, press − while holding CTRL (Windows) or COMMAND (Mac).

Setting Strokes and Fills in the Toolbar

To set the stroke or fill of a shape, click the stroke or fill color picker in the Toolbar. Make sure to select your stroke and fill colors before drawing the shape. If you have already drawn a shape on the Stage and want to change its color, select the shape and change the colors using the color pickers in the Property Inspector.

Clicking the Default Color button in the Toolbar sets the stroke to black and the fill to white. The button to the right of that button swaps your current stroke fill colors. The No Color button (white box with a diagonal red line) is used to remove the stroke or fill of a shape.

The Snap To Objects Button

The Snap To Objects button toggles whether Flash will constrain movement and scaling of objects to a certain amount of pixels set in View | Snapping | Edit Snapping. This button is required for connecting an animation to a motion path, which I will explore in more detail later in this chapter.

Merge Drawing vs. Object Drawing

The Object Drawing button appears at the bottom of the Toolbar when you have any shape drawing tool selected. When the Object Drawing button is deselected, the next shape you draw will be drawn in Merge Drawing mode. In Merge Drawing mode, overlapping shapes that occupy the same layer (discussed later in this chapter) will become one combined shape. Object Drawing allows you to draw shapes in a group while preserving the ability to modify the shape. Object Drawing shapes that overlap and occupy the same layer will not combine like their Merge Drawing brethren.

Which drawing mode should you use? Most people familiar with Adobe Illustrator prefer Object Drawing mode because Object Drawing is closer to drawing in Illustrator. Merge Drawing is great if you need to make unique shapes. Throughout the rest of this book, you will primarily be working in Merge Drawing mode, but I recommend using the mode you feel most comfortable with. Figure 1-3 shows what the Toolbar looks like with Object Drawing mode off and on.

EXERCISE 1-1: Using the Flash Drawing Tools

This exercise will give you some practice using the basic Flash drawing tools you will be working with throughout this book.

1. Open Flash.

2. Create a new Flash document or Flash file by choosing File | New.

NOTE If you are using Flash CS3, you will have the option to choose a New Flash File ActionScript 3.0 or ActionScript 2.0. For programming Wii games, you need to use ActionScript 2.0, which I will discuss in detail in the next chapter.

FIGURE 1-3

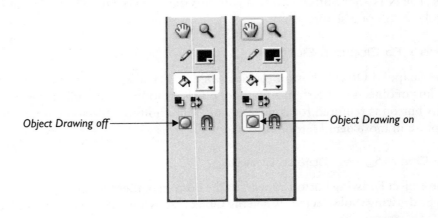

Object Drawing off —————

————— Object Drawing on

Object Drawing mode off and on

Flash Fundamentals

3. If you do not see the Toolbar, choose Window | Tools to open the Toolbar.

4. In the Toolbar, select the Rectangle tool from the flyout menu that contains the other shape drawing tools and choose any stroke color and any fill color. Make sure Object Drawing mode is turned off. Notice the Property Inspector changes when you select the Rectangle tool to give you options for drawing rectangles.

5. Click and drag on the Stage to draw a rectangle of any size, such as the one shown here.

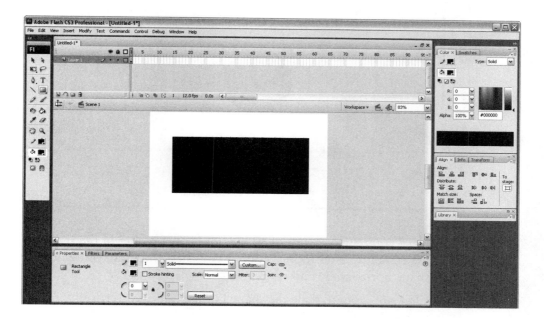

6. In the Toolbar, select the Selection tool.

7. Select the fill of the rectangle on the Stage by single-clicking the rectangle's fill.

8. Select the stroke and fill of the rectangle by double-clicking the rectangle's fill.

9. Press DELETE on your keyboard to delete the shape from the Stage.

10. In the Toolbar, select the Oval tool under the flyout menu of the Rectangle tool.

11. Click and drag on the Stage to draw an oval of any size.

12. In the Toolbar, select the Free Transform tool.

13. Click and drag to create a selection area around the entire shape on the Stage. Notice the boxes that surround the shape, as shown in the following illustration.

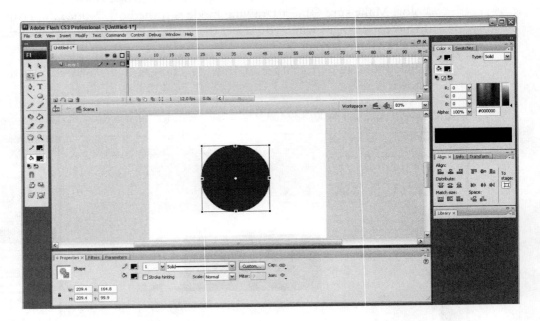

14. Place your cursor over one of the boxes on a corner of the shape. Notice the cursor updates to show that if you click and drag, you will scale the shape horizontally and vertically.

15. Click and drag to scale the shape horizontally and vertically. Hold SHIFT on your keyboard while dragging and notice how the shape maintains its proportions.

16. Place your cursor just outside one of the corner boxes until your cursor turns into a rotating arrow.

17. Click and drag to rotate the shape. Hold SHIFT on your keyboard to constrain the rotation to 45-degree angles, as shown next.

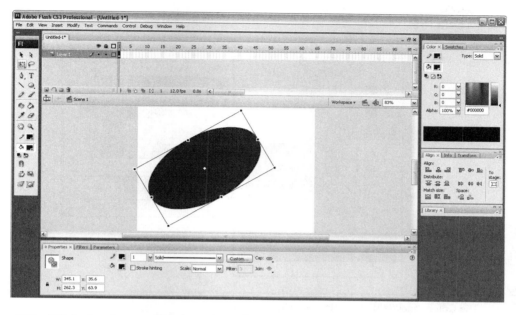

18. With the shape still selected, in the Property Inspector change the fill color of the shape by using the Fill color picker.

19. Close the document. You do not need to save your changes.

UNDERSTANDING IMPORTANT PANELS

The Toolbar contains all kinds of tools for drawing in Flash. Another set of tools Flash has to help you develop content are called *panels*. There are many panels in Flash, but again, because my purpose here is to create Wii games, I will only focus on the panels you will use most as a game designer.

The Color and Color Swatches Panels

The Color panel and the Color Swatches panel (shown in Figure 1-4) help you work with and manage color. The Color panel is the only place in the Flash authoring environment where you can create a custom gradient. The Color Swatches panel is used to store colors and gradients.

FIGURE 1-4

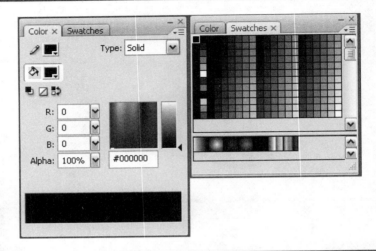

The Color panel (left) and Color Swatches panel (right)

EXERCISE 1-2: Creating a Custom Gradient

In this exercise, you'll create your own custom gradient using the Color panel.

1. Create a new blank Flash document.

2. Draw a circle on the Stage with a stroke of any color and a fill of any color.

3. In the Toolbar, choose the Selection tool.

4. On the Stage, single-click the fill of the circle you created in Step 2.

5. With the fill of the circle selected, find the Color panel. If it is hidden, choose Window | Color to show the panel.

6. In the top left of the Color panel, select the Fill icon (shown here) to tell Flash you are modifying a fill.

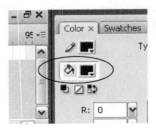

7. In the Type drop-down menu inside the Color panel, select Radial. This will apply a radial gradient to your fill from the last gradient you created. The default gradient is black and white.

8. Now you're going to change the outer gradient color to black and change the inner gradient color to green. To change the color of a gradient, double-click one of the gradient slider color pickers (shown here) in the Color panel and choose a color.

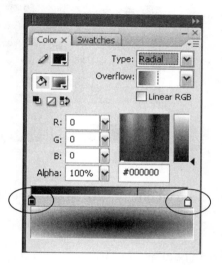

9. Once you have set the gradient colors, you can transform the gradient using the Gradient Transform tool. With the fill still selected, choose the Gradient Transform tool from the Free Transform tool flyout menu in the Toolbar. Notice the fill on the Stage has handles to transform the gradient you created.

10. Click and drag the inner circles of the Gradient Transform handles to move the origin of the gradient.

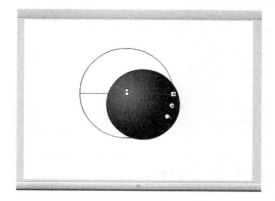

11. With the gradient still selected, go to the Swatches panel. If you do not see that panel, choose Window | Swatches.

12. In the Swatches panel, save the gradient by clicking in the blank area to the right of the gradient swatches area. Your new gradient will appear in the swatches, as shown here.

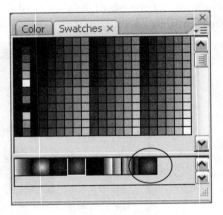

13. Close the file. You do not need to save your changes.

The Align Panel

In Flash, objects can be aligned relative to each other or relative to the Stage. The ability to align objects to the Stage makes it easy to place an object directly in the horizontal or vertical center of the Stage. The Align panel also allows you to space objects evenly and scale a set of objects so that they are all the same width or height.

EXERCISE 1-3: Using the Align Panel

Now you'll get some practice using the Align panel to align some objects.

1. Open Flash and create a new Flash file.

2. On the left side of the Stage, draw a rectangle roughly 150 pixels wide with any stroke and fill.

 You can check and adjust the size of a shape in the Property Inspector once the shape is selected.

3. On the right side of the Stage, draw an oval roughly 150 pixels wide with any stroke and fill color.

4. Using the Selection tool, click and drag a selection area around the box shapes to select them.

5. With both shapes selected, open the Align panel. If you do not see the Align panel, choose Window | Align.

6. In the Align panel, make sure To Stage is highlighted, as shown in the illustration. This will make the alignment of your shapes relative to each other instead of the Stage.

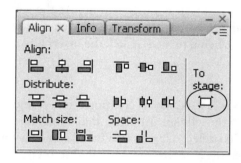

7. In the Align panel, click the Align Vertical Center button (shown here). Notice the alignment of the shapes on the Stage.

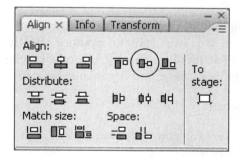

 If you roll your mouse over any of the buttons in the Align panel, Flash will tell you the name of that button.

8. In the Align panel, click the To Stage button. The next align button you click will align the shapes relative to the Stage.

9. In the Align panel, click the Align Horizontal Center button. The shapes align to the horizontal center of the Stage.

10. Close the file. You do not need to save your changes.

WORKING WITH LAYERS

Up to this point, you have only worked with the X and Y or horizontal and vertical positioning of objects. Layers control the Z position or stacking of objects. It is essential to understand the basics of working with layers when creating Flash content.

Creating Layers

Creating layers in Flash is fairly simple. At the top of the screen, you will see the Timeline. Near the bottom-left corner of the Timeline is the Insert Layer button (it looks like a page being turned). Click the Insert Layer button to create a new layer.

Deleting Layers

Deleting layers is just as easy as creating them. A few buttons to the right of the Insert Layer button, you will see a button that looks like a trash can. That is the Delete Layer button. To delete a layer, select the layer you want to delete. You know a layer is selected when the layer becomes highlighted. Then, click the Delete Layer button to delete the layer.

Managing Layers

When working in Flash, you will often create many layers. In order to avoid confusion and clutter, it is important to practice effective layer management. Effective layer management involves naming layers, changing the stacking order of layers, showing and hiding layers, and organizing layers into layer folders.

Naming Layers

Flash names layers for you with names like Layer 1, Layer 2, etc. If you choose to keep the default names, you could only imagine how hard it would be to find and edit content with many layers. I always recommend naming your layers, unless you are not planning on saving or publishing the file. To name a layer, double-click the layer name (not the layer icon) and type the new layer name.

Changing the Stacking Order of Layers

Just as you have control over the horizontal and vertical positioning of objects, you also have control over their stacking order. The stacking order of layers is based on the layer position in the Timeline. The top layer is in front of everything, and the bottom layer is behind everything. To change the order of layers, click on the left side of the layer and drag the layer up or down.

Showing and Hiding Layers

At the top of the Timeline, you will see three icons: an eye, a lock, and a box. These icons, along with the buttons below them, control the visibility, locking, and display of the layers as outlines, respectively.

To hide a layer, click the button below the eye on the right side of the layer you want to hide. The button turns to a red X, indicating the layer is hidden. To hide all layers, click the Show/Hide All Layers button (eye icon). The buttons below the eye turn into red Xs, indicating the layers are hidden.

To show a hidden layer, click the red X on the hidden layer you want to show. To show all layers, click the Show/Hide All Layers button. If only some of the layers are hidden, you will have to click the button twice to show all the layers.

Locking and Unlocking Layers

Locking a layer prevents editing any artwork on that layer. This will help you to not accidentally edit artwork or add content to a layer unintentionally.

To lock a layer, click the button below the Lock/Unlock All Layers button (lock icon) on the right side of the layer you want to hide. The button turns to a lock icon, indicating the layer is locked. To lock all layers, click the Lock/Unlock All Layers button. You will see lock icons on all layers, indicating all layers are locked.

To unlock a locked layer, click the lock icon on the locked layer you want to unlock. To unlock all layers, click the Lock/Unlock All Layers button. If only some of the layers are locked, you will have to click the button twice to unlock all the layers.

Organizing Layers Using Layer Folders

The more layers you have in a Flash file, the more difficult it becomes to find a layer you want to edit, even if your layers are named properly. In Flash, you can organize layers into folders to easily find the content you are looking for.

To create a layer folder, click the Insert Layer Folder button at the bottom of the Timeline. You can name a layer folder in the same way you name a layer.

To place layers into folders, click and drag a layer from the left side (in order to avoid accidentally hiding or locking the layer) and drop the layer on top of the correct layer folder.

To expand or collapse a layer folder, click the arrow to the left of the layer folder icon. When the arrow is pointing down, the folder is expanded; when the arrow is pointing right, the folder is collapsed.

Different Types of Layers

There are a few different types of layers in Flash. So far, you have looked at normal layers and layer folders. The other types of layers are masks and guides. Mask and guide layers give you more design control by allowing you to add different effects to your Flash applications.

Mask Layers and Masked Layers

A *mask* layer reveals content in a *masked* layer. For example, if you wanted to create the effect of looking through a telescope in Flash, you would create a circular area to represent the telescope viewing area. That circle would be a mask, and everything viewed with the telescope would be masked.

To create a mask, you need two things: the mask itself and the content to be revealed, or masked content. The mask layer needs to be in a separate layer directly above the masked content. Next, you must tell Flash which layer is the mask and which layer is masked. The fastest way to do this is to right-click (Windows) or CTRL-click (Mac) the mask layer and select Mask. When you do this, you will notice the layer icons change, and the masked layer indents a little.

NOTE To preview masked content in Flash, you need to show and lock the mask layer as well as the masked layer. This is to preview the mask while you are working in the Flash file. When you create a Flash movie from a Flash file (which I will discuss later), the mask effect will show, regardless of which layers are locked or hidden.

Guide Layers

Guides are used in two different ways: to guide designing content for a Flash application, or to guide an animation. For now, I'll just talk about turning a layer into a design guide. To turn a layer into a guide, right-click (Windows) or CTRL-click (Mac) the layer you want to use as a guide and select Guide. The guide layer works like a normal layer when you are working in Flash, but guide layers do not show up in your Flash movie—only in the .FLA file.

 TIP Turning a layer into a guide layer is also great if you have a layer you may or may not use later on. That way, you can sort of temporarily disable that layer.

The Layer Properties Window

You can get a little more control about what type of layer you want in the Layer Properties window. To open the Layer Properties window, double-click the layer icon (not the layer name) of the layer you want to modify. Using the Layer Properties window, you can set multiple layers to be masked. You will look at using the Layer Properties window in the following exercise.

EXERCISE 1-4: Working with Layers

In this exercise, you will use everything you have learned about layers to create an ocean scene viewed through a telescope.

1. Open Flash and create a new Flash file.

2. In the Timeline, click the Insert Layer button to create a new layer.

3. Name the top layer **Boat** and name the bottom layer **Water**.

4. Drag the Water layer above the Boat layer.

5. Lock the Boat layer.

6. Select the Water layer. Notice the pencil icon in the middle of the layer, indicating that is the layer you are currently drawing on.

7. Use the Brush tool and the Paint Bucket tool to draw some waves on the water layer. They don't have to be anything fancy. Just waves, as shown here.

8. Lock the Water layer and unlock the Boat layer.

9. On the Boat layer, draw a boat. Feel free to be a little creative here.

10. Lock both layers. Create a new layer above the Water layer. Name the new layer **Telescope**.

11. On the Telescope layer, draw a circle roughly 300 pixels in diameter, with no stroke and a bright green fill.

 When creating a mask, it is best to pick a color you aren't using on the Stage. That way, if you forget to set that layer as a mask, it is easy to catch.

12. Set the Telescope layer to be a mask layer by right-clicking (Windows) or CTRL-clicking (Mac) the Telescope layer and selecting Mask. Notice the Boat layer is not masked.

13. Double-click the layer icon on the left side of the Boat layer (not the layer name). Make the Boat layer masked by selecting Masked in the Layer Properties window, as shown next, and then click OK.

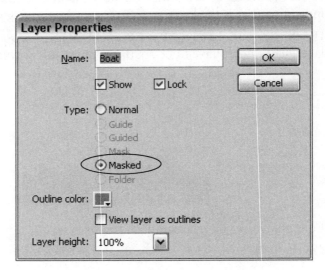

14. Notice that the Boat layer is now masked by the Telescope layer. If it is not masked, make sure to lock the Boat layer.

NOTE If you wanted to make the telescope effect a little more realistic, you could create a background layer below the Boat layer with a rectangle the size of the Stage using any color you'd like for the background. Then, you could make that layer masked as well. For the finishing touch, you could deselect everything by clicking in the gray area off the Stage and set the background color of your Flash file to Black in the Property Inspector.

15. Close the file. You do not need to save your changes.

WORKING WITH SYMBOLS

Symbols are reusable assets and fundamental building blocks in Flash. To understand symbols, imagine you are designing a Flash game with lots of clouds in the background. You have designed dozens of levels, each filled with dozens of clouds. To save time when designing the clouds, you simply copied the same cloud over and over, changing the scale of the cloud each time so the different clouds look unique. After setting up all of your clouds, you realize you could draw a better cloud if you put your mind to it. The more you think about the original cloud, the more it bothers you. You think of changing it, but the tediousness of the task is more than you can handle. Your conundrum brings you to a point of insanity so intense that you decide to give up game design altogether.

That's why you want to use symbols. Using symbols, you can create one "master" symbol, and create links to or copies of the symbol (called *instances*). Each copy of the master symbol can have a unique scale, rotation, and transparency, but it is still linked to the master symbol. When you change the art of the master symbol, all of the instances automatically update.

In addition to helping you save time, using symbols saves loads of file size over creating copies of shapes or other graphics. When you use symbols, Flash adds the file size of the original symbol to your movie, but each instance of that symbol takes up very little file size because it is only a copy of the original.

Now that I've discussed the benefits of using symbols, I'll talk about what types of symbols you will be working with to create Wii games.

Graphic Symbols

Graphic symbols are primarily used for graphics you want to reuse that do not animate. One important thing about graphic symbols is that you cannot use ActionScript to control them. When creating Wii games (or any Flash games for that matter), it is good to use graphic symbols for backgrounds that you need to recycle but that do not animate. Because of the limitations of graphic symbols, I will not use them too much throughout this book.

Button Symbols

Button symbols are great when you want to add simple interactivity to a Flash application. Using button symbols, you can easily add mouse rollover and click effects to a graphic. The downside with using button symbols is that they don't allow for the complex interactivity you need to create games.

Movie Clip Symbols

Movie clip symbols are the type of symbols you will be working with throughout this whole book. Movie clip symbols can hold animations and support the most complex interactivity you can create in Flash. Most important, movie clips give you all the tools you need to create Wii games.

Creating Symbols

There are two different ways to create symbols. You can either create a symbol on a blank Stage, or you can convert art you have already created to a symbol. Throughout this book, I will discuss the benefits of using one over the other. For now, the most important thing to remember is that there are two different ways to create them.

To create a symbol on a blank Stage, choose Insert | New Symbol. You will then see the Create New Symbol dialog box. Choose the type of symbol you want to create and click OK. Flash then gives you a blank Stage to create a new symbol, as shown in Figure 1-5.

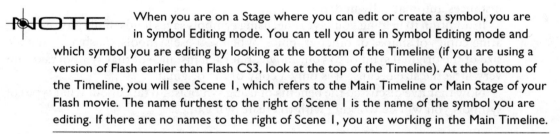

NOTE   When you are on a Stage where you can edit or create a symbol, you are in Symbol Editing mode. You can tell you are in Symbol Editing mode and which symbol you are editing by looking at the bottom of the Timeline (if you are using a version of Flash earlier than Flash CS3, look at the top of the Timeline). At the bottom of the Timeline, you will see Scene 1, which refers to the Main Timeline or Main Stage of your Flash movie. The name furthest to the right of Scene 1 is the name of the symbol you are editing. If there are no names to the right of Scene 1, you are working in the Main Timeline.

FIGURE 1-5

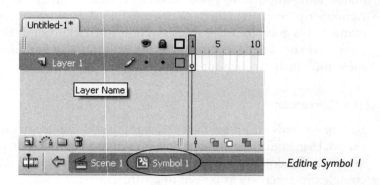

Symbol Editing mode

All of the symbols you create are stored in the Library panel. You can access the Library panel by choosing Window | Library. In the Library, you can quickly edit, rename, and organize your symbols.

Remember that symbols are stored in the Library, and instances are what you see on the Stage.

If you want to convert art you have already drawn to a symbol, select the artwork on the Stage and choose Modify | Convert To Symbol. You will then see the Convert To Symbol dialog box (not to be confused with the Create New Symbol dialog box). Choose the type of symbol and the registration (X/Y origin). Then click OK to convert the art you selected to a symbol. You will then see a blue box around your artwork on the Stage, indicating it is an instance of a symbol. If you select the instance on the Stage, you will see information about the instance in the Property Inspector.

TIP   You may have noticed that the keyboard shortcut to Modify | Convert To Symbol is F8. This is one of the most useful Flash keyboard shortcuts to memorize, since you will be converting art to a symbol pretty often.

Editing Symbols

There are two ways to edit symbols. One way is to edit the symbol in place, meaning while viewing its surrounding elements. Another way to edit a symbol is to isolate it from everything else so that you are viewing only elements that are part of the symbol. Both ways are commonly used, and I will go into more detail on why you would use one over the other throughout this book.

To edit a symbol in place, double-click the symbol on the Stage. You will know you are in Symbol Editing mode because you will see the name of the symbol you are editing furthest to the right of Scene 1 at the bottom of the Timeline. For an example, refer to Figure 1-5. When you are in Edit in Place mode, you will also see the other elements that are on the Stage with your symbol, but not part of your symbol. Those elements will look semitransparent or faded.

You can edit a symbol by itself by double-clicking the symbol icon (not the name of the symbol) in the Library. You can tell you are in Symbol Editing mode because you will see the name of your symbol to the right of Scene 1 at the bottom of the Timeline. Refer to Figure 1-5 for an example.

Double-clicking the name of a symbol in the Library will allow you to change the symbol's name.

Any changes you make while you are in Symbol Editing mode will change all instances of the symbol you are editing.

Naming Symbols

When you create a symbol, you can specify a name for that symbol. Always name your symbols so that you can find them in case you need to modify them. Symbol names should not have any spaces or special characters (characters other than numbers and letters) and must always begin with a letter. A common naming convention for symbols is to begin the symbol name with a prefix that represents its symbol type using lowercase letters and name the symbol using an uppercase letter. Example: if you created a cloud shape and converted it to a movie clip symbol, a good name for that symbol would be "mcCloud." That way, you can look at the symbol in the Library and tell its type (movie clip, or mc for short), and know that it contains a cloud graphic. Because symbols in the Library are listed in alphabetical order, Flash will keep your symbol types grouped for you if you use this naming convention.

Making Instances of Symbols

Once you have created a symbol, you can easily create as many instances of that symbol as you want by dragging them from the Library onto the Stage. Each symbol instance can have a unique position, scale, and rotation without affecting other instances of that symbol. If you make any changes to a symbol via Symbol Editing mode, the changes will apply to all instances of that symbol.

EXERCISE 1-5: Creating and Editing Symbols

Understanding symbols is crucial when working in Flash. In this exercise, you will get practice creating, naming, and editing symbols.

1. Open Flash and create a new Flash file.

2. Use the drawing tools in the Toolbar to draw a cloud on the Stage.

3. Using the Selection tool, draw a selection area around the cloud to select it.

4. Press F8 on your keyboard to convert the cloud to a symbol.

5. Name the cloud **mcCloud**, choose Movie Clip for the type, and click top-left registration, as shown next. Click OK when you are done.

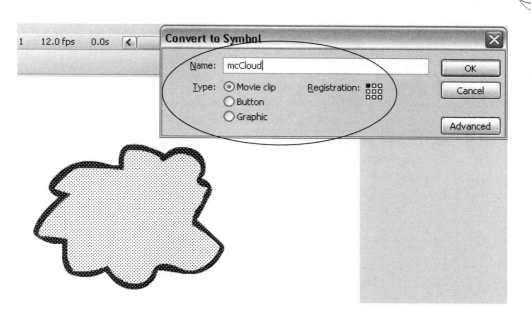

NOTE The default registration for symbols is top left. Top left is also the X/Y origin on the Stage. To keep things consistent, it is usually best to give all symbols top-left registration. I will discuss exceptions to this later on in this book.

6. Create three more instances of the mcCloud symbol by dragging the symbol out of the Library onto the Stage.

7. Using the Free Transform tool, scale each instance differently.

 Even though each instance has a unique scale, all of the instances are linked to the symbol in the Library.

8. Edit one of the clouds in place by double-clicking it on the Stage. Notice at the bottom of the Timeline that you are now in Symbol Editing mode, editing the mcCloud symbol. Also notice the other clouds look a little dimmer.

9. Inside the mcCloud symbol, draw some eyes on the cloud, as shown in the illustration. Notice how the other instances on the Stage automatically update as you draw the eyes.

10. Return to the Main Timeline by clicking Scene 1 at the bottom of the Timeline.

11. Now, you will edit the symbol from the Library, so the symbol is isolated. Double-click the icon to the left of the mcCloud symbol name in the Library to enter Symbol Editing mode. Notice in the bottom of the Timeline to the right of Scene 1, Flash is showing that you are in Symbol Editing mode editing the mcCloud symbol.

12. Use the Brush tool to draw a face on the cloud.

13. Return to the Main Timeline by clicking Scene 1 at the bottom of the Timeline. Notice how all the mcCloud instances on the Stage have updated to reflect the change you made to the symbol.

14. Close the file. You do not need to save your changes.

CREATING ANIMATIONS

Flash is a great program for creating animations. Animation is created by playing a sequence of still images called *frames*. The speed of an animation depends on how many frames per second (FPS) the movie is playing, also known as *frame rate*. In

Flash, animation can be created in the Timeline or by using ActionScript. There are three types of animation in Flash: frame-by-frame animation, shape tween animation, and motion tween animation. Through the rest of this chapter, I will show you how to use these different animation techniques to create animations.

Understanding the Timeline

Before creating animations, it is important to understand how the Timeline works. The Timeline is used to create animation and/or navigation in Flash. It is divided up into frames, which will play when your Flash movie is running. There are three different types of frames in Flash: regular frames, keyframes, and blank keyframes.

Understanding Regular Frames

Frames are areas in the Timeline where there is no change in art. Let's say you wanted to create an animated image gallery in Flash. Each image would stay on the screen for two seconds without moving or changing, and then it would animate off the screen. In this case, you would use regular frames while the art is not animating. One advantage to using regular frames is that you can save on file size because Flash does not re-draw the art. The limitation to using frames is that because they specify no change in art, you cannot draw on them.

To create frames, click in the area of the Timeline where you want to create a frame and choose Insert | Timeline | Frame, or use the keyboard shortcut F5. I prefer using the keyboard shortcut, but you won't hurt my feelings if you don't. When you create frames, the Timeline extends to the frame you selected. In the Timeline, regular frames are blocks of medium gray.

The last regular frame before a change in art has a gray background with a white rectangle inside it (see Figure 1-6).

FIGURE 1-6

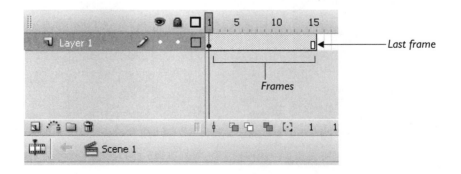

Regular frames have a gray background, and the last regular frame has a white rectangle.

Understanding Keyframes

In order to animate, you need to make changes in art. This is where *keyframes* come in. A keyframe is a special kind of frame you can use to create or change art. You are already familiar with keyframes. All the drawing you have done so far has been on keyframes. In fact, you can only draw on keyframes.

To create a keyframe, click in the area of the Timeline where you would like to create a keyframe and choose Insert | Timeline | Keyframe, or use the keyboard shortcut F6. This is another shortcut I recommend memorizing, since you will be creating keyframes often. When you create a keyframe, you will see a black dot inside the frame. The black dot inside the frame means there is art in that keyframe (see Figure 1-7).

Understanding Blank Keyframes and Blank Frames

Blank keyframes are keyframes that do not contain art. They are particularly useful when working with ActionScript and can be used to save on file size.

To create a blank keyframe, select the place in the Timeline where you would like to create it and choose Insert | Timeline | Blank Keyframe, or use the keyboard shortcut F7, which I also recommend. A blank keyframe has a white background with a black outline of a circle inside. Frames that are blank look like regular frames but have a white background (see Figure 1-8).

Selecting Frames

Selecting a frame is simple: click the frame you want to select. When the frame is selected, the background of that frame turns black.

FIGURE 1-7

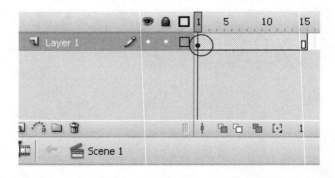

Keyframes that contain art have a black dot.

FIGURE 1-8

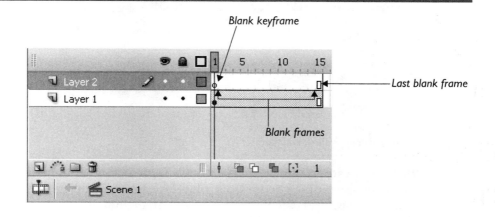

Different types of blank frames

To select multiple frames, use the Selection tool. Make sure nothing in the Timeline is selected by clicking in the Pasteboard (the gray area outside the Stage), and click and drag the frames in the Timeline you want to select. When frames are selected, the background of those frames changes to black.

Moving and Copying Frames

To move frames, you must first have one or more frames selected. After you have a frame selection, click and drag your selection to move it. To make a copy of your selection, hold ALT (Windows) or OPTION (Mac) while dragging and you will see a plus sign by your cursor indicating you are about to copy the frames. Release the mouse button before releasing the key on the keyboard to copy the frame(s).

Deleting Frames

To delete frames, select the frame or frames you want to delete and choose Edit | Timeline | Remove Frames or press the keyboard shortcut SHIFT-F5 (which I also recommend memorizing, by the way). The frames you selected will then be deleted.

Understanding the Playhead

The Playhead is the semitransparent rectangle at the top of the Timeline, shown in the following illustration. You can look at it to see which frame you are currently viewing, or click and drag it to preview an animation.

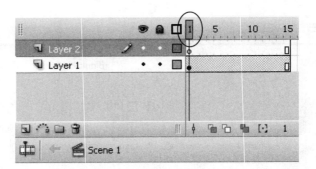

Previewing an Animation

When you create an animation, you usually want to test the animation along the way. To test an animation, choose Control | Test Movie. By default, the animation will endlessly loop. You can control playback of an animation, including looping, by using ActionScript, which I'll discuss in the next chapter.

NOTE The keyboard shortcut for Control | Test Movie is CTRL-ENTER (Windows) or COMMAND-RETURN (Mac). You will use this command frequently while developing Wii games, so I recommend memorizing it. If you are feeling overwhelmed trying to memorize every keyboard shortcut I mention, it's okay to forget them all . . . except this one.

Frame-by-Frame Animation

Now that you have a general idea of how the Timeline works, I can talk about creating a frame-by-frame animation. *Frame-by-frame* animations are animations where you define every frame of the animation using any combination of frames, keyframes, or blank keyframes.

EXERCISE 1-6: Creating a Frame-by-Frame Animation

In this exercise, you will create a simple frame-by-frame animation of a stick figure jumping up and down.

1. Open Flash and create a new Flash file.

2. Using the drawing tools in the Toolbar, draw a stick figure on the Stage roughly 150 pixels high and 75 pixels wide. Notice the Timeline changes once you draw art on the Stage to show you are working in a keyframe as opposed to a blank keyframe.

3. Select frame 2 in the Timeline and press F6 on your keyboard to create a new keyframe. Notice the new keyframe is a copy of the last keyframe.

4. In the Timeline, make sure the Playhead is on frame 2. Select the stick figure on the Stage and move it up a little (10–20 pixels).

5. Repeat Steps 3 and 4 on frame 3 instead of frame 2. The stick figure jumps up for two frames. Next, you will make the stick figure land by copying frame 2.

6. Select frame 2. Once it is selected, the background of the frame turns black.

7. Hold ALT (Windows) or OPTION (Mac) and click and drag frame 2 to copy it. Release your mouse on frame 4. Notice while you are dragging that there is a plus sign by your cursor, indicating releasing the mouse will create a copy of your selection.

NOTE As I discussed earlier, Flash will automatically loop animations. You are placing the second frame at the end here because that is when the stick figure is in the middle of its jump. This will make the stick figure look like it is bouncing. If you want a quick preview of this animation, you can drag the Playhead from frame 1 to frame 4.

8. Preview the movie by pressing CTRL-ENTER (Windows) or COMMAND-RETURN (Mac) on your keyboard. Watch the stick figure jump up and down in the preview window. Sweet!

9. Close the file. You do not need to save your changes.

NOTE Frame-by-frame animations are not limited to moving the same object up and down. They are really only limited to your creativity. Try thinking of another simple animation and use the animation techniques I've talked about to create it in Flash.

Shape Tween Animation

Shape tween animation is used to morph shapes into different shapes. For example, if you wanted to morph a letter into another letter, you would use a shape tween. The word *tween* is simply a shortened version of "in between." Tween animations are created defining a start keyframe and an ending keyframe, and telling Flash to animate the frames in between.

Shape Tween Rules

Note these few restrictions on shape tween animations:

) You need to be working with basic shapes. You cannot perform a shape tween on a symbol or a group.

) Though you can have many shapes animate on the same layer using a shape tween, any part of a layer where you define a shape tween must not contain any grouped objects or symbols.

Creating a Shape Tween

To create a shape tween, define a starting keyframe by drawing a shape. Then, create a keyframe two or more frames after the starting keyframe and draw the ending shape. Once you have starting and ending keyframes set up, in the Timeline, select any frame in between the starting and ending keyframes and select Shape from the Tween drop-down menu in the Property Inspector. That's it!

EXERCISE 1-7: Creating a Shape Tween Animation

In this exercise, you will create a simple shape tween by making a circle morph into a star.

1. Open Flash and create a new Flash file.

2. On the Stage, draw a circle with any stroke and fill colors.

3. In the Timeline, create a blank keyframe on frame 30. This frame will hold the star you'll create in the next step.

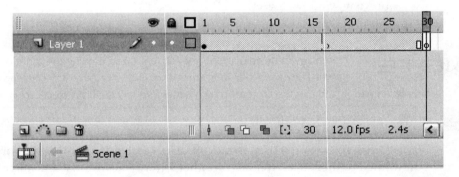

4. On frame 30, draw a star on the Stage.

NOTE To draw a star, use the PolyStar tool hidden in the flyout menu of the Rectangle tool. After you select the PolyStar tool, click the Options button in the Property Inspector and choose Star in the Style drop-down menu.

5. To create the shape tween, select any frame in between the two keyframes you want to tween and choose Shape from the Tween drop-down menu in the Property Inspector, as shown next.

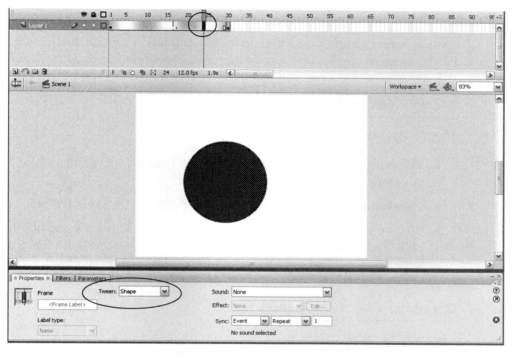

6. You will know that you have created a successful shape tween if you see an arrow with a green background in the frames where Flash is creating a tween for you, as shown in the following illustration (although you'll have to imagine the green background behind the arrow!). If you see a broken line instead of an arrow, Flash is telling you that you are disobeying the laws of the shape tween. If that happens, try this exercise again from the beginning.

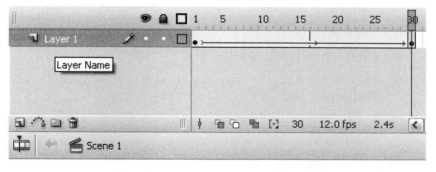

7. To preview the shape tween, press CTRL-ENTER (Windows) or COMMAND-RETURN (Mac) on your keyboard. Nice!

8. Close the file. You do not need to save your changes.

Motion Tween Animation

Motion tweens are the most common form of animation in Flash, because they require you to use symbols. Because motion tweens use symbols, they take up much less file size and system resources than the other types of animation you have created so far.

Motion Tween Rules

Motion tweens have these limitations:

❯ You must use symbols. If you do not use symbols, the animation will either not work properly or not work at all.

❯ The starting and ending keyframes must contain the same symbol.

❯ When working with motion tweens, you can animate only one object on each layer. That is not to say you can't animate hundreds of objects at the same time; you just need to use a different layer for each object you want to motion tween.

Creating a Motion Tween

To create a motion tween, you need to specify starting and ending keyframes of the animation using the same symbol. Then follow the same steps for creating a shape tween, but choose Motion instead of Shape in the Tween drop-down menu in the Property Inspector. If you rotate, scale, move, or otherwise change the instance on the first or last keyframe, Flash will animate the change for you.

EXERCISE 1-8: Creating a Motion Tween Animation

In this exercise, you'll create a simple motion tween.

1. Open Flash and create a new Flash file.

2. On the Stage, draw a ball roughly 100 pixels in diameter.

3. Select the ball on the Stage and convert it to a symbol by using the keyboard shortcut F8.

4. In the Convert To Symbol dialog box, name the symbol **mcBall**, choose Movie Clip for the type, and click OK.

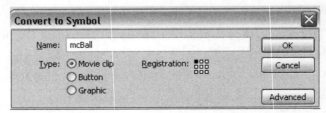

 You do not need to use movie clips when creating a motion tween. Any
symbol type will work in the same way.

5. In the Timeline, select frame 5 and press F6 on your keyboard to create a
keyframe.

6. On frame 5, drag the instance of mcBall up. This position will represent the
peak height of the ball.

7. Select frame 1. After frame 1 is selected, click and drag it to frame 10 while
holding the ALT (Windows) or OPTION (Mac) key on your keyboard to
create a copy of frame 1.

8. Click in between the first two keyframes in the Timeline and choose Motion
for the Tween type in the Property Inspector, as shown next. Flash then
creates a motion tween for you.

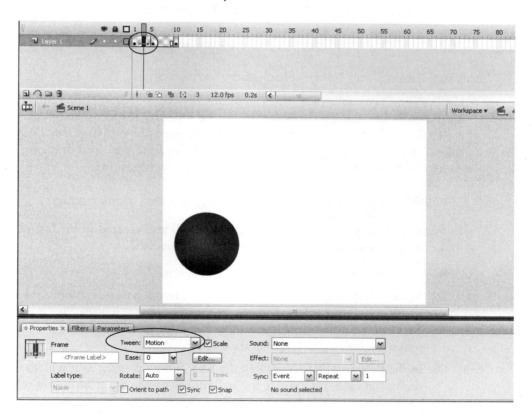

NOTE The visual cue that Flash has created a successful motion tween is the arrow with a purple background in the frames where the tween is occurring. A broken arrow indicates one of the motion tween rules has been disobeyed. If you see a broken line instead of an arrow, make sure you have only one instance of the mcBall movie clip on each keyframe. If you cannot find the problem, try this exercise from the beginning.

9. Repeat Step 4 in the second set of keyframes to create the motion tween of the ball coming down.

10. Test the movie (CTRL-ENTER or COMMAND-RETURN). Watch the ball move up and down. Cool!

NOTE Notice the animation of the ball looks a bit robotic. There are a few things you can do to fix this. One of them is applying something called easing. *Easing* refers to animation slowing down and speeding up. You can use easing to make the ball look much more like a bouncing ball. You'll do this in the next exercise.

11. Save the file, or keep it open. You will use it in the next exercise.

Applying Easing for More Realistic Animation

Using easing, you can have a little more control over your animations and make them a little more lifelike. You apply easing in the Property Inspector once you have created a tween. For basic easing, you can drag the Ease slider up or down. Dragging the Ease slider up makes your animation slow toward the end, and dragging the Ease slider down makes your animation slower near the beginning.

EXERCISE 1-9: Applying Easing to an Animation

In this exercise, you will apply easing to the ball you created in the last exercise to make the bouncing of the ball look much more realistic.

1. Open the file you created in the last exercise.

2. In the Timeline, click in between the first two keyframes. Notice the Property Inspector shows values you can change to control tweens. Because the first part of the animation is the ball moving upward, you will apply easing to make the ball slow down on its way up.

3. In the Property Inspector, drag the Ease slider up as far as it will go to make the tween ease out. Notice the ball moves on the Stage after you release the Ease slider.

 The term "ease out" refers to the animation going slower at the end, and the term "ease in" refers to an animation going slower at the beginning.

4. Click in between the last two keyframes in the Timeline and drag the Ease slider all the way down to make the ball ease in on its way down.

5. Test the movie. Notice the effect of the easing you applied makes the animation a little more realistic. However, it looks a little like the ball is sticking to the floor because the first and last keyframes are the same. You will fix this in the next steps.

6. In the Timeline, select frame 9. Press F6 on your keyboard to convert that frame to a keyframe. Now, you have a keyframe of the ball right before it lands.

7. Select the last keyframe in the Timeline (frame 10); hold SHIFT and press F5 on your keyboard to remove that frame.

8. Test the movie. The animation is looking a lot better. Still though, it doesn't feel right. When a ball bounces, it flattens a little. If you add that, the animation will look a lot better. On frame 1, use the Free Transform tool to squash the ball a little, as shown here.

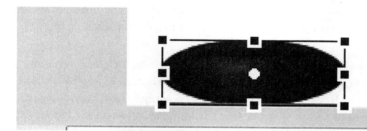

9. Test the movie. Notice the animation feels more realistic now. Great!

10. Save the file, or leave it open for the next exercise.

Storing Animation in a Movie Clip

Up to this point, you really haven't used movie clips to their full potential. Movie clips, as their name implies, can hold animations. They can act as self-contained Flash movies. This may sound a little confusing, but just know that anything you can create on the Main Timeline can be stored in a movie clip.

EXERCISE 1-10: Placing Animation in a Movie Clip

In this exercise, you will place the ball animation you created in the last exercise inside of a movie clip.

1. Open the file you worked with in the last exercise.

2. Click in the gray area outside the Stage to make sure everything is deselected.

3. In the Timeline, click and drag from frame 1 to frame 9 to select all the frames. When the frames are selected, they have a black background.

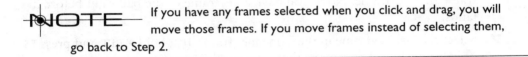 If you have any frames selected when you click and drag, you will move those frames. If you move frames instead of selecting them, go back to Step 2.

4. Right-click (Windows) or CTRL-click (Mac) your selection of frames and choose Cut Frames from the menu. The frames disappear. You will paste them in the next steps.

5. Create a new symbol by choosing Insert | New Symbol. Name the new symbol **mcAnimation**, choose Movie Clip for its type, and click OK. When you click OK, you are in the Timeline of mcAnimation.

NOTE Insert | New Symbol creates a symbol from scratch, not from your selection. When you choose Insert | New Symbol, Flash takes you to the new, empty symbol's timeline, which is a blank stage. Up to this point, you have been using the keyboard shortcut F8 to create symbols. F8 is the keyboard shortcut for Modify | Convert To Symbol, which creates a symbol from your selection and does not automatically take you into the symbol's timeline.

6. Select frame 1, and right-click (Windows) or CTRL-click (Mac) frame 1 and choose Paste Frames from the menu. Your animation is now stored in the movie clip mcAnimation instead of the Main Timeline.

7. Return to the Main Timeline by clicking Scene 1 at the bottom of the Timeline.

8. Deselect everything, then select frames 2 through 9, and press SHIFT-F5 to remove all frames after frame 1.

9. From the Library, drag an instance of mcAnimation onto the Stage.

10. Test the movie. Notice the animation plays even though there is only one frame on the Main Timeline.

NOTE ———— Storing animations, layers, and all types of artwork inside of movie clips is a very common practice. In this case, storing the animation in a movie clip gives you the ability to quickly move the animation on the Stage. You even have the power to animate this movie clip on the Main Timeline, so the ball can move from side to side while it is bouncing. You will look a lot more into storing content in movie clips throughout the rest of this book.

---

11. Close the file. You do not need to save your changes.

Now that you have a good foundation of Flash knowledge, you are ready to start learning ActionScript to add interactivity to your Flash movies.

OTHER FLASH RESOURCES

Because this chapter is only designed to teach you the bare necessities of Flash, I only discuss tools that you will absolutely need when creating Wii Flash games. Though you can always review this chapter, Flash is an enormous application and there is plenty more to learn if you are interested. Here are some of my favorite web sites for learning Flash:

❭ **Lynda.com**   This site has loads of video training material, and more Flash training than any other web site I've seen. The quality of the training is also outstanding. It is set up so that you pay a monthly fee to gain access to thousands of training videos and hundreds of videos of Flash training. It is definitely worth checking out, if only for a month.

❭ **ChadAndToddCast.com**   This is my podcast web site, and here you can find lots of free training in all Adobe software. You can also send requests to receive free video training to answer any question you have.

❭ **YouTube.com**   This site actually has a lot of great Flash training. You will have to search for it, but it is free.

There are tons of Flash podcasts that have beginning and advanced techniques. If you search on any podcast web site, or in iTunes, you should be able to find quality training quickly.

I also recommend picking up a basic Flash book. Before you buy the book, browse through it to make sure the wording is easy to understand.

CHAPTER 2

ActionScript 2.0 Essentials

IN this chapter, I will talk about some basic programming concepts in ActionScript 2.0. You will use your knowledge of Flash and the concepts you learn in this chapter to create games that are playable on the Wii. As you build games throughout this book, you may want to occasionally come back to this chapter to review the concepts you learned. Learning a programming language can be extremely challenging and can take a lot of time, but it will feel more and more natural to you as you work at it.

Just like the last chapter, this chapter does not contain everything there is to know about ActionScript 2.0. Rather, this chapter will teach you the basic concepts of ActionScript 2.0 and give you the skills you need to build Flash games for the Wii. At the end of this chapter, there are some resources where you can learn more about ActionScript 2.0.

UNDERSTANDING ACTIONSCRIPT 2.0

ActionScript 2.0 is the language used to program Wii Flash games. It is very similar to JavaScript, but you don't need to know JavaScript to learn ActionScript 2.0.

Where Do I Place the Code?

There are several places you can place ActionScript code. You can place it directly on movie clips or buttons, in keyframes in the Timeline or keyframes within movie clips, or in external files. I do not recommend placing code directly on movie clips or buttons, as this creates code that can be difficult to maintain. Placing code in external files and placing it in the Timeline are both good practices. For simplicity's sake, in this book I will place all code within keyframes in the Timeline.

How Do I Place Code in the Timeline?

Code can be placed in the Timeline using the Actions panel. The Actions panel can be accessed by choosing Window | Actions or by pressing the keyboard shortcut F9 (Windows) or OPTION-F9 (Mac). Before you open the Actions panel, always make sure you have the frame where you want to supply ActionScript selected.

There are two ways to write ActionScript in the Actions panel: Normal mode and Script Assist mode. To toggle between the two, click the Script Assist button in the Actions panel (see Figure 2-1). Normal mode requires you to type out all your code by hand, and Script Assist mode is more of an intuitive interface where Flash writes much of the code for you. Though I do not discourage the use of Script Assist, its capabilities are limited, so I will use Normal mode for the code in this book. Once you have an understanding of how ActionScript 2.0 works, and some practice typing the code, it may be faster for you to use Normal mode than Script Assist.

FIGURE 2-1

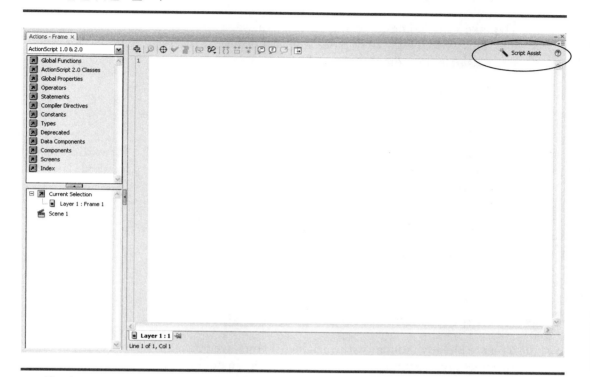

The Actions panel and Script Assist button

The area in the left side of the Actions panel is called the Toolbox. The Toolbox is for helping you write code and is used in conjunction with Script Assist. You can show or hide the Toolbox by clicking the arrow that divides the Toolbox and the Scripting pane. The Scripting pane is the main area of the Actions panel where you write code.

Making Comments in Your Code

As you write more and more ActionScript, it is always best to place comments in your code so that you or someone else can easily navigate through the ActionScript you write. Comments are not processed as ActionScript code, so you can write comments as messages to yourself or others in plain English. . .or any other language, for that matter. You can also place code in a comment to temporarily disable it. In ActionScript, comments have a gray color so that they are easily distinguishable from ActionScript code.

Making Single-Line Comments

To make a single-line comment, type two forward slashes (//) at the beginning of the line. This will tell Flash to skip that line of code when processing ActionScript. This is what a single-line comment looks like:

```
// This is a single-line comment
```

Making Multiline Comments

To create a multiline comment, begin the commented area with a forward slash and an asterisk (/*), and end the comment with an asterisk and then a forward slash (*/). A multiline comment looks like this:

```
/*
Comment line 1
Comment line 2
*/
```

WORKING WITH VARIABLES

You are already familiar with variables if you have taken an Algebra class. In math, variables represent numbers whose value you do not know. Working with variables allows you to create equations that will work regardless of whether you know the value of the variable.

In ActionScript, *variables* are used to hold data. For example, you could create a variable called score that could represent the number of points a player has in a game. Storing the player's points in the score variable enables you to work with the player's points without having to know the exact number of points the player has.

Variables do not always contain numbers. They can contain true or false values, text, or any other type of data you can work with in Flash. In this section, you will take a look at how to create variables in Flash.

Defining Variables

To create or define a variable, type **var** in the Scripting pane in the Actions panel. After var, type a space and then type the name of your variable. Variable names should begin with a lowercase letter and only contain letters and numbers. To create a variable called score, you would type

```
var score
```

Setting Values

Variables can hold data, but in order for that to happen you must tell Flash what data the variable will hold. To set a value of a variable, use the equal sign (=) and then type the value of the variable. Placing spaces before or after the equal sign is optional, but you may find it easier to read your code if you use a space. If you wanted to give a value of 0 to a variable called score, you would type

```
var score = 0;
```

NOTE The semicolon at the end of the code works similar to a period in a sentence; it marks the end of a statement. If you forget to put semicolons at the end of statements in your ActionScript code, you will not usually get an error and your code will run properly. However, it is a best practice to always end every ActionScript statement with a semicolon.

Sometimes, you will not give a value to a variable at the same time you create it. I'll talk about those times when examples come up, starting in the next chapter. In these cases, you can declare a variable on one line and give the variable a value on another line. If you wanted to write the preceding code on separate lines, you would type

```
var score;
score = 0;
```

Declaring a Data Type

An excellent way to check for errors in your code is to tell Flash what type of data a variable will hold. This is called *declaring* a *data type*. That way, if you put a number in a variable that is supposed to hold text, Flash will tell you that you made a mistake in your code. This will help a lot when you start writing large blocks of code. To declare a data type for a variable, type a colon after the variable name and then the data type of the variable. The data type for a number is called Number, the data type for text is called String, and the data type for true or false is called Boolean. If you wanted to create a variable called myName with a value of "Todd" (or your own name), and you wanted to tell Flash that variable has a String data type, you would type

```
var myName:String = "Todd";
```

NOTE The value of a string can be any combination of letters, spaces, special characters, and numbers. When you give the value of a string, you put the value in quotes. Code in quotes has a green color, so string values can be easily recognized among the other elements of your code.

There are many different data types, and I will discuss more of them later on.

EXERCISE 2-1: Creating Variables

Now you will get some practice creating variables.

1. Open Flash and create a new Flash file. If you are working in Flash CS3, make sure the Flash file is an ActionScript 2.0 file.

2. Select the first keyframe of Layer 1 and open the Actions panel by pressing F9 (Windows) or OPTION F9 (Mac).

3. In the Actions panel, make sure Script Assist is turned off and the Toolbox is hidden.

4. In the Scripting pane, create a variable by typing

```
var
```

CAUTION Notice the word var is blue. That's because var is a keyword in Flash. *Keywords* are reserved ActionScript words that have special meaning. When you create a variable, avoid choosing names that turn blue after you type them. This could create errors that keep your code from running properly.

5. Type a space, and then name the variable **myName**. Your code should look like this:

```
var myName
```

6. Give the variable a data type of String. Notice that the word String turns blue, because it is a keyword in Flash. Your code should look like this:

```
var myName:String
```

7. Set the myName variable's value to your name. Remember that the value of a string should be in quotes. Notice that the quotes and the value within the quotes turn green. Green is the default color for string values in Flash. Your code should look like the code next, with your name instead of Todd.

```
var myName:String = "Todd";
```

8. Close the file. You do not need to save your changes.

UNDERSTANDING INSTANCE NAMES

In order to change values and control movie clips using ActionScript, the movie clip you want to control needs an *instance name*. A movie clip's instance name makes it unique from other copies (or instances) of the same symbol (the item stored within

ActionScript 2.0 Essentials

FIGURE 2-2

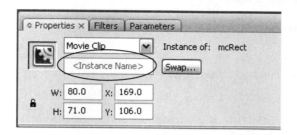

The Instance Name field in the Property Inspector

the Library). To give a movie clip instance (or a button instance) an instance name, select the instance on the Stage and type in the Instance Name field in the Property Inspector (shown in Figure 2-2). When naming instances, follow the same rules you follow when creating variables.

 If you end movie clip instance names with _mc, Flash will give you access to code hinting, which will make typing your code much easier.

WORKING WITH PROPERTIES

Properties are variables that are attached to objects. You are already familiar with properties. When you create a movie clip and change its X or Y position, you are modifying its properties. You can also modify an object's properties using ActionScript. To modify an object's properties with ActionScript, you use something called *dot syntax*. In ActionScript, dot syntax is used to communicate to something within something else. For example, the property that controls the X position of a movie clip is called _x. If you wanted to modify the X position of a movie clip with an instance name of my_mc and set it equal to 10, you would type

```
my_mc._x = 10;
```

Here, the dot in the code (after my_mc) tells Flash to look for something called _x inside of my_mc. Then, you can give a value to the property using the equal sign just as when you give a value to a variable.

EXERCISE 2-2: Modifying Movie Clip Properties Using ActionScript

In this exercise, you will control some different properties of a movie clip by using ActionScript.

1. Open Flash and create a new Flash file (ActionScript 2.0).

2. Using the Rectangle tool, draw a rectangle on the Stage.

3. With the Selection tool, select the rectangle and convert it to a movie clip by using the keyboard shortcut F8.

4. Name the movie clip **mcRect**, and make its registration point at the top left, as shown in the following illustration. When you are done, click OK.

5. Make sure you are in the Main Timeline by clicking Scene 1 at the bottom of the Timeline.

6. Select the movie clip on the Stage and, in the Instance Name field in the Property Inspector, type **rect_mc** (as shown in Figure 2-3).

 Always remember to give instance names to any symbols you plan to modify using ActionScript.

7. Create a new layer and name it **actions**. Make sure the actions layer is at the top.

 Having your code in a layer at the top is a best practice and makes your code easy to maintain.

8. Select the first keyframe of the actions layer and open the Actions panel by pressing F9 (Windows) or OPTION F9 (Mac).

9. In the Actions panel, click in the Scripting pane and type

```
rect_mc._x = 10;
```

FIGURE 2-3

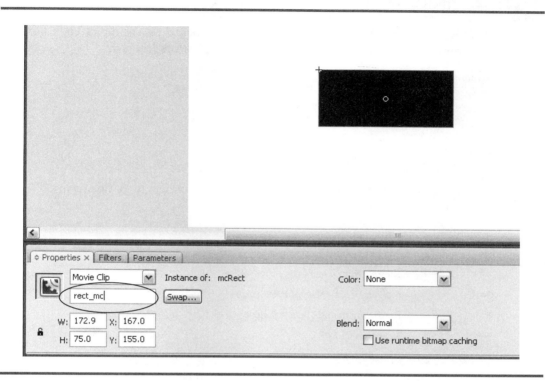

The Instance Name field in the Property Inspector

TIP   Because this movie clip has an instance name ending with _mc, Flash gives you code hinting when you type a dot. Code hinting is Flash's way of helping you write ActionScript code. This shows you properties you can modify on a movie clip. The properties you can modify begin with an underscore (_).

10. If you look at the movie clip on the Stage, you will notice its X position does not update. That is because the ActionScript you type does not run until the Flash movie is playing.

11. Press CTRL-ENTER (Windows) or COMMAND-RETURN (Mac) to test the movie. Notice the rect_mc instance moves 10 pixels from the left edge of the Stage. The values of properties you set in code override the values on the Stage. Nice!

12. Close the file. You do not need to save your changes.

WORKING WITH NUMBERS

In ActionScript, performing basic mathematical operations is simple. The following table outlines some of the basic mathematical operators in Flash.

Symbol	Use	Example
+	Addition	1 + 2 = 3
–	Subtraction	2 – 1 = 1
*	Multiplication	1 * 2 = 2
/	Division	2 / 1 = 2

There are also a few other ways to work with numbers in ActionScript. The following table shows a few examples of this.

Symbol	Use	Example	Result
+=	Add to a number's current value	a += 3	a + 3
–=	Subtract from a number's current value	a –= 3	a – 3
*=	Multiply by a number's current value	a *= 3	a * 3
/=	Divide by a number's current value	a /= 3	a / 3
++	Increment by 1	a ++	a + 1
--	Decrement by 1	a --	a – 1

WORKING WITH STRINGS

When working with strings, plus signs (+) concatenate, or connect, two strings. The following code demonstrates two strings being connected:

```
var firstName:String = "Todd";
var lastName:String = "Perkins";
var fullName:String = firstName + lastName;
// fullName is "ToddPerkins"
```

In order to create spaces when using concatenation, you need to concatenate a space. This is demonstrated in the following code in the var fullName line:

```
var firstName:String = "Todd";
var lastName:String = "Perkins";
var fullName:String = firstName + " " + lastName;
// fullName is "Todd Perkins"
```

You will see more examples of string concatenation as you start creating games.

UNDERSTANDING FUNCTIONS AND METHODS

When you create Wii Flash games, you will write many lines of code. Functions allow you to reuse parts of your code so that you don't have to keep writing the same lines over and over again. Methods are also functions, but they are functions attached to objects. I will talk more about methods in the next section.

Using Simple Functions

If you have experience working with Flash before reading this book, you may already be familiar with functions. Functions are needed to control the playback of a Flash movie. If you wanted a Flash movie to stop playing instead of looping endlessly, you would use the stop function. To run a function, type the function name and opening and closing parentheses. If running the function is the end of your ActionScript statement, type a semicolon after the parentheses. The code to run the stop function and make your Flash movie stop playing is

```
stop();
```

You can place this code at any keyframe in your actions layer and Flash will stop the movie when the Playhead reaches that frame.

EXERCISE 2-3: Using the stop Function

In this exercise, you will learn how to use the stop function to stop the playback of your Flash movies.

1. Open Flash and create a new Flash file (ActionScript 2.0).

2. Draw a rectangle on the Stage.

3. Select the rectangle and convert it to a movie clip.

NOTE Though this exercise does not require the movie clip to have a particular name, you should still avoid giving this movie clip a name with spaces or special characters. If you don't remember what characters are special characters, you can think of special characters as the characters that are used to represent curse words (%&#!, etc.). Like many people, Flash might get upset if you swear at it.

4. In the Main Timeline, select frame 10 in the Timeline and press F6 on your keyboard to create a keyframe.

5. In frame 10, select the movie clip on the Stage and move it to a different area of the Stage. In the next step, you will create a motion tween.

6. In the Timeline, select any frame between frame 1 and frame 10, and in the Property Inspector, set the Tween type to Motion (as shown in Figure 2-4).

7. Test the movie and preview the animation. Notice the animation loops endlessly. In the next steps, you will use ActionScript to stop the movie when it reaches the last frame. Close the preview window when you are done.

FIGURE 2-4

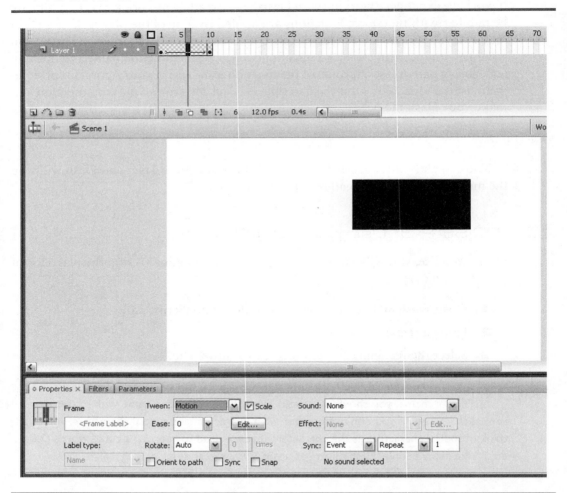

Creating the motion tween

The keyboard shortcut to test the movie is CTRL-ENTER (Windows) or COMMAND-RETURN (Mac).

8. Create a new layer above Layer 1 and name the new layer **actions**.

9. In the actions layer, select frame 10 and press F7 on your keyboard to create a blank keyframe.

10. Select frame 10 of the actions layer and open the Actions panel by pressing F9 (Windows) or OPTION-F9 (Mac).

11. In the Scripting pane of the Actions panel, type

```
stop();
```

12. Test the movie. Watch the movie play and stop on the last frame. Cool!

 You do not have to save the file in order to preview the ActionScript you wrote.

13. Close the file. You do not need to save your changes.

Defining and Using Custom Functions

Up to this point, I have only discussed the code to run a function. Defining a function refers to the area of code where you tell Flash a function's name and what it does. Running a function refers to using a function that either you created or is built into Flash. Follow these steps to create, or declare, a custom function:

1. To create a function, you need to use the function keyword. In the same way that the var keyword tells Flash you are going to create a variable, the function keyword tells Flash you are going to create a function.

2. After the function keyword, you need to type a space and give your function a name. Function names have the same restrictions as variable and instance names.

3. After the function name, type opening and closing parentheses. These correspond to the opening and closing parentheses used when you are running the function.

4. After the parentheses, type a colon and the type of data the function will return. I will talk more about functions returning values later in this section. If your function does not return a value (and many of the functions you create will not), the return data type is Void. This step is optional, but it is a best practice to include it.

5. The last step in creating a function is to tell Flash what the function does. After all of the code in the previous steps, place the code that runs when you run the function in opening and closing curly braces ({}). These can be on the same line or on separate lines, although it may be easier for you to read your code if the brackets are on their own lines.

A function called myFunction that sets the X position of a movie clip called my_mc to 10 looks like Figure 2-5.

To run a custom function that you created, type the function name and opening and closing parentheses. Figure 2-6 shows Flash running a function.

NOTE It doesn't matter where you write the code to run the function as long as it is defined in the same frame as when you run it. When you run a function, Flash will search for the function definition in the same frame where you run the function. If there is a definition for that function, Flash will run the function.

You can create variables inside the curly braces of a function, but the variable is known and can only be used inside of that function. This concept will make more sense once you start creating games, and I will discuss it in greater detail then.

FIGURE 2-5

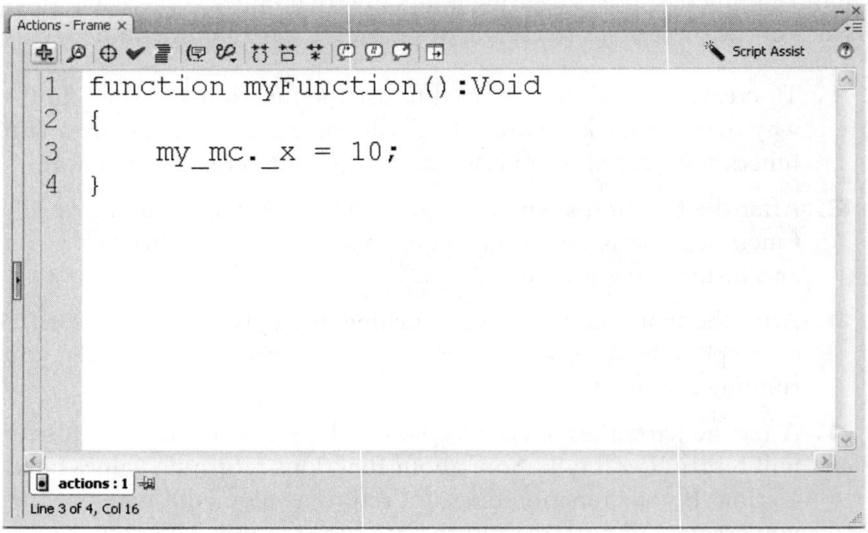

```
Actions - Frame ×

1  function myFunction():Void
2  {
3      my_mc._x = 10;
4  }

actions : 1
Line 3 of 4, Col 16
```

A simple function called myFunction

FIGURE 2-6

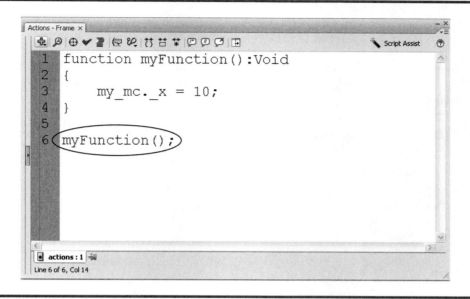

Running a function called myFunction

ActionScript 2.0 Essentials

EXERCISE 2-4: Creating and Using a Custom Function

In this exercise, you will create and use a simple custom function.

1. Open Flash and create a new Flash file (ActionScript 2.0).

2. On the Stage, draw a rectangle with a black fill and convert it to a movie clip named mcRect.

3. Give the rectangle an instance name of **rect_mc**.

4. Create a new layer named **actions**. Make sure it is at the top.

5. Select the first keyframe of the actions layer and open the Actions panel.

6. In the Actions panel, click in the Scripting pane and type

```
function setValues():Void
{

}
```

7. Inside the curly braces of the setValues function, type

```
rect_mc._x = 10;
rect_mc._y = 10;
rect_mc._alpha = 50;
```

 The _y property controls a movie clip's Y position, and the _alpha property controls the opacity of a movie clip from 0 to 100 (0 is invisible, 100 is fully opaque).

8. Below the closing curly brace of the setValues function, run the setValues function by typing

```
setValues();
```

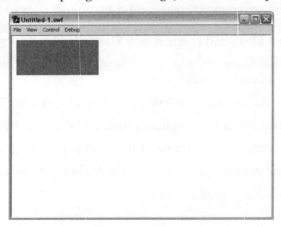

9. Test the movie. Notice in the preview window, shown in the following illustration, that the rectangle is 10 pixels from the left edge of the Stage, 10 pixels from the top edge of the Stage, and semitransparent. Nice!

10. Save the file, and keep it open for the next exercise.

Understanding Parameters

At the beginning of this section I mentioned that functions are reusable blocks of code. One way to make a function reusable is by using something called *parameters*. Parameters are values that can change each time you use a function.

To understand parameters, let's take a look at some of Flash's built-in functions that use parameters. If you want your Flash movie to navigate to a certain frame when you click a button, you would use the gotoAndPlay or gotoAndStop function to control the navigation of your movie. If you wanted your movie to play from the first frame, you would type

```
gotoAndPlay(1);
```

In this example, the number 1 is a parameter passed in to the gotoAndPlay function. Each time you use the gotoAndPlay function, you can pass in a different parameter, depending on the frame you want to play. You will use the gotoAndPlay function often when you start creating games.

NOTE The gotoAndStop function works the same as the gotoAndPlay function, but when the movie gets to the frame you pass in, the movie stops instead of playing.

Another function that uses a parameter is called trace. The trace function (also known as trace statement) is used when writing code to test if certain parts of the code are working. When you use the trace function, the value you pass in shows up in the Output window when you test the movie. The Output window, shown in Figure 2-7, is used to show you trace statement messages and errors when testing your Flash movies. For example, if you wanted to write a note to yourself to appear in the Output window by using the trace function, you could type

```
trace("note to self: Hi self!!!");
```

When you trace a string, the message shows up in the Output window exactly as you typed it. You can also use a trace statement to check the value of a variable. If you created a variable called myName and gave it a string value of "Todd", you could

FIGURE 2-7

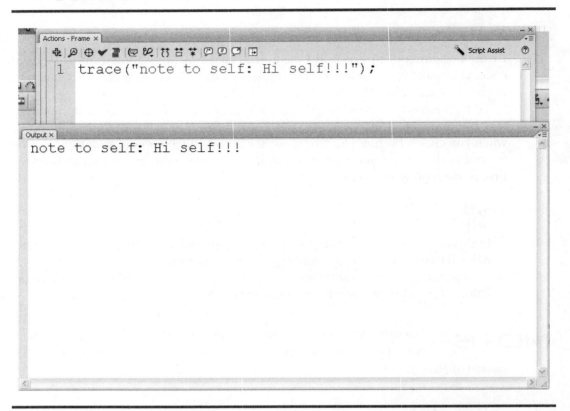

Trace statement showing up in the Output window

trace myName and the value of the variable would show up in the Output window (see Figure 2-8).

Some functions have multiple parameters. If a custom or prebuilt function has multiple parameters, the values are all passed in the parentheses when you run the function, and they are separated by commas.

Creating Functions with Parameters

Making functions that accept parameters is only a little more complex than making functions that do not accept parameters. To make a function accept parameters, you need to do two things: create the parameters when you define the function, and pass in the parameters when you run the function.

ActionScript 2.0 Essentials

FIGURE 2-8

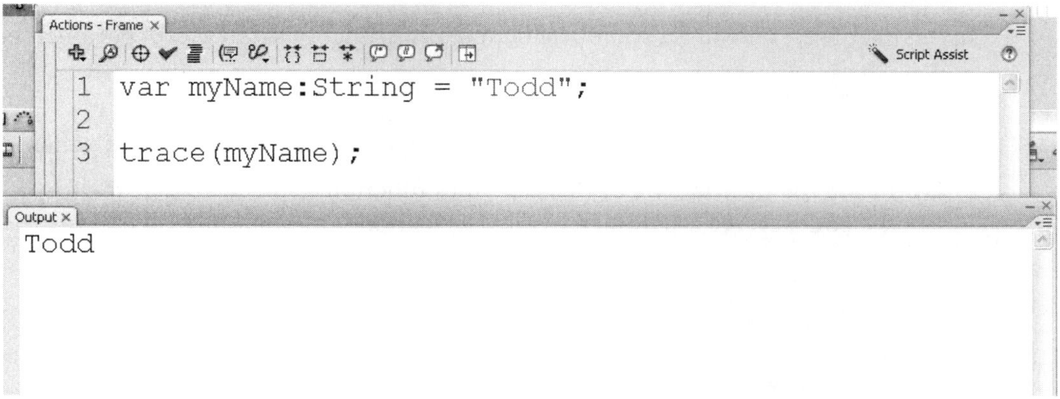

```
Actions - Frame ×                                          Script Assist   ?
1  var myName:String = "Todd";
2
3  trace(myName);
```

```
Output ×
Todd
```

Tracing the value of a variable

Creating parameters inside a function is similar to declaring variables without giving them values. The only difference is that you declare the variables inside of the parentheses of the function declaration, separated by commas instead of semicolons. If you had a function called myFunction, and you wanted the function to accept a parameter called myParam, that had a data type of String, you would type

```
function myFunction(myParam:String):Void
{

}
```

Once you have defined a function that accepts parameters, you need to pass in parameters when you run the function. The parameters you pass in must have the same data type you specified when you defined the function. For example, if you wanted to run the function defined in the code in the last paragraph, you would type

```
myFunction("Any value will work, as long as it is a String!");
```

Notice the value passed in is a string (you can tell because it's in quotes). Why does it have to be a string? It has to be a string because the function is looking for a string to give a value to the myParam parameter. Take a minute to look over the code and think about how it works.

EXERCISE 2-5: Writing and Using Functions with Parameters

In this exercise, you will get some practice creating functions that accept parameters.

1. Open the file you worked with in the last exercise.

2. Select the first keyframe of the actions layer and open the Actions panel.

3. Inside the parentheses of the setValues function you declared at the top of the code, create a parameter called xPosition with a Number data type.

```
Actions - Frame ×                                                    Script Assist
1  function setValues(xPosition:Number):Void
2  {
3      rect_mc._x = 10;
4      rect_mc._y = 10;
5      rect_mc._alpha = 50;
6  }
7
8  setValues();

actions : 1
Line 1 of 8, Col 36
```

4. Inside the curly braces of the setValues function, find the line where you set the _x property of rect_mc to 10 (shown in the following illustration), and replace the 10 with xPosition.

```
Actions - Frame ×                                                    Script Assist
1  function setValues(xPosition:Number):Void
2  {
3      rect_mc._x = xPosition;
4      rect_mc._y = 10;
5      rect_mc._alpha = 50;
6  }
7
8  setValues();

actions : 1
Line 3 of 8, Col 25
```

 At this point, the xPosition parameter does not have a value. The value of the parameter will be whatever value you pass in when you run the setValues function.

ActionScript 2.0 Essentials

5. At the bottom of the code, find the line where you run the setValues function. Inside the parentheses, type 50, as shown next. The number that you type here will be the X position of the rect_mc movie clip when you preview the movie.

```
function setValues(xPosition:Number):Void
{
    rect_mc._x = xPosition;
    rect_mc._y = 10;
    rect_mc._alpha = 50;
}

setValues(50);
```

6. Test the movie. Notice the rect_mc movie clip is 50 pixels from the left edge of the Stage, just as you passed in when you ran the setValues function. Nice!

7. Close the preview window, and change the value passed into the setValues function. Take a minute to review how the code is working, and test the movie again.

8. When you are finished, close the file. You do not need to save your changes.

Understanding Return Values

Some functions give values back after they run. This is called *returning a value*. The Math class, or Math object, has many properties and methods that perform various mathematical operations. Many of the Math methods are functions that return values. One example of a function that returns a value is the Math.random method. This function is attached to the Math object, so it is called a method instead of a function. The Math.random method gives you a random number between 0 and 1, but not including 1. You would see a random decimal number in the Output window if you typed this code and tested the movie:

```
trace(Math.random());
```

Notice this line of code ends with two closing parentheses. The first one is for the Math.random method, and the second is to close the trace statement.

When the Math.random method runs, Flash does some work behind the scenes and returns a number. Once you start creating games, you will use and create many different functions that return values.

Creating Functions That Return Values

Creating functions that return values takes two steps. First, you tell Flash what type of data a function will return. Then, inside the curly braces where you define the function, you use the return keyword to return the data.

Setting a Return Data Type

The return data type is set after the colon in the first line of the definition of a function. Up to this point, you have not created functions that return values, so you have used Void as the return data type. You can set the return data type by replacing Void with a type of data (i.e., String, Number, Boolean, etc.). In the code that follows, the function myFunction has a return data type of String.

```
function myFunction():String
{

}
```

Returning a Value

To make a function return a value, you must use the return keyword inside the function definition. In the example that follows, the function myFunction returns a string value of "Hello!".

```
function myFunction():String
{
    return "Hello!";
}
```

It's important to note that when a function has a return data type, you must also return the data inside the function using the return keyword. The type of data returned must match the return data type.

EXERCISE 2-6: Creating a Function with Return Data

In this exercise, you will get some practice creating functions that return data, and see how that data can be used.

1. Open Flash and create a new Flash file (ActionScript 2.0).

2. Change the name of Layer 1 to **actions**.

3. Select the first keyframe of the actions layer and open the Actions panel.

4. In the Scripting pane, create a function called sayHello that returns a string by typing

```
function sayHello():String
{

}
```

 In the preceding code, String is capitalized because it's referring to a data type. This is also the case with all other data types.

5. In order for this function to return a string, you must use the return keyword (all lowercase) inside the function. The return keyword should turn blue if it is typed correctly. Make this function return "Hello!" The code should look like this:

```
function sayHello():String
{
    return "Hello!";
}
```

6. Run this function inside a trace statement to make sure it is working. Make sure the trace statement is below the closing curly brace of the function definition. The code should look this:

```
function sayHello():String
{
    return "Hello!";
}
trace(sayHello());
```

7. Test the movie, and notice the message that appears in the Output window. When you are finished, close the preview window.

8. Now, you will make this function reusable by having it accept a parameter. Create a parameter called person with a data type of String. The code should look like this:

```
function sayHello(person:String):String
{
    return "Hello!";
```

```
}
trace(sayHello());
```

9. In the trace statement, pass in a person's name as a string to the sayHello function. The code should look like the code that follows, but the name does not have to be Todd.

```
function sayHello(person:String):String
{
    return "Hello!";
}
trace(sayHello("Todd"));
```

10. Inside the sayHello function, place the person parameter in the return line using concatenation. Remember to put a space after "Hello", to tell Flash there should be a space between "Hello" and the person's name. The code should look like this:

```
function sayHello(person:String):String
{
    return "Hello " + person + "!";
}
trace(sayHello("Todd"));
```

11. Before you test the movie, take a minute to look at how the code is working. Ask yourself the following questions: How is the name in the trace statement being sent to the sayHello function? What is the return line of code doing with the person parameter? What will happen when I test the movie?

12. Test the movie and watch what displays in the Output window.

13. When you are finished, close the file. You do not need to save your changes.

Working with Methods

As I mentioned earlier, *methods* are functions that are attached to objects. To use an object's methods, type the object name, a dot, and the name of the method, with the appropriate parameters passed in parentheses. One method available to use on movie clips is the stop method. If you wanted to stop the playback of a movie clip instance called my_mc, you would type the following code:

```
my_mc.stop();
```

You will work more with methods and learn about different methods later on, when you start creating games.

WORKING WITH EVENTS AND EVENT HANDLERS

We are going to work with events and event handlers often when creating Wii Flash games. *Events* are things that happen, such as when a button gets clicked. *Event handlers* are special functions that run when an event takes place, instead of running when you specify in the code. You do not need to write code for events to take place, but you need to create event handlers if you want something to happen when an event occurs.

Writing Event Handlers

Because event handlers are functions, much of the syntax for creating them is identical to that of creating functions. Most of the event handlers you will be working with do not have parameters or return values. When creating an event handler, you need to tell Flash the object that received the event, state the name of the event, and set that equal to a function. Setting something equal to a function is something you haven't done at this point. The syntax for setting something equal to a function is a little bit different from using the function keyword first. What follows is an example of setting something equal to a function.

Instead of writing

```
function myFunction(parameter:String):Void
{

}
```

you would write

```
myFunction = function(parameter:String):Void
{

}
```

This way of writing functions is acceptable for creating non–event handler functions, but I prefer using this method only when creating event handler functions. That way, I can quickly differentiate between the two.

Here is an example of how an event handler looks in code, with the object being objectName and the event being eventName:

```
objectName.eventName = function():Void
{

}
```

NOTE The dot after objectName tells Flash that eventName is connected to objectName. Just as objects have properties, as discussed earlier in this chapter, many objects also have events associated with them. Writing an event handler allows you to run code when an event happens. Without an event handler, the event still occurs, but no code will run.

In Flash, almost all events begin with "on." For example, the event name for clicking a movie clip (or a button) is onRelease. If you wanted to run a trace statement when you clicked a movie clip called my_mc, you would type

```
my_mc.onRelease = function():Void
{
    trace("you clicked my_mc!");
}
```

There are several events that you will be working with as you create Wii Flash games. Most of the events we will use are connected to movie clips. The following table outlines the movie clip events you will be using most often.

Event Name	Event
onRelease	When the mouse is pressed and released on a movie clip
onPress	When the mouse is pressed down on a movie clip
onRollOver	When the mouse rolls over a movie clip
onRollOut	When the mouse rolls out of a movie clip
onEnterFrame	Runs repeatedly with the frame rate of the Flash movie

EXERCISE 2-7: Writing Event Handlers

In this exercise, you will write an event handler that reacts to a mouse click.

1. Open Flash and create a new Flash file (ActionScript 2.0).
2. On the Stage, draw a rectangle and convert it to a movie clip named **mcRect**.
3. In the Main Timeline, select the movie clip on the Stage, and type **rect_mc** for its instance name in the Property Inspector.
4. Create a new layer above Layer 1 and name the new layer **actions**.
5. Select the first keyframe of the actions layer and open the Actions panel.
6. In the Actions panel, click in the Scripting pane, and type

```
rect_mc.onRelease = function():Void
{
    trace("you clicked on rect_mc!");
}
```

7. Test the movie. Click the rectangle on the Stage. Notice the message that shows up in the Output window each time you click the button (shown in Figure 2-9). Nice!

8. Try using another event from the last table, and see what happens. Note that if you use the onEnterFrame event, you may have trouble closing the Output window because messages continue to appear in it. This is because the onEnterFrame event happens as long as the Flash movie is playing. To stop the messages from appearing, close the preview window.

9. Close the file. You do not need to save your changes.

FIGURE 2-9

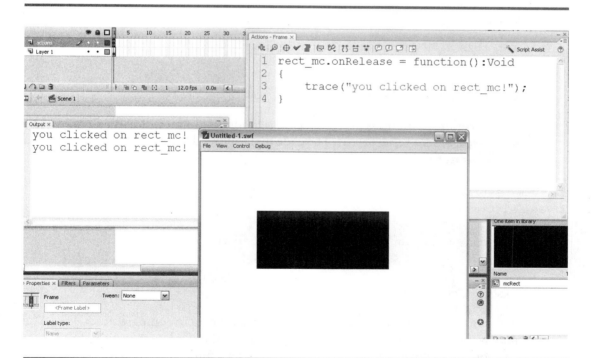

The working event handler

WORKING WITH CONDITIONAL STATEMENTS

A *conditional statement* is an if/then statement. In other words, you have power to run a block of code only if a certain condition is true. You also have power to run a block of code only if a condition is not true. You can even set up multiple conditions that get checked in a particular order, and have a block of code run for the first condition that is true.

Creating a Conditional Statement

Conditional statements, or if statements, have three parts: the conditional keyword, the condition, and what to do if the condition is true. The condition is placed in parentheses and evaluated as true or false (a Boolean value), and the code that executes if the condition is true is placed in curly braces. The code that follows demonstrates a basic conditional statement:

```
if(condition)
{
    // Run this code if the condition is true
}
```

Using Boolean Variables in a Conditional Statement

When working with Boolean variables in a conditional statement, using the variable name represents a value of true. The code that follows demonstrates a variable called administrator inside a conditional statement:

```
var administrator:Boolean = true;
if(administrator)
{
    //This code will run because administrator is true
}
```

Using Conditional Operators

Sometimes you will want to use a conditional statement to compare two values. You may want to know if a number variable is greater than or less than another number variable. Sometimes you will want to test whether a number is equal to another number. To do this, you need to use conditional operators. Here is a list of the most common conditional operators:

Operator	Meaning	Example
>	Is greater than	if(a > b)
<	Is less than	if(a < b)
==	Is equal to (different from one equal sign used when setting values)	if(a == b)
>=	Is greater than or equal to	if(a >= b)
<=	Is less than or equal to	if(a <= b)
!=	NOT equal to	if(a != b)

The following code example demonstrates a conditional statement using conditional operators:

```
if(3 <= 4)
{
    // This code will run because 3 is less than or equal to 4
}
```

Writing an else Statement

An else statement must follow an if statement, and the code inside the curly braces of an else statement will run only if its accompanying if statement's condition is evaluated as false. Because else statements run when an if statement's condition is false, they do not require a condition. The following code demonstrates an else statement:

```
if(3 > 4)
{
    // This code will not run because the condition is false
}
else
{
    This code will run because the if statement's condition is false
}
```

Writing an else if Statement

If you want to create a hierarchy of conditions, you can use else if statements. In other words, you can have Flash check if a condition is true, and if it is not true check another condition, and if that condition is not true, Flash can check yet another condition. You get the point. To create an else if statement, you must first have an if statement. The following code demonstrates an example of an else if statement:

```
if(condition 1)
{
```

```
// run if condition 1 is true
}
else if(condition 2)
{
// run if condition 1 is false and condition 2 is true
}
else if(condition 3)
{
// run if condition 1 and 2 are false and condition 3 is true
}
else
{
// run if conditions 1, 2, and 3 are false
}
```

riting Compound Conditional Statements

Conditions in a conditional statement can be broken up into expressions. You can check if multiple expressions are true within one condition. A conditional statement with more than one expression is also called a *compound* conditional statement. In a compound conditional statement, you can check if one expression and another expression are both true, or check if one expression or another expression is true. The conditional operator for "and" is two ampersands (&&). The conditional operator for "or" is two vertical pipes (||).

NOTE Vertical pipes are created by holding SHIFT and pressing backslash (\) on the keyboard.

The following code demonstrates compound conditional statements.

```
if(a > 0 && a < 5)
{
    // This will run if a is greater than zero AND less than five
}

if(a == 0 || a == 5)
{
    // This code will run if a is equal to zero OR if a is equal to five
}
```

ActionScript 2.0 Essentials

EXERCISE 2-8: Writing Conditional Statements

In this exercise, you'll get some practice writing conditional statements yourself.

1. Open Flash and create a new Flash file (ActionScript 2.0).

2. Change the name of Layer 1 to **actions**.

3. Select the first keyframe of the actions layer and open the Actions panel.

4. In the Actions panel, click in the Scripting pane and create a conditional statement that evaluates whether 3 is greater than 2 by typing the following code:

```
if( 3 > 2)
{
    trace("condition 1 is true");
}
```

5. Test the movie. Notice the message, shown in Figure 2-10, that comes up in the Output window.

FIGURE 2-10

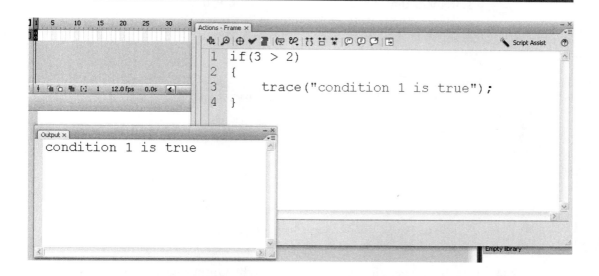

The trace statement appearing in the Output window

6. Change the code in the if statement to read if 3 is less than 2, so the condition will be false. Your code should match this snippet:

```
if( 3 < 2)
{
    trace("condition 1 is true");
}
```

7. Below the if statement, write an else statement. Inside the else statement, trace "all conditions are false". Your code should look like this:

```
if( 3 < 2)
{
    trace("condition 1 is true");
}
else
{
    trace("all conditions are false");
}
```

8. Test the movie. Notice the message in the Output window indicating all conditions are false. Close the preview window when you are finished.

9. Between the if statement and the else statement, create a compound else if statement that is true if 3 is less than 2 OR if 3 is greater than 2. Inside the else if statement, trace "condition 2 is true". Your code should look like this:

```
if( 3 < 2)
{
    trace("condition 1 is true");
}
else if( 3 < 2 || 3 > 2)
{
    trace("condition 2 is true");
}
else
{
    trace("all conditions are false");
}
```

10. Test the movie. Notice the message in the Output window indicating condition 2 is true. Close the preview window and look over the code again to make sure you understand how it is working.

11. Close the file. You do not need to save your changes.

UNDERSTANDING LOOPS

A *loop* is a block of code that runs a certain number of times. Loops help you to perform tasks where you repeat yourself. Using loops, it is just as easy to run a block of code one time as it is to run a block of code a thousand times. You will use loops often when you create games later on.

Writing a For Loop

There are a few different types of loops, but the one you will be working with most is called a *for* loop. The following code shows a basic for loop that will run 20 times.

```
for(var i:Number = 0; i < 20; i ++)
{
    // this is the code that is looped
}
```

A *for* loop begins with the for keyword. Then, in parentheses there are three elements, separated by semicolons.

The first element is the loop variable. In this case, there is a variable called i that is a number data type with a value of zero. This number is known as the loop index. The loop index can be used inside the loop. I will talk about using the loop index later.

The second element states how long the loop will run. The code in the preceding sample will run as long as the i variable is less than 20. Because the i variable has an initial value of zero, the loop will run 20 times. If you tested the movie with this code in your actions layer, you would see the numbers 0 through 19 in your Output window. This is because the variable i has an initial value of 0, and the loop stops running once i is equal to 20. Each time a loop runs is called an iteration.

The third element tells Flash what to do if the condition in the middle is not true after the block of code in the curly braces runs. In this case, the i variable will increment by 1.

It is important to note that a loop runs a certain number of times, but it is instantaneous in actual time. In other words, if you used a loop that ran 20 times, and added 1 to the X position of a movie clip each time the loop ran, you would not see the movie clip animate. Instead, you would see the movie clip 20 pixels from its starting point.

EXERCISE 2-9: Creating a For Loop

In this exercise, you will create a simple for loop to see a loop in action.

1. Open Flash and create a new Flash file (ActionScript 2.0).

2. Change the name of Layer 1 to **actions**.

3. Select the first keyframe of the actions layer and open the Actions panel.

4. In the Scripting pane, create a loop that runs 10 times by typing this code:

```
for(var i:Number = 0; i < 10; i++)
{

}
```

5. Inside the curly braces of the loop, trace the value of i. Your code should match what is shown here:

```
for(var i:Number = 0; i < 10; i++)
{
    trace(i);
}
```

6. Test the movie. Notice the values that appear in the Output window, shown in the illustration, are 0 through 9.

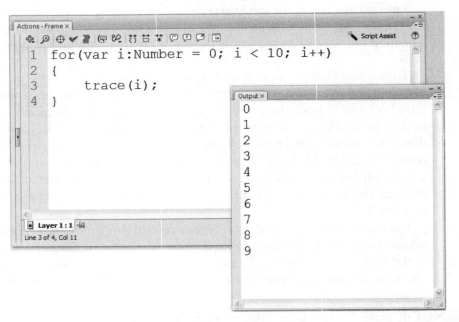

7. Close the file. You do not need to save your changes.

In the next section, I will discuss arrays, and how to use a loop to capture data from an array.

UNDERSTANDING ARRAYS

Arrays are a little different than anything you've worked with up to this point, and you'll use them often when creating games. Earlier in this chapter, I discussed how variables are containers that hold data. *Arrays* are containers that can hold *multiple* data values.

Creating an Array

The Array data type is also called a class. A *class* refers to the behavior of an object. You already have experience working with classes. Classes are similar to symbols. When you create an instance of a movie clip, you are actually creating an instance of the MovieClip class. To create an instance of a class that is not visible, like the Array class, you type the keyword "new," a space, and the name of the class followed by parentheses. Once you create an instance of the Array class, you can access its properties and methods in the same way you access the properties and methods of a movie clip. The following code shows an example of creating a new instance of the Array class called my_ary.

```
var my_ary:Array = new Array();
```

As discussed earlier, arrays hold multiple data values. The values of an array are stored in numerical order. Items in an array can be referenced by their numerical position, which in an array is called an index number. The first index of an array is always zero, and array indices are always referenced using square brackets ([]).

Adding to an Array

There are a few different ways to add data to an array. One way is to set the value of a particular index of an array. The following code demonstrates the data "Some text" being added to an array called my_ary at index 0, and the data "Some more text" added to the array at index 1.

```
var my_ary:Array = new Array();
my_ary[0] = "Some text";
my_ary[1] = "Some more text";
```

Data inside an array is not limited to strings. In fact, arrays can hold any type of data, and even different types of data.

You can also create an array and add data to it using one line of code. To do this, instead of using the new keyword to create an array, you type square brackets and the values of the array, separated by commas. The following code demonstrates some numeric values being added to an array called my_ary on the same line the array is created.

```
var my_ary:Array = [7,3,15,6,12];
```

Another way to add data to an array is to use the push method of the Array class. The push method adds an item to the last index of an array. If the array has no indices, the data is placed at index zero. The following code shows the push method adding the data "Pushed text" to an array instance called my_ary at index zero.

```
var my_ary:Array = new Array();
my_ary.push("Pushed text");
```

Capturing Data from an Array

There are several different ways to capture data from an array. One way is to reference the data by its index in the array. The code that follows demonstrates tracing data at index one of an array called my_ary.

```
var my_ary:Array = [7,3,15,6,12];
trace(my_ary[1]);
// Traced value is 3
```

In this code, the value in the Output window would show 3, because the first value in the array, which is 7 in this case, is at index zero.

Another helpful tool for working with arrays is the length property. The length property of an array gives you the number of items in the array (not the last index number). You can then use this information in a code loop (or a for loop) to use the data in each index of an array, which you will do often when you create games. The following code shows a loop that runs for each index of the array my_ary and traces the value of each index.

```
var my_ary:Array = [7,3,15,6,12];
for(var i:Number = 0; i < my_ary.length; i++)
{
    trace(my_ary[i]);
}
// The Output window would then show each of the values in the array
```

EXERCISE 2-10: Working with Arrays

In this exercise, you will get some practice working with arrays by creating a simple array and tracing different values of data in that array.

1. Open Flash and create a new Flash file (ActionScript 2.0).

2. Change the name of Layer 1 to **actions**, select the first keyframe of the actions layer, and open the Actions panel.

3. In the Scripting pane, create an array called my_ary and give the array some text values by typing the following code:

```
var my_ary:Array = ["text1", "text2", "text3", "text4"];
```

4. Add another value to the array using the push method. Your code should look similar to this:

```
var my_ary:Array = ["text1", "text2", "text3", "text4"];
my_ary.push("text5");
```

5. Below all the code you have written, trace the value of index 4 of the array by typing the name of the array and placing 4 inside square brackets. Your code should look similar to this:

```
var my_ary:Array = ["text1", "text2", "text3", "text4"];
my_ary.push("text5");
trace(my_ary[4]);
```

6. Test the movie. Notice the value that appears in the Output window matches the fifth item in the array, which is index 4. With the preceding code, the Output window would show "text5".

7. Close the window and the Flash file. You do not need to save your changes.

UNDERSTANDING DOT SYNTAX AND COMMUNICATION

Dot syntax is Flash's method of communication. You have actually been using dot syntax throughout this chapter to set property values and use methods. To reference a property or a method attached to an object, you typed the object name and a dot (.) and then the property or method name. You can also use dot syntax to communicate between different objects, like movie clips.

Understanding Communication Between Objects

In the last chapter, I discussed how movie clips can be placed in other movie clips. Using dot syntax, it is possible to modify properties or use methods of any movie clip with an instance name, even if that movie clip is nested within another movie clip. When a movie clip is nested within another movie clip, the child movie clip is treated as a property of the parent movie clip. The following code demonstrates an example of modifying the X position of the movie clip child_mc that is within the movie clip parent_mc.

```
parent_mc.child_mc._x = 10;
```

Here, the X position of the child_mc movie clip is set to 10. It's important to note that positioning of children inside a parent movie clip is relative to the parent movie clip, as shown in Figures 2-11 and 2-12.

FIGURE 2-11

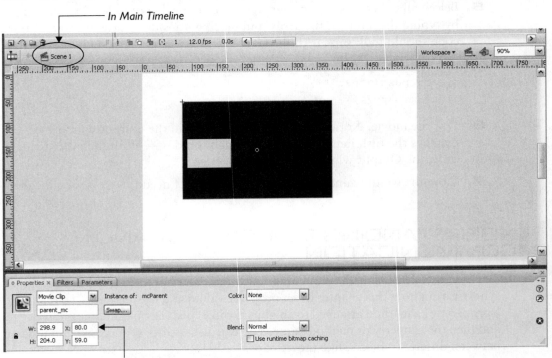

Positioning of a parent movie clip

FIGURE 2-12

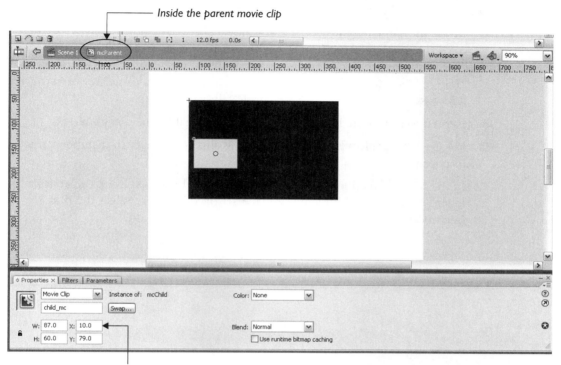

X position of child movie clip is 10, even though it is further to the right than the parent Movie Clip.

Positioning of a child movie clip

EXERCISE 2-11: Communicating to a Child Movie Clip

In this exercise, you will get practice communicating between movie clips. Understanding this concept is key to using ActionScript 2.0.

1. Open Flash and create a new Flash file (ActionScript 2.0).

2. On the Stage, draw two rectangles with different fills, one larger than the other, and turn them into movie clips. Name the larger one **mcParent** and name the smaller one **mcChild**. Make sure to give both symbols top-left registration.

3. Enter the Timeline of mcParent by double-clicking the parent movie clip on the Stage. Make sure that you see mcParent in the Timeline, indicating you are editing the mcParent movie clip.

4. Inside the Timeline of the mcParent movie clip, drag an instance of mcChild onto the Stage, placing it in the center of the larger rectangle. Give the mcChild movie clip an instance name of **child_mc**. Note the X position of child_mc, shown in Figure 2-13. You will change this using ActionScript in a few steps.

5. Return to the Main Timeline by clicking Scene 1 in the Timeline.

6. On the Stage, select the mcParent movie clip and give it an instance name of **parent_mc**.

7. In the Main Timeline, create a new layer called **actions**. Lock the actions layer, so you don't accidentally place art on that layer. Select the first keyframe of the actions layer and open the Actions panel.

FIGURE 2-13

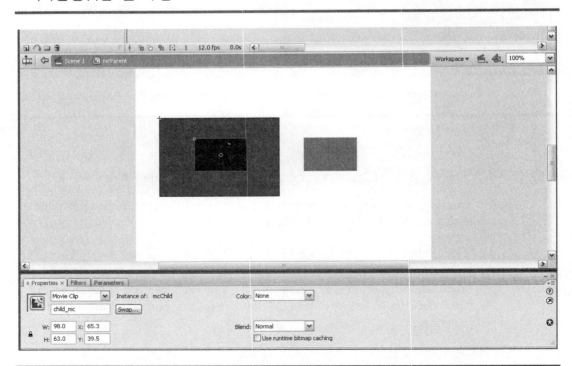

The child_mc instance inside the mcParent movie clip

ActionScript 2.0 Essentials

8. In the Actions panel, type the following code:

```
parent_mc.child_mc._x = 0;
```

9. Test the Movie. Notice the child_mc movie clip is on the left edge of its parent movie clip, parent_mc, as shown in Figure 2-14. This is because the X position of a child is relative to its parent.

10. Save the file, or keep it open for the next exercise.

Understanding Communication from Children to Parents

Using dot syntax, you can also communicate from a child to a parent. Each movie clip has a property that holds its parent movie clip, called _parent. If a movie clip with an instance name of child_mc were nested within another movie clip, you could change the X position of the parent movie clip using the following code:

```
child_mc._parent._x = 10;
```

FIGURE 2-14

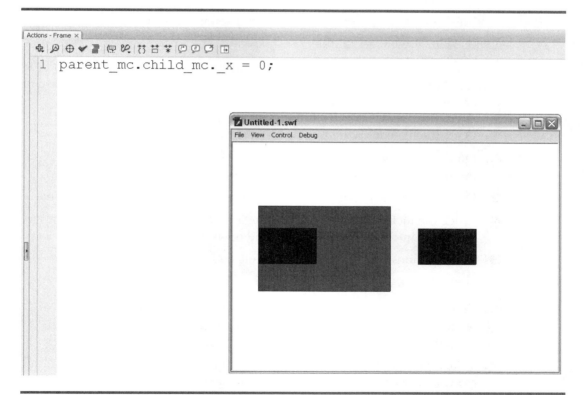

The child_mc movie clip's X position is zero, relative to its parent movie clip, parent_mc.

NOTE All children inside a parent movie clip will move along with the parent when the parent movie clip is moved. This is because the parent movie clip acts as a container, and when you move the container, everything within the container moves with it.

One advantage to using the _parent property is that you do not have to know the instance name of the parent movie clip. Another advantage that you will see throughout the rest of this book is using _parent will make the code you write more reusable.

TIP You can use _parent repeatedly to refer to grandparents and great-grandparents of a movie clip and so on. If there were a movie clip named child_mc, which was nested within a movie clip called parent_mc, which was nested within a movie clip called grandParent_mc, which was nested within a movie clip called greatGrandParent_mc, you could reference the great-grandparent movie clip from within parent_mc by typing child_mc._parent._parent._parent. Here, the first _parent refers to parent_mc, the second to grandParent_mc, and the third to greatGrandParent_mc.

EXERCISE 2-12: Communicating Between Children and Parents

In this exercise, you will get practice communicating from a child movie clip to its parent movie clip using the _parent property. You will also look at placing ActionScript inside of a movie clip's timeline.

1. Open the file you created in the last exercise.

2. On the Main Timeline, select the first keyframe of the actions layer, open the Actions panel, and delete the code you wrote.

3. Double-click the parent_mc movie clip on the Stage to enter its Timeline.

4. Inside the mcParent movie clip, create a new layer called **actions**. Select the first keyframe of the actions layer and open the Actions panel.

5. In the Actions panel, type the following code:

```
child_mc._parent._x = 0;
```

6. Test the movie. Notice the parent movie clip is moved to the left of the Stage, and the child_mc movie clip is still in its same location relative to the parent movie clip, as shown in Figure 2-15.

7. Take a minute to look over your code and make sure you understand how the code is working. Note that using the name _parent is a property of child_mc, and is different than the instance name of the parent movie clip

ActionScript 2.0 Essentials

FIGURE 2-15

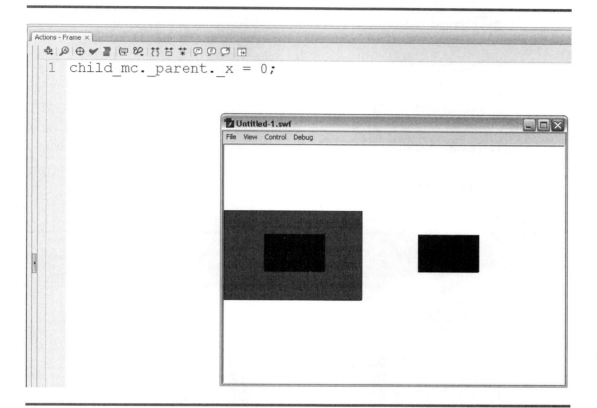

```
Actions - Frame ×
1   child_mc._parent._x = 0;
```

Positioning of the parent_mc movie clip after testing the movie

on the Main Timeline, which is parent_mc. Using the _parent property does not require you to know the name of the parent movie clip.

8. Save the file, or keep it open for the next exercise.

Understanding _root

The name _root refers to a very useful tool in ActionScript, because it represents the Main Timeline. In fact, _root, or the Main Timeline, is actually a movie clip that acts as a container for your entire Flash movie. Understanding that the Main Timeline is a movie clip will be of more use later on. If you place code inside of a movie clip, no matter how many other movie clips that movie clip is nested within, you can use _root to reference the Main Timeline. This is a very effective way to communicate from one movie clip to another.

EXERCISE 2-13: Communicating Using _root

In this exercise, you will get practice communicating between movie clips using _root.

1. Open the file you worked with in the last exercise.

2. In the Main Timeline (or Scene 1), select the unnamed instance of mcChild on the Stage and give it an instance name of **child2_mc** (as shown in Figure 2-16).

3. Double-click the movie clip parent_mc on the Stage to enter its Timeline.

4. Inside the mcParent movie clip, select the first keyframe of the actions layer and open the Actions panel.

FIGURE 2-16

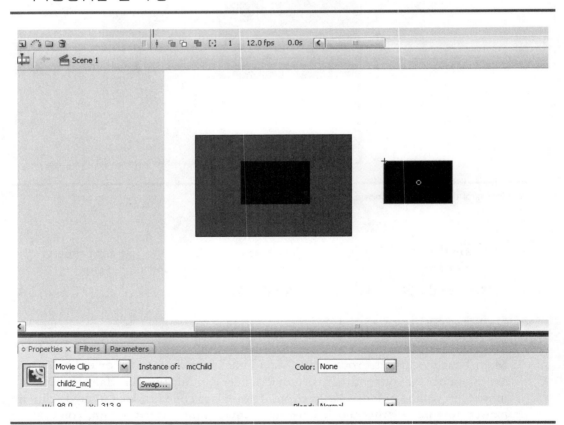

Naming the instance of mcChild on the Main Timeline

ActionScript 2.0 Essentials

5. In the Actions panel, delete all the code and replace it with the following code:

```
_root.child2_mc._x = 0;
```

6. Test the movie. Notice the position of the movie clip child2_mc is at the left edge of the Stage, as shown in Figure 2-17. Because _root references the Main Timeline, you can use this method to communicate to an object on the Main Timeline. You can even use this technique along with the other communication techniques you have learned up to this point to communicate to any object from any object, as long as the objects you are communicating through have instance names.

7. Save the file, or keep it open for the next exercise.

FIGURE 2-17

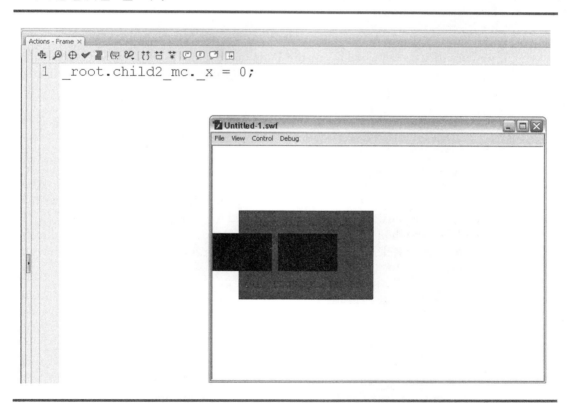

The movie clip child2_mc is at the left edge of the Stage.

Understanding the this Keyword

One of the most challenging concepts to grasp when using ActionScript is the meaning of the "this" keyword. The "this" keyword is relative; its meaning changes, depending on where it is in the code. It refers to the object where the this keyword resides. For example, on the Main Timeline, the this keyword represents the Main Timeline. Inside a movie clip, the this keyword represents that movie clip. If the this keyword is inside an event handler attached to a movie clip, the this keyword represents the movie clip to which the event handler is attached.

Using the this Keyword on the Main Timeline

If you use the this keyword on the Main Timeline, outside an event handler, "this" refers to the Main Timeline. For example, the following code, when the movie plays, would give you a value of _level0, which is the same as _root.

```
trace(this);
```

Using the this Keyword Inside a Movie Clip

If you use the this keyword inside the Timeline of a movie clip, this refers to each instance of that movie clip. For example, if you placed the following code inside a frame in a movie clip's Timeline, you would see _level0, a dot, and then the instance name of the movie clip.

```
trace(this);
```

Using the this Keyword in an Event Handler

There is one massive trap with understanding the this keyword. When you write an event handler, or any type of function attached to an object, the this keyword refers to the object on which the function is being created. For example, the code that follows shows an onRelease event handler for a movie clip called my_mc that traces the value of this.

```
my_mc.onRelease = function():Void
{
    trace(this);
}
```

Here, the value in the Output window will show the movie clip my_mc. This is because the code inside the curly braces is connected to my_mc. Remembering this will help you greatly in working with the this keyword.

EXERCISE 2-14: Using the this Keyword

In this exercise, you will get practice using the this keyword to communicate to different movie clips. You will also get practice using the this keyword in different contexts.

1. Open the Flash file you used in the last exercise.

2. On the Main Timeline, double-click parent_mc to enter its Timeline.

3. Select the first keyframe of the actions layer, open the Actions panel, and delete the code that you have previously written.

4. Type the following code in the Actions panel:

```
this._x = 0;
```

5. Test the movie. Notice the parent_mc movie clip's X position is at the left edge of the Stage, as shown in the following illustration. In this case, the this keyword represents parent_mc.

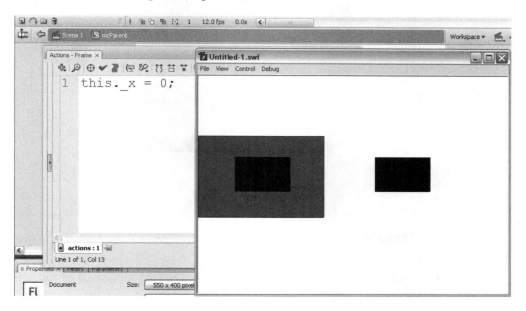

NOTE   The this keyword, when placed within a movie clip, represents each instance of that movie clip. If you were to place many instances of mcParent on the Main Timeline, each instance would have an X position of zero when the movie is played. Code within a movie clip affects all instances of that movie clip because it is a change made directly on a symbol via Symbol Editing mode, rather than to one particular instance.

6. Return to the Main Timeline by clicking Scene 1 in the Timeline.

7. On the Main Timeline, select the first keyframe of the actions layer and open the Actions panel.

8. In the Actions panel, type the following code:

```
this.child2_mc._y = 0;
```

9. Test the movie. You should then see the child2_mc movie clip at a Y position of zero, as shown next. This is because the this keyword, in this instance, refers to the Main Timeline, and the child2_mc movie clip is on the Main Timeline. This code would look the same if the this keyword were replaced by _root, because here, both represent the Main Timeline.

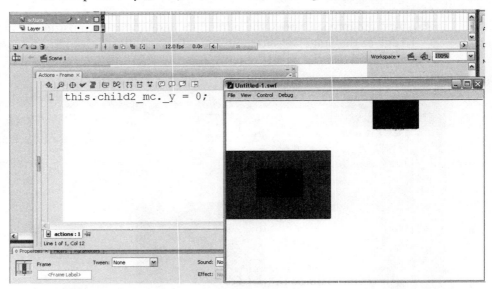

10. On the Stage of the Main Timeline, double-click the parent_mc movie clip to enter its Timeline.

11. Inside the Timeline of mcParent, select the first keyframe of the actions layer and open the Actions panel.

12. In the Actions panel, beneath the code you already wrote, create an onRelease event handler for the child_mc movie clip by typing the following code:

```
child_mc.onRelease = function():Void
{

}
```

13. Inside the curly braces of the event handler, type **this._y = 0;** . Your code should match the code shown:

```
child_mc.onRelease = function():Void
{
    this._y = 0;
}
```

14. Before you test the movie, predict what will happen. What does the this keyword mean here?

15. Test the movie. Click the child_mc movie clip inside the parent_mc movie clip. Notice that the child movie clip moves to a Y position of zero, as in the following illustration, showing that in the code you just wrote, the this keyword represents child_mc.

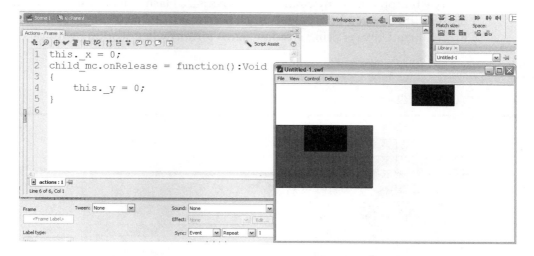

16. Examine all the code you wrote in this exercise. Notice that the this keyword represents three different objects. Make sure you understand which object the this keyword represents in each context and why.

17. Save the file, or keep it open for the next exercise.

Using the Insert Target Path Button

If the syntax to communicate to a particular movie clip ever seems confusing, you can use the Insert Target Path button in the Actions panel to have Flash write the path for you. The Insert Target Path button will give you the path to any object with an instance name in your Flash file. This is a very quick and effective way to communicate from one object to another, without requiring you to remember each object's instance name.

When you click the Insert Target Path button, you will see the Insert Target Path window (shown in Figure 2-18). In the Insert Target Path window, you will see all the objects in your Flash movie that you can communicate with via ActionScript. You can click the buttons to the left of instances that have nested movie clips to expand or collapse the view inside that movie clip. You can then navigate to the instance you wish to communicate with and click OK. Flash will then give you the path to the instance you want to communicate with.

If you use the Insert Target Path button and see objects in your Flash movie that are in greater than and less than signs, Flash is telling you those objects do not have instance names. If you try to create a path to any of those objects. Flash will prompt you to give instance names to them.

You can choose either the relative or absolute path to a movie clip by clicking the radio buttons at the bottom of the window. However, I recommend never using the relative button under any circumstances because Flash will not use the this keyword properly if you attempt to place a target path inside an event handler. For that reason I recommend always using absolute paths (_root) when working with this feature.

FIGURE 2-18

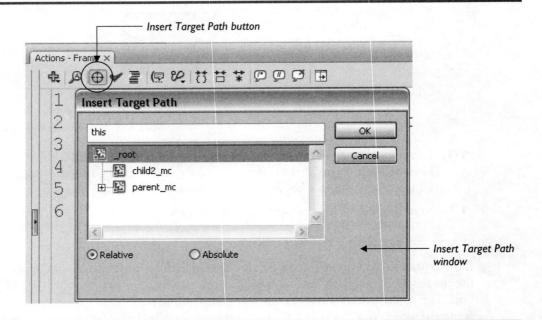

The Insert Target Path button and window

ActionScript 2.0 Essentials

EXERCISE 2-15: Using the Insert Target Path Button

In this exercise, you will get practice communicating between movie clips using the Insert Target Path button.

1. Open the file you worked with in the last exercise.

2. On the Main Timeline, select the first keyframe of the actions layer and open the Actions panel.

3. In the Actions panel, delete the code that is already there.

4. Click the Insert Target Path button to open the Insert Target Path window.

5. In the Insert Target Path window, expand the parent_mc movie clip by clicking the plus (+) button or the delta button to the left of it. Then, select child_mc. Choose the Absolute radio button, as shown here, and click OK.

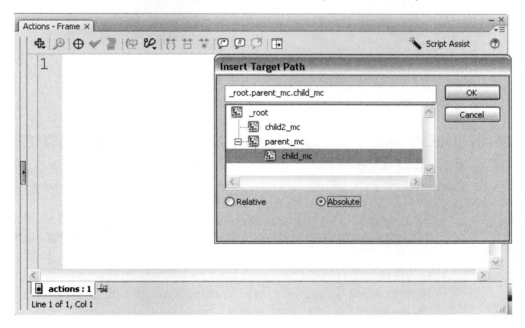

6. Notice that Flash writes out the entire path to child_mc for you, including _root.

NOTE — Here, you do not need _root because this code is already on the Main Timeline. Leaving it in the code is completely optional in this case, but if the code were inside a movie clip's Timeline, leaving _root would be necessary.

7. After the path Flash wrote for you, set the X position to 0. Your code should match the code shown:

```
_root.parent_mc.child_mc._x = 0;
```

8. Test the movie. Notice the X position of the child_mc movie clip is zero. Nice!

9. Close the file. You do not need to save your changes.

OTHER ACTIONSCRIPT 2.0 RESOURCES

Right now, you know enough ActionScript 2.0 to create simple Wii games. If you want to learn ActionScript 2.0 in greater detail, check out the following resources:

- ❯ **Kirupa.com** This site has loads of free Flash tutorials from basic design to advanced ActionScript. Here, you will also find tutorials in other software and programming languages.

- ❯ **Lynda.com** There are many hours of top-notch ActionScript training here. I highly recommend this site for learning ActionScript, and all kinds of other technologies. You can even watch a lot of content for free!

- ❯ **Actionscript.org** This site is an amazing resource for Flash developers. It's a massive forum where you can find the answer to just about any ActionScript question imaginable.

- ❯ **ChadandToddCast.com** This is my podcast, and here you can find loads of free ActionScript training. You can even send in your questions to be answered in video podcast form.

CHAPTER **3**

Creating Your First Wii Game

NOW

that you understand the basics of Flash and ActionScript, you are ready to start creating Wii games! In this chapter, you will learn how to create a template in Flash that you will use as a basis of all of the Wii games you will make throughout the rest of this book. You will also learn how to upload your game to a web server and play it on the Wii.

CREATING A WII GAME TEMPLATE IN FLASH

Because you will have the same settings in Flash for all the games you create, it makes sense to build a template so that you do not have to do the same steps repeatedly. There are a few steps to making a game in Flash that is playable on the Wii. First, you need to create the game using Flash Player 7, which you can set up in Publish Settings. You will also need to set a specific size so that the game will be full screen when you play it on a Wii. Once you have these settings specified in Flash, you can build your Wii game just as you would build any other Flash application. When your game is finished, all you have to do is upload it to a web server and you can play it on your Wii. Sweet!

EXERCISE 3-1: Setting Correct Publish Settings

In this exercise, you will begin creating your Wii game template by modifying some settings in the Publish Settings dialog box. You will also set the size of your Flash movie to be the appropriate size for Wii games.

1. Open Flash and create a new Flash file (ActionScript 2.0).

2. Choose File | Publish Settings to open the Publish Settings dialog box.

3. In the Publish Settings dialog box, click the Flash tab. For Version, select Flash Player 7, as shown in the following illustration. This step is the most important step in creating a Wii Flash game. Without this step, your game may not work on the Wii. This is because the Internet Channel only supports content made for Flash Player 7.

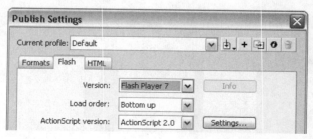

4. Click the HTML tab. Choose Percent for Dimensions, as shown here, to make the Flash movie scale to the full browser window size. Setting this option will make playing the game in a browser similar to playing it on a Wii, so you can test your game accurately before putting it on a web server.

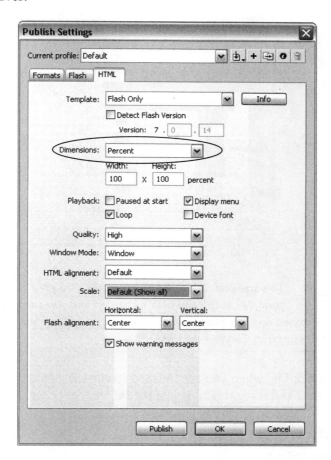

5. When you are finished, click OK to close the Publish Settings dialog box.

6. Make sure everything is deselected on the Stage, and click the Size button in the Property Inspector to launch the Document Properties dialog box.

7. In the Dimensions area of the Document Properties dialog box, shown next, enter **790 px** for the width and **610 px** for the height.

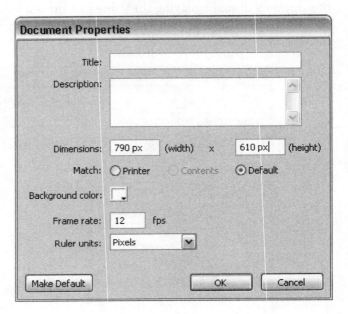

NOTE   This size could vary slightly, depending on your television. You will test it on your Wii at the end of this chapter, and you can adjust it as necessary. Also, this size is based on having the Internet Channel navigation menu hidden. You can hide the menu in the Internet Channel settings.

8. Click OK when you are finished to close the Document Properties dialog box, and leave this file open for the next exercise.

EXERCISE 3-2: Using Comments to Create an ActionScript Template

In this exercise, you will create an actions layer to store ActionScript to control your games, and use comments to set up organization for your ActionScript.

1. Make sure you are working with the same file from the last exercise.

2. Change the name of Layer 1 to **actions**.

3. Select the first keyframe of the actions layer and open the Actions panel.

4. In the Actions panel, type two forward slashes (//) to create a single-line comment. Notice the forward slashes turn gray, indicating that anything written on this line will not be processed as ActionScript. That way, you can write notes to yourself to keep your code organized. This will help a lot as your code becomes more complex.

5. After the slashes, type some minus signs (–) and type **IMPORT AND INCLUDE STATEMENTS**. After that, type some more minus signs to make this area an obvious section of code. The area below this comment will be used to import ActionScript classes, which I discuss later.

6. Go down two lines, and create a commented area called **DECLARE VARIABLES AND CREATE OBJECTS**.

7. Repeat Steps 5 and 6 to create commented areas for **DEFINE FUNCTIONS**, **DEFINE EVENT HANDLERS**, and **RUN IMMEDIATELY**. Your code should match the following illustration.

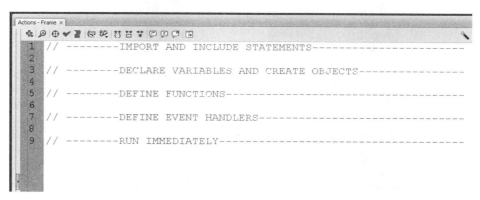

8. Keep this file open for the next exercise.

EXERCISE 3-3: Saving and Using the Template

In this exercise, you will save your file as a template and create a file from that template.

1. Make sure you are working with the file from the last exercise.

2. Choose File | Save As Template to open the Save As Template dialog box.

3. In the Save As Template dialog box, shown next, name your template **Basic Wii Game**. For Category, type **Wii Games**. For Description, type a description of your template.

4. When you are finished, press Save to save the file as a template. Next, you will create a file from that template.

5. Close the file. Don't worry about saving the file; it is already saved as a template in Flash.

6. Choose File | New to create a new Flash file. In the dialog box, choose the Templates tab to select a template. Choose the Wii Games category and select the Basic Wii Game template, as shown here.

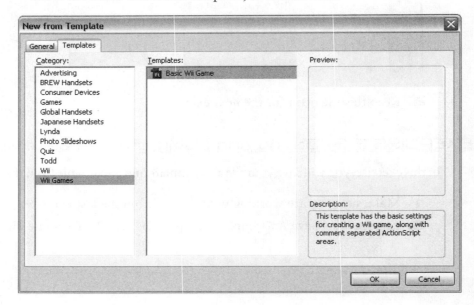

7. Click OK to create a new Flash file from the template. When the new file is created, notice the ActionScript in the actions layer, the size of the movie, and the publish settings are all the same as when you set them up. From now on, you can just create a new file from this template instead of changing those settings each time. Cool!

8. Close the file. You do not need to save your changes.

CREATING YOUR FIRST WII FLASH GAME

Now that you have a template set up, you are ready to create your first Wii Flash game! The first game you create will be a simple spotlight game, where you will use a spotlight to find a hidden object.

Before you write the ActionScript to create the game, you might want to preview the finished game. You can preview the finished game by opening first_final_commented.fla in the Chapter 3 exercise files folder. Once you have the file open, test the movie to preview the game. This is the way the game works: you have to use the spotlight to find and click on the face before the time runs out. You can click on the face after you win or lose to play again. In the .FLA file, notice that the first keyframe of the actions layer contains all the ActionScript for the game. The code is commented for you to see how it works.

Building a Game Plan

Whenever you decide to create a game, it is a good idea to chart out your plans by writing them down somewhere. If you don't do that, I recommend at least thinking about what exactly you want your game to do. Does the game involve racing against some sort of a timer? How will you win the game? How will you lose the game? This list shows the plan I will follow to create this game:

> Create and organize basic art elements.

> Add mouse and mask interactivity.

> Determine a win.

> Determine a lose using a timer.

> Randomize placement of the face.

> Upload the game to a web server.

The basic idea behind this plan is simple: first, get the game working, and then add the frills. Usually this is the best route, because it ensures you will not waste time creating artwork for a game that doesn't work properly. Having a good plan before you start will save loads of time in the long run.

Now that you have a game plan, you are ready to start creating the game.

EXERCISE 3-4: Examining the .FLA File

In this exercise, you will take a look at the artwork already created for you.

1. Open first.fla from the Chapter 3 exercise files folder. Save the file as first_{your name}. Notice there are three layers on the Main Timeline: actions, spotlight mask, and all.

2. Select the green circle on the spotlight mask layer. Notice it is an instance of mcMask, and its instance name is mask_mc. This movie clip will be used as a mask for the all layer.

3. Deselect the artwork on the Stage by clicking in the Pasteboard (the gray area off the Stage), and notice in the Property Inspector that the background color of this movie is black.

4. Select the white block on the Stage, and notice it is an instance of the mcAll movie clip and its instance name is all_mc.

5. Double-click all_mc to enter its Timeline. There are two elements on the Stage: an instance of mcFace called face_mc and an instance of mcBG called bg_mc.

6. In the mcAll movie clip, double-click face_mc to enter its Timeline. Notice there are four layers: actions, words, face, and shadow (see the following illustration). There are also three frames.

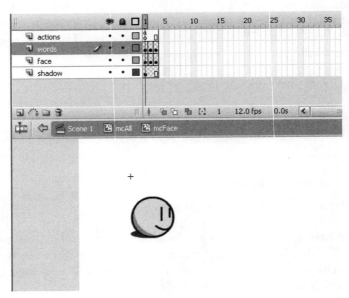

7. Select the actions layer and open the Actions panel. There is a stop action to stop the movie from playing.

8. Move the Playhead through the different frames to preview the art in each frame. Frame 1 is the face in its normal state, frame 2 is for a win, and frame 3 will show if you lose the game. Notice there is an invisible bubble on frame 1 of the words layer (you can select it by selecting frame 1 of the words layer). This is for random placement of the movie clip, which I will do later on.

9. Return to the Main Timeline, select the first keyframe of the actions layer, and open the Actions panel. The code is the same code you wrote when you created the template.

10. Save the file, and keep it open for the next exercise.

EXERCISE 3-5: Adding Mouse and Mask Interactivity

In this exercise, you will write the ActionScript to add mouse and mask interactivity to the game.

1. Make sure you are working in the file from the last exercise.

2. On the Main Timeline, select the first keyframe of the actions layer and open the Actions panel.

3. In the DEFINE FUNCTIONS section of the code, create a skeleton of a function called startGame. This is where you will add all the code to start a game. Your code should look similar to this snippet:

```
function startGame():Void
{

}
```

4. In the RUN IMMEDIATELY section of code, run the startGame function.

```
startGame();
```

5. Now you will define what the startGame function does. Inside of the curly braces where you defined the startGame function, type **mask_mc.startDrag(true);**. This will make the mouse drag the mask_mc movie clip. Your code should look like this:

```
function startGame():Void
{
    mask_mc.startDrag(true);
}
```

NOTE The startDrag method is a method of the MovieClip class that allows you to drag a movie clip. Passing in true as you did in the preceding code tells Flash to lock the registration point of the movie clip to the position of your mouse. If you pass in a value of false, the object that is being dragged is locked to your mouse at the location where the mouse was when you started dragging it.

6. Test the movie, as shown in the following illustration. Notice you are dragging the mask_mc movie clip, and that the registration point of the movie clip (which is in the center in this case) is locked to the mouse position. Close the preview window when you are done.

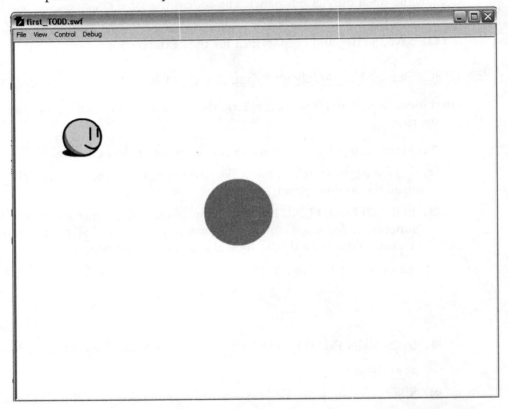

7. In the Actions panel, below the code you wrote in Step 5, write the code that will hide the mouse by typing **Mouse.hide();**.

```
function startGame():Void
{
    mask_mc.startDrag(true);
    Mouse.hide();
}
```

 Hiding the mouse cursor will not hide the mouse cursor on the Wii. It will work for testing in Flash and on web browsers installed on computers, though, so if anyone wants to play your game from a computer, they will not see the mouse.

8. Test the movie. Notice you no longer see the mouse cursor. Nice!

9. The last step is to set the mask_mc movie clip as a mask for the all_mc movie clip. You can do this in ActionScript by using the setMask method. The setMask method masks the movie clip that calls it using the mask passed in parentheses. Below the last code you wrote, type **all_mc.setMask(mask_mc);**. The completed code should match this snippet:

```
function startGame():Void
{
    mask_mc.startDrag(true);
    Mouse.hide();
    all_mc.setMask(mask_mc);
}
```

10. Test the movie. You should see the mask working as shown in the following illustration, so all you see of the all_mc movie clip is what is revealed by the mask_mc movie clip (its mask). Cool! Now you are ready to determine a win.

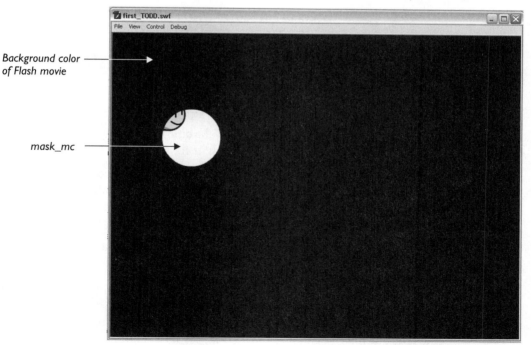

Background color of Flash movie

mask_mc

11. Save the file, and keep it open for the next exercise.

EXERCISE 3-6: Determining a Win

In this exercise, you will determine a win of the game when the face_mc movie clip is found and clicked. You will also add the interactivity to be able to play the game again.

1. Make sure the file you have been working with is open.

2. Select the first keyframe of the actions layer and open the Actions panel.

3. In the EVENT HANDLERS section, define an onRelease event handler for the face_mc movie clip. Remember that the face_mc movie clip is inside the all_mc movie clip. Your code should match this:

```
all_mc.face_mc.onRelease = function():Void
{

}
```

4. Inside the curly braces of the code you just wrote, make the face_mc movie clip go to and stop at its winning frame (frame 2) by typing **all_mc.face_mc.gotoAndStop(2);**.

```
all_mc.face_mc.onRelease = function():Void
{
    all_mc.face_mc.gotoAndStop(2);
}
```

TIP You could have used the this keyword here to refer to all_mc.face_mc, because this is an event handler for that movie clip. Here, I wrote out the full path because I am going to copy this code and paste it somewhere else later on.

5. Test the movie. Notice the "You Win!" bubble appears when you click the face, but the mask is still applied. You will fix that in the next step.

6. Below the last code you wrote, unmask the all_mc movie clip. You can do this by using the setMask method again and passing in null instead of a movie clip name. Type **all_mc.setMask(null);**.

```
all_mc.face_mc.onRelease = function():Void
{
    all_mc.face_mc.gotoAndStop(2);
    all_mc.setMask(null);
}
```

7. Test the movie, and click the face_mc movie clip. Notice that the mask is removed, but now you can see the mask_mc movie clip. You will fix this in the next step.

8. Hide the mask_mc movie clip by setting its _visible property to false. To do this, type **mask_mc._visible = false;** below the last code you wrote. Your code should match the code that follows:

```
all_mc.face_mc.onRelease = function():Void
{
    all_mc.face_mc.gotoAndStop(2);
    all_mc.setMask(null);
    mask_mc._visible = false;
}
```

9. If you tested the movie now, everything would work right, but you would lose the mouse cursor when you clicked the face_mc movie clip. To show the mouse again, use the show method of the Mouse class. Below the code you typed in the last step, type **Mouse.show();.**

```
all_mc.face_mc.onRelease = function():Void
{
    all_mc.face_mc.gotoAndStop(2);
    all_mc.setMask(null);
    mask_mc._visible = false;
    Mouse.show();
}
```

10. Test the movie, and click the face_mc movie clip. The mask disappears and hides, as shown in the following illustration, and the mouse shows. Great! The last thing you will add in this exercise is the ability to play the game again once you win. You'll do that in the next few steps.

11. The goal is that once the game is finished, you can click the face_mc movie clip to play again. To do this, you need to add some logic using conditional statements. The first step is to create a variable that will hold whether the game is finished. Go to the DECLARE VARIABLES AND CREATE OBJECTS section of your code and type this code:

```
var gameFinished:Boolean = false;
```

 Remember that Boolean is a true or false data type, and neither true nor false should have quote marks written around them.

12. Now, you will write the logic inside the face_mc event handler that tests to see if the game is finished. The game will be finished when the gameFinished variable has a value of true. Above all the code inside the face_mc.onRelease event handler, write a conditional statement that checks to see if gameFinished is true. Your code should look like this (new code is bold):

```
all_mc.face_mc.onRelease = function():Void
{
    if(gameFinished)
    {

    }
    all_mc.face_mc.gotoAndStop(2);
    all_mc.setMask(null);
    mask_mc._visible = false;
    Mouse.show();
}
```

13. Below the closed curly brace of the conditional statement, write an else statement, wrapping the four lines below it in curly braces.

```
all_mc.face_mc.onRelease = function():Void
{
    if(gameFinished)
    {

    }
    else
    {
        all_mc.face_mc.gotoAndStop(2);
        all_mc.setMask(null);
        mask_mc._visible = false;
        Mouse.show();
```

```
        }
    }
```

14. So far, you have only defined what will happen if the gameFinished variable is false, or in other words, when the if statement is not true. Before you do that, you will need to set gameFinished to true. You will do that within the else statement, above the previously written code.

```
all_mc.face_mc.onRelease = function():Void
{
    if(gameFinished)
    {

    }
    else
    {
        gameFinished = true;
        all_mc.face_mc.gotoAndStop(2);
        all_mc.setMask(null);
        mask_mc._visible = false;
        Mouse.show();
    }
}
```

15. If the game is finished and you click face_mc, you want to start a new game by using the startGame function. Run the startGame function inside the if statement.

```
all_mc.face_mc.onRelease = function():Void
{
    if(gameFinished)
    {
        startGame();

    }
    else
    {
        gameFinished = true;
        all_mc.face_mc.gotoAndStop(2);
        all_mc.setMask(null);
        mask_mc._visible = false;
        Mouse.show();
    }
}
```

16. Test the movie. Notice that when you click face_mc the second time, the winning message still displays. This is because the movie clip is still on frame 2. In addition, if you click the movie clip a third time, nothing happens. This is because you never changed gameFinished back to false. You will fix both of these problems in the next step.

17. In your code, find the DEFINE FUNCTIONS section. Inside the curly braces of the startGame function, set the gameFinished variable to false and make the face_mc movie clip go back to frame 1. The complete startGame function should look like this:

```
function startGame():Void
{
    gameFinished = false;
    all_mc.face_mc.gotoAndStop(1);
    mask_mc.startDrag(true);
    Mouse.hide();
    all_mc.setMask(mask_mc);
}
```

18. Test the movie, and click the face_mc movie clip multiple times to toggle winning the game and starting a new one. Sweet! True, the game isn't too challenging. You will fix this by creating a way to lose using a timer. After that, you will randomize the position of the face so that it is different each time.

19. Keep the file open for the next exercise.

EXERCISE 3-7: Determining a Lost Game

In this exercise, you will create a timer that counts down when the game starts. You will lose the game if the timer runs out before you find the face.

1. Make sure you are working in the file from the last exercise.

2. On the Main Timeline, select the first keyframe of the actions layer and open the Actions panel.

3. In the CREATE VARIABLES section of the code, below the gameFinished variable, create a new variable called timer, with an Object data type, equal to a new instance of the Object class. Your code should match this:

```
var timer:Object = new Object();
```

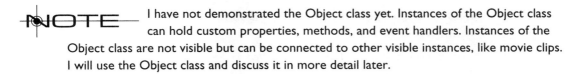

NOTE I have not demonstrated the Object class yet. Instances of the Object class can hold custom properties, methods, and event handlers. Instances of the Object class are not visible but can be connected to other visible instances, like movie clips. I will use the Object class and discuss it in more detail later.

4. Below that line of code, create a variable called seconds with a Number data type and a value of 5. This will represent the number of seconds before the timer runs out.

```
var seconds:Number = 5;
```

5. On the next line, create a variable called frameRate, with a Number data type and a value of 12. This represents the number of frames per second the movie is playing. Your timer will work by counting down one frame at a time, and you will use this variable with the number of seconds to calculate how many frames to count down.

```
var frameRate:Number = 12;
```

6. On the next line, create a variable called timeLeft, with a Number data type and a value of seconds multiplied by frameRate. This will give the number of frames left to count down.

```
var timeLeft:Number = seconds * frameRate;
```

7. Now that you have the variables created, you can define the function that will make the timer count down. In the EVENT HANDLERS section of code, below the all_mc.face_mc.onRelease event handler, create the skeleton of an event handler function called timer.countDown.

```
timer.countDown = function():Void
{

}
```

NOTE The term countDown is not a built-in event or function name in Flash. You are creating it with these lines of code. Here, you will define what happens for the timer to count down. Then, you will attach this event handler to the main timeline so that the timer will count down as the movie plays.

8. The first thing you want to happen for the timer to count down is to subtract 1 from the timeLeft variable. You can do this by using the mathematical operator, --. Your code should match the code shown next (new code in bold):

```
timer.countDown = function():Void
{
    timeLeft --;
}
```

9. When the timeLeft variable goes to or below zero, the time is out and the game is lost. In order to do something after the timer is out, create a conditional statement that checks to see if the timeLeft variable is less than or equal to zero.

```
timer.countDown = function():Void
{
    timeLeft --;
    if(timeLeft <= 0)
    {

    }
}
```

10. Inside the curly braces of the conditional statement, you will place code that tells Flash what happens when the game ends. You actually wrote this code in the last exercise. Remember what you wrote for when you win the game? This is exactly what you want to happen when you lose the game, except you want the face_mc movie clip to go to the losing frame. Copy the code from inside the curly braces of the else statement in the all_mc.face_mc.onRelease event handler by selecting it and choosing Edit | Copy. Paste the code in the conditional statement you just wrote by clicking in the appropriate area of code and choosing Edit | Paste. Then just have the face_mc movie clip go to and stop at frame 3 instead of frame 2.

```
timer.countDown = function():Void
{
    timeLeft --;
    if(timeLeft <= 0)
    {
        gameFinished = true
        all_mc.face_mc.gotoAndStop(3);
        all_mc.setMask(null);
        Mouse.show();
        mask_mc._visible = false;
    }
}
```

11. If you tested the movie right now, the timer wouldn't work. You need to attach it to something that runs over and over with the frame rate of the Flash movie. The name of the event is onEnterFrame, and you will attach the timer.countDown function to the onEnterFrame event of the main timeline, or _root. At the bottom of the code inside the startGame function, add this line of code:

```
_root.onEnterFrame = timer.countDown;
```

TIP — This code tells Flash that _root.onEnterFrame is the same as timer.countDown, which will make the timer.countDown event handler execute along with the frame rate of the Flash movie (12 times per second). Another way to write this is to set _root.onEnterFrame equal to a function, and to define the function then and there. Writing the code this way will make the code easier to optimize, because you will have more control to start and stop the onEnterFrame event.

12. Test the movie. Allow the time to run out, and then click the face_mc movie clip to restart the game. What the heck!? The movie seems to be freaking out! The problem is that you never reset the timeLeft variable, so once it goes to zero, it stays at zero. You will have to reset the timer. You'll do this in the next step.

13. On the line above the code you wrote in Step 11, reset the timeLeft variable to its initial value (seconds * frameRate).

```
timeLeft = seconds * frameRate;
```

 Though the timeLeft variable changes as the timer counts down, the seconds and frameRate variables stay the same.

14. Test the movie. You may notice that if you win and then let the time run out, the face tells you that you lost. This is because you need to stop the _root.onEnterFrame from running by deleting it when you win the game. To do this, add the code that follows to the end of the else statement inside the all_mc.face_mc.onRelease event handler. All the code should be blue if typed properly.

```
delete _root.onEnterFrame;
```

 This code stops the timer.countDown event handler from running, because its running is dependent on _root.onEnterFrame.

15. Test the movie. Allow the time to run out, and then click the face_mc movie clip to restart the game. It works! Congratulations, you made your first working game! Next step: randomizing the position of the face.

Using Math.random to Generate Random Numbers

The Math class is similar to the Mouse class in that you can access its properties and methods directly from the class without creating an instance of it. The random method is a method of the Math class that generates a random number between 0 and 1, but not including 1. The numbers generated are decimal numbers that can be multiplied with another number to produce random numbers in a particular range. For example, the code that follows generates a random number between 0 and 10, but not including 10:

```
Math.random() * 10;
```

The number you multiply Math.random by is the range of numbers you want. Here, the range is from 0 to 9, which is a range of ten numbers. If you wanted to have the same range of numbers but shift the values, you could add to the product of Math.random() * 10. For example, the code that follows would give you a random number between 1 and 10, instead of 0 to 9:

```
Math.random() * 10 + 1;
```

Here, the minimum number is no longer 0, it's 1. In addition, the maximum number is no longer 9, it's 10. Because multiplication takes place before addition in math (according to the order of operations), the range of values is shifted by 1. You can use this to create a formula. The formula for generating a random number is shown in this line of code:

```
Math.random() * range + minimumValue;
```

Now what if you wanted to create code that gave you a random number based on a minimum number and a maximum number? For example, say you wanted code that would generate a die roll, giving you a random number between 1 and 6. To find the range, you could subtract the minimum value from the maximum value. Then, add the minimum value to the product of Math.random() * range. The code that follows shows an example of this; it would give you a value of a number between 1 and 6:

```
var min:Number = 1;
var max:Number = 6;
var range:Number = max - min;
Math.random() * range + min;
```

Now that you understand the theory behind random numbers, you can apply this to generate a random position of the face_mc movie clip.

Understanding Random Placement of a Movie Clip

You know how to get random numbers within a certain range, but how do you determine the values in that range? What if you want to have at least 25 pixels of space between the movie clip and the edge of the Stage? Figure 3-1 shows the goal.

FIGURE 3-1

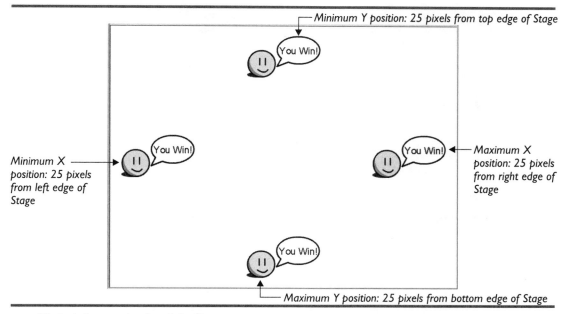

25 pixels from each edge of the Stage

Though you could place instances on the Stage and chart down the values you want, it is better to use ActionScript to do the calculations. That way, if the size of the movie clip or the Stage ever changes, you will not need to change your code.

Finding minimum values is fairly simple. If the movie clip has top-left registration, the minimum amount is the amount of space, or padding, you want the object to have between the edges of the Stage. To find the maximum amounts is a little more challenging, but not too crazy. The width and height of the Stage are held in the Stage.width and Stage.height properties, respectively. However, if you used these values for the maximum values, the movie clip might end up off the Stage. The maximum value you want for the X position is the Stage width, minus the width of the movie clip (held in the _width property), minus any padding. This is shown in Figure 3-2.

Using this same formula, you could calculate the Y position using Stage.height and the _height property. Now try putting this theory into practice.

FIGURE 3-2

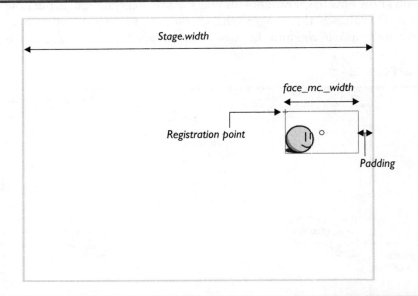

Maximum X position

EXERCISE 3-8: Randomizing the Position of the Face

In this exercise, you will randomize the position of the face each time you play the game.

1. Make sure you are working in the file from the last exercise.

2. On the Main Timeline, select the first keyframe of the actions layer and open the Actions panel.

3. In the DECLARE VARIABLES AND CREATE OBJECTS section, below the other variables, create a variable called padding, with a Number data type and a value of 25. This will represent the amount of space between the face_mc movie clip and the edge of the Stage. Your code should match this line of code:

```
var padding:Number = 25;
```

4. Next, create a variable called maxX, with a Number data type. This will represent the maximum X position of face_mc. The value is Stage.width – all_mc.face_mc._width – padding.

```
var maxX:Number = Stage.width - all_mc.face_mc._width - padding;
```

5. On the next line, create a variable called maxY with a Number data type. This will represent the maximum Y position of face_mc. The value of this variable should be the same as the last line, but with height in place of width in both places.

```
var maxY:Number = Stage.height - all_mc.face_mc._height - padding;
```

6. Next, you will define a function that will generate a number within a random range. Create a function called randomRange below the startGame function in the DEFINE FUNCTIONS section. The function will accept two parameters, min and max, both numbers. Note that multiple parameters are separated by commas. The function will also return a Number.

```
function randomRange(min:Number,max:Number):Number
{

}
```

7. Within this function, you will create a variable to represent the range. The variable will have a Number data type and a value of max minus min. Your code should match the code that follows (new code is bold):

```
function randomRange(min:Number,max:Number):Number
{
    var range:Number = max - min;
}
```

NOTE The max and min parameters will not have a value until you run this function, which you will do in a few more steps. Also, variables created within a function can only be used in that function, and nowhere else in your code. Why would you want to do that? For one thing, the range variable will only be used in this function. For another, the value of the range variable is dependent on the values passed in via the min and max parameters.

8. On the next line of code, create a variable called randomNumber with a Number data type. This variable will represent the random number generated when this function runs. The value will be Math.random() * range + min.

```
function randomRange(min:Number,max:Number):Number
{
    var range:Number = max - min;
    var randomNumber:Number = Math.random() * range + min;
}
```

9. The last thing you need to do is return the randomNumber variable using the return keyword.

```
function randomRange(min:Number,max:Number):Number
{
    var range:Number = max - min;
    var randomNumber:Number = Math.random() * range + min;
    return randomNumber;
}
```

TIP You learned about functions that return values in the last chapter.

10. Now, this function will give you a random number within the range you pass in via the min and max parameters. All you have left to do is to set the X and Y positions of the face_mc movie clip. To do this, inside the startGame function, at the top of the code in curly braces, set the _x property of face_mc to randomRange(padding,maxX) and the _y property to randomRange(padding,maxY).

```
function startGame():Void
{
    all_mc.face_mc._x = randomRange(padding,maxX);
    all_mc.face_mc._y = randomRange(padding,maxY);
    gameFinished = false;
    all_mc.face_mc.gotoAndStop(1);
    mask_mc.startDrag(true);
    Mouse.hide();
    all_mc.setMask(mask_mc);
    timeLeft = seconds * frameRate;
    _root.onEnterFrame = timer.countDown;
}
```

NOTE Because the randomRange function returns a number, the values of randomRange(padding,maxX) and randomRange(padding,maxY) are random numbers within the ranges passed in the parameters.

11. Test the movie, and try to find face_mc before the time runs out. Notice it is in a random position each time, but it never touches the edges. Nice! Congratulations, your first game is complete! Now you can upload it to a web server.

Uploading Your Game to a Web Server

In order to play your game on the Wii, it must be accessible via the Internet Channel. This means your game needs to be on the Internet for you to play it. If you do not have your own web site, you can easily get one for free. These two sites offer free web hosting:

❯ www.x10hosting.com

❯ www.zendurl.com

These are just a few of the sites that offer free web hosting. You can search for free web hosting online to find more resources.

Once you have a web site, make sure to save all of the information the provider gives you regarding putting files on your site. This information will likely be some sort of a site address, and/or a user name and a password. Keep it handy, because you will be using it soon.

When you have a web site to place files on, you can put your game online. There are a few different ways to do this. If you do not know how to upload files to a web server, the next section will explain how to do so using a method called FTP.

Uploading Your Game Online Using FTP

FTP (File Transfer Protocol) is a way to move files from your computer to another computer. Sending a file to another computer is also called uploading. In order to play your Wii Flash game, the files on your computer need to be uploaded to the computer hosting your web site. There are many different ways to send a file by FTP.

On the PC, you can use Internet Explorer to upload files using FTP. On a Mac, Fetch is a great FTP program. Both Mac and PC versions of Adobe Dreamweaver have built-in FTP capabilities.

One of the most convenient (not to mention free) ways to send files using FTP is by using a plug-in for your web browser. A decent FTP plug-in for Firefox is called FireFTP. You can download Firefox at www.mozilla.com and FireFTP at https://addons.mozilla.org/en-US/firefox/addon/684, or you can do a web search for FireFTP.

EXERCISE 3-9: Using FireFTP to Upload Your Game

In this exercise, you will put your game on your web site using FireFTP.

1. Open the game .FLA file you created in Flash.

2. Choose File | Publish to create the SWF, HTML, and JavaScript pages you will be uploading.

3. Open Firefox, and click the FireFTP button. If you do not see that button, Choose Tools | Add-ons, select FireFTP from the Add-ons menu, and click Enable to enable the FireFTP add-on.

4. In the FireFTP window, click the Manage Accounts button and choose New to open the Account Manager dialog box, shown at right. Here, you will type in the information to connect to your web site so that you can upload files.

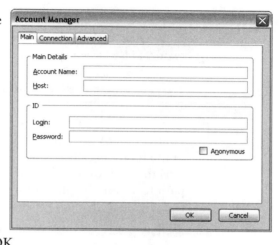

5. In the Account Manager dialog box, enter an account name and the FTP information you received from your web host (host, login, and password). When you are finished, click OK.

6. Select your account from the Account drop-down menu and click the Connect button; then enter your login and password information to create a connection.

7. On the left side of the screen, choose the folder that contains the files for your game. On the right side of the screen, choose the folder where you want to upload your files.

8. Drag and drop the game's SWF, HTML, and AC_RunActiveContent.js files into the window on the right side of the screen to upload the files. The files will appear on the right side of the screen when they have finished uploading, as shown in the following illustration.

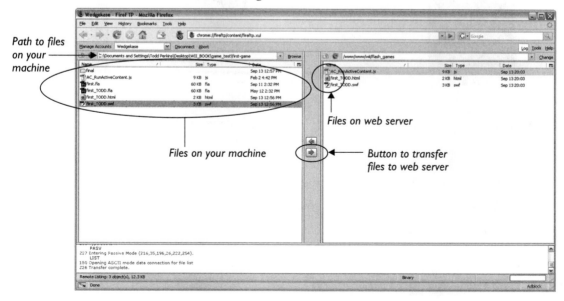

NOTE AC_RunActiveContent.js is a JavaScript file that Flash creates for you to help your Flash application run better in the Internet Explorer browser. If Flash didn't create that file for you, you can change your Publish Settings by choosing Flash Only from the Flash tab in the Publish Settings window. Once you update your Publish Settings, choose File | Publish and Flash will create the file for you.

9. That's it, now your game is ready to play on the Wii. You can test it on your computer by navigating to the HTML file in a web browser as shown in the following illustration. Notice the web address is my domain name plus the path to the file. The address in your browser should match the path to where the files are stored on your web site. All you have to do now is navigate to this page using the Internet Channel on a Wii.

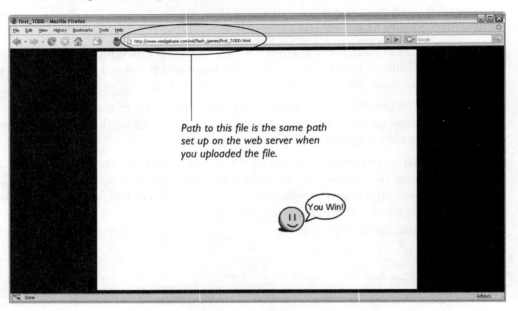

Path to this file is the same path set up on the web server when you uploaded the file.

EXERCISE 3-10: Playing Your Game on a Wii

In this exercise, you will use the Internet Channel to play your game on the Wii.

1. On your Wii, navigate to the Internet Channel from the Wii menu.

2. In the Internet Channel, browse to the location of your game.

3. Play your game.

4. Congratulations! You just played a game *you* created on your Wii. Now that you have made a simple game, read on to see more advanced features to make games with better interactivity.

CHAPTER 4

Creating Enemies:
A Meteor
Shooting Game

NOW that you have created a basic Wii Flash game, you are ready to create something a little more exciting and a little more complicated. In this chapter, you will build a meteor shooting game. Here, you will learn how to dynamically create enemies, pick up some advanced timeline navigation techniques, build a custom cursor, and create and use an energy bar. Get ready to have some fun!

PLANNING YOUR GAME

As usual, before you begin writing code to create your game, and even before you begin creating the graphics for your game, it is best to have a nice game plan. This is called beginning with the end in mind. Following that principle, let's briefly talk about what features your game will have.

> Custom mouse cursor

> Mouse/Wii remote click interactivity

> Meteors that move

> Meteors that explode when hit (clicked on)

> Energy bar that moves down when meteors get too close

> Losing the game if Energy runs out

> Ability to play the game multiple times

> Winning the game

If at any point you would like to preview the finished game, the name of the file is shooter_final.fla.

PREPARING YOUR GAME FLA FILE

Once you have a decent plan for your game, it's time to begin prepping your main .FLA file. What do you do to prep the file? There are a few different ways to do this. One method is to create an element, write the code for that particular element, then move to the next element, and so on until your game is complete. Another method is to develop all graphical content first, and then write all the code for all of the elements. Both ways are effective, but for this game you will use the first method. That way, you will have the element fresh in your mind when you write the code that controls that element. This is great when you are working with complex movie clips, which you will do somewhat for this game.

The first thing you'll do to prep your game is create a new file based on the template you created in the last chapter.

EXERCISE 4-1: Creating a File from the Basic Wii Game Template

Now you'll create a Flash file using the template you created.

1. Make sure Flash is open.

2. From the Welcome screen, in the Create From Template area, click the More button.

3. In the New From Template dialog box, shown here, choose Wii Games for the Category, select the Basic Wii Game template, and click OK.

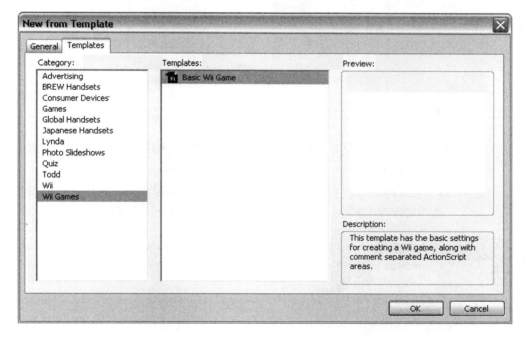

4. Make sure nothing is selected, and in the Property Inspector change the Background Color to Black.

5. Save the file as **shooter_{your name}.fla**.

6. Keep the file open for the next exercise.

EXERCISE 4-2: Creating the Background

Now, you'll create a sweet starry background for your game using movie clips.

1. Make sure you are working in the same file from the last exercise.

2. In the Timeline, create a new layer below the actions layer. Name the layer **BG**.

3. In the Toolbar, select the PolyStar tool.

4. In the Property Inspector, click the Options button.

5. In the Tool Settings dialog box, shown here, choose Star for the Style and click OK.

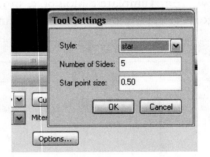

6. Choose a fill color for the star. I picked a medium gray (#999999).

7. In the BG layer, draw a small star on the Stage.

8. Select the star you just drew and convert it to a movie clip symbol by pressing the keyboard shortcut F8, or by choosing Modify | Convert To Symbol.

9. In the Convert To Symbol dialog box, choose Movie Clip for the Type, type **mcStar** in the Name field, choose top left for registration, and click OK.

 You do not necessarily need to create the exact same graphics as I do. Feel free to create different graphic elements or to change the graphics once the game is complete.

10. Drag some instances of the mcStar movie clip from the Library to the Stage to create a starry background, such as I've done in the following illustration.

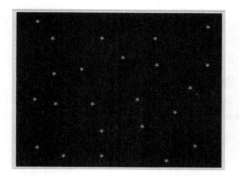

11. Save the file. You can leave it open for the next exercise.

EXERCISE 4-3: Designing a Custom Mouse Cursor

In this exercise you'll design a custom crosshair cursor for the mouse. If you are working in the shooter_start file, you will only need to write the code in this exercise.

1. Make sure you are working in the file from the last exercise.

2. Above the BG layer, create a new layer and name it **cursor**.

3. On the cursor layer, draw your custom cursor in the gray area off the Stage. You may want to zoom in close to do this. You also may want to give your custom cursor a black outline, as shown in my example, so that it's easier to see when you roll over objects.

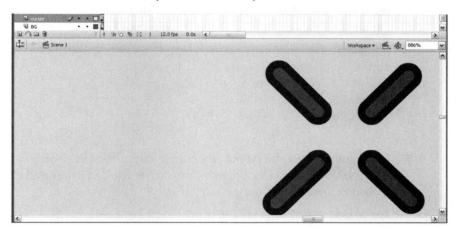

4. Select your cursor graphic on the Stage and convert it to a symbol by choosing Modify | Convert To Symbol or with the keyboard shortcut F8.

5. Name the symbol **mcCursor**, choose Movie Clip for its Type, and choose center for its registration.

6. On the Main Timeline, select the instance of mcCursor that you just created and in the Property Inspector, type **cursor_mc**.

7. Select the first keyframe of the actions layer and open the Actions panel by choosing Window | Actions.

8. In the Actions panel, in the DEFINE FUNCTIONS section, create the skeleton of a function called startGame. Your code should match this:

```
function startGame():Void
{

}
```

9. In the startGame function, write the code to hide the mouse.

```
function startGame():Void
{
    Mouse.hide();
}
```

10. Next, write the code to drag the cursor movie clip. For this, use the startDrag method and pass in a value of true. The startDrag method drags the movie clip that runs the method. In this case, the movie clip will be cursor_mc. Passing in true locks the registration point of a movie clip (which for mcCursor is the center) to the position of the mouse cursor.

```
function startGame():Void
{
    Mouse.hide();
    cursor_mc.startDrag(true);
}
```

11. Last, you will set the cursor_mc movie clip's _visible property to true. You will use this value later on when you write the code that makes it possible to win or lose the game.

```
function startGame():Void
{
    Mouse.hide();
    cursor_mc.startDrag(true);
    cursor_mc._visible = true;
}
```

12. In the RUN IMMEDIATELY section of your code, run the startGame function.

```
startGame();
```

13. Test the movie by choosing Control | Test Movie or by using the keyboard shortcut CTRL-ENTER (Windows) or COMMAND-RETURN (Mac). Move your mouse around in the Flash Player window and watch the cursor move. Nice!

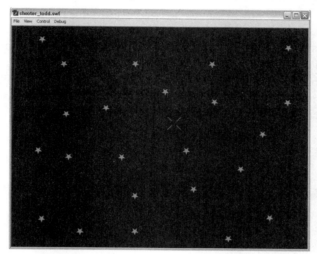

14. Save the file, and keep it open for the next exercise.

Understanding Frame Labels

In the next section, you will set up something called *frame labels*. If you are new to Flash, this concept might be unfamiliar to you. Creating a frame label essentially gives a particular frame a name. Frame labels have several important benefits. One of them is that they help you and other designers find elements in your .FLA files easier, because frames can have intuitive names that tell what is happening on the Stage. But the best part about using frame labels is that you can change the art and move the frames in your .FLA file without having to change your ActionScript code.

To create a frame label, all you need to do is select a keyframe and type the label name in the Property Inspector. It is a best practice to create a separate layer for frame labels and to place all frame labels in blank keyframes.

The following exercise will give you practice creating frame labels.

EXERCISE 4-4: Creating Enemies

In this exercise, you will create your meteor enemies. If you are working in shooter_start.fla, you can skip to the next exercise, or use this exercise to review the content inside the mcMeteor movie clip.

1. Make sure you are working in the file from the last exercise.

2. Choose Insert | New Symbol (not Modify | Convert To Symbol) to create a new blank symbol.

3. In the Create New Symbol dialog box, enter **mcMeteor** for the Name, choose Movie Clip for the Type, and click OK.

4. On the Stage inside of mcMeteor, draw a meteor roughly 100 pixels wide and 100 pixels high. If you want to have a black outline around your meteor, you may want to temporarily change the Background Color in the Property Inspector. If you do, make sure to change the Background Color back to black when you are done. It's okay if your meteor isn't as amazing as the meteor I came up with here, which seems to resemble a chocolate chip cookie.

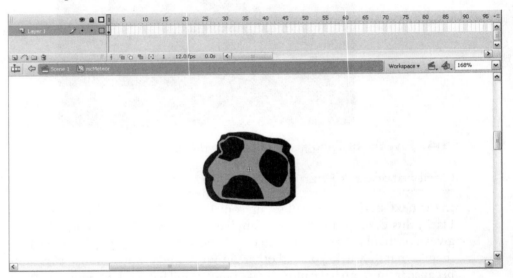

5. Still inside the mcMeteor movie clip, select the meteor and use the Align panel (Window | Align) to center the meteor to the middle of the Stage horizontally and vertically. The registration point should then be in the center of the meteor, as shown in the following illustration.

6. Next, you'll break the meteor up into four quarters and animate the meteor exploding. First, make sure your meteor is a basic shape. You can tell that your meteor is a basic shape when you select it. If your meteor has white dots on it when it's selected, it's a basic shape. If your meteor has rectangles around it, it's a grouped object. To convert a grouped object into a basic shape, select the object and press COMMAND (Mac) or CTRL (Windows) repeatedly until you see all the rectangles disappear. Once you have a basic shape, using the Lasso tool, select the upper-right quarter of the meteor on the Stage, as shown here.

7. Convert your selection to a movie clip by pressing F8 on your keyboard. Name the movie clip **mcPiece1**, choose top-left registration, and make sure to select Movie Clip for the Type.

8. Once you have created the movie clip, make sure it is selected on the Stage and choose Modify | Arrange | Lock to lock the mcPiece1 movie clip on the Stage.

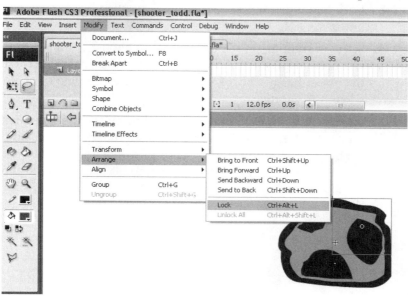

9. Repeat Steps 6–8 for the other three quarters of the meteor.

10. Unlock all the pieces of the meteor by choosing Modify | Arrange | Unlock All. When all the pieces are selected, you may notice that you can see lines that separate the pieces, as shown in the following illustration. This happens occasionally when creating objects in this way. Fortunately, there's a pretty simple work-around.

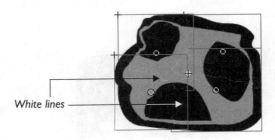

White lines

11. Change the name of Layer 1 to **BG**.

12. Select all the movie clips on the BG layer and copy them by choosing Edit | Copy.

13. Create a new layer and paste the movie clips in the same place in the new layer by choosing Edit | Paste In Place.

14. Lock and hide the top layer by clicking the Lock Layer and Hide Layer buttons.

15. Select everything on the BG layer, and choose Modify | Break Apart. This will change all of the movie clips back into editable vector art. You can tell the object has been broken apart, because you won't see blue rectangles when it is selected.

16. Next, you'll put each of the movie clips on the top layer in separate layers. Lock the BG layer, and select all the movie clips on the top layer. Right-click (Windows) or CTRL-click (Mac) your meteor and choose Distribute To Layers, as shown next, to place each movie clip in a separate, named layer. Cool! You can delete the extra empty, unnamed layer if there is one.

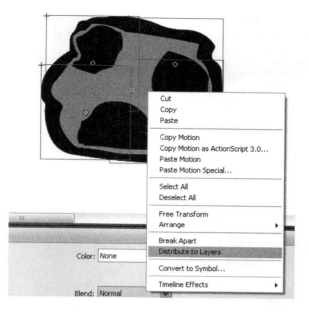

17. Now, you'll animate the meteor exploding. Select frame 10 of the mcPiece4 layer; then hold SHIFT on your keyboard and select frame 10 of the mcPiece1 layer to select four frames, as shown here.

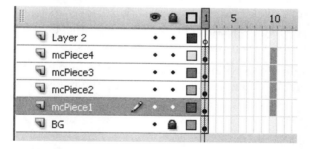

18. Press F6 on your keyboard or choose Insert | Timeline | Keyframe to convert the frames you selected to keyframes.

19. On frame 10, move all the meteor pieces away from the center. Select all the pieces by single-clicking (double-clicking will get you in Symbol Editing mode) and choose Alpha from the Color drop-down in the Property Inspector. Then, drag the Alpha Amount slider down to 0%.

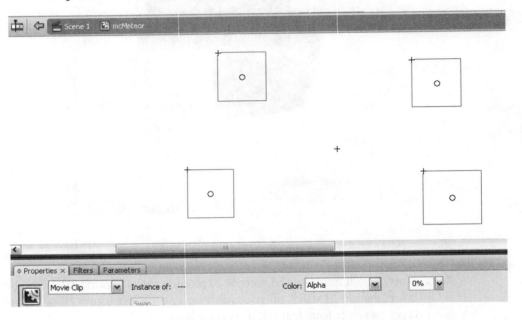

20. Next you'll create a motion tween. Select frame 5 of the mcPiece4 layer and SHIFT-click frame 5 of the mcPiece1 layer to select a range of frames. In the Property Inspector, choose Motion in the Tween drop-down to create motion tweens for all the meteor pieces.

21. In the Property Inspector, choose CW in the Rotate drop-down, shown here, to make the pieces spin when the meteor explodes.

22. Scrub the Playhead to preview the animation.

23. Change the name of the top layer to **labels**.

24. Select frame 2 of the labels layer and press F7 on your keyboard to create a blank keyframe.

25. With frame 2 of the labels layer selected, type **explode** in the Frame field in the Property Inspector, as shown in the following illustration.

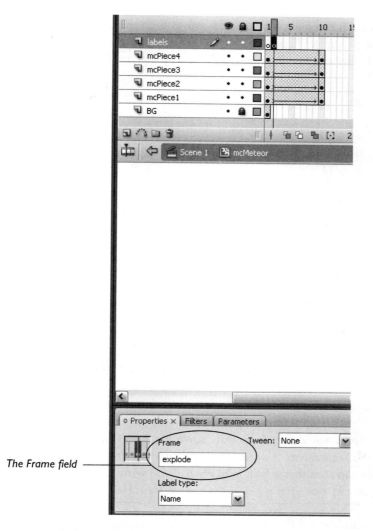

The Frame field

26. Extend the Timeline in the labels layer to frame 10 by selecting frame 10 and pressing F5 on your keyboard. This will make it easy to see the name of the frame label in this layer.

27. Above the labels layer, create a new layer called **actions**.

28. Select the first keyframe of the actions layer and open the Actions panel. In the Actions panel, write a stop action to stop the movie clip from playing. You will use ActionScript later on to play this movie clip whenever a meteor is clicked.

```
stop();
```

29. Once a meteor explodes, you want to unload that movie clip so that it won't slow down the Flash Player. To do this, create a blank keyframe on frame 10 of the actions layer, open the Actions panel, and type **this.unloadMovie();**.

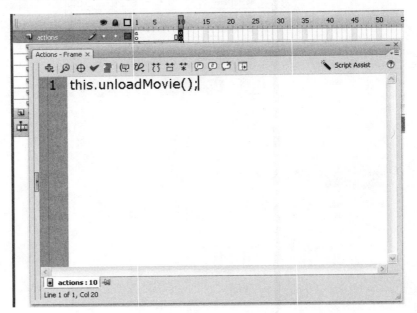

NOTE — The code this.unloadMovie(); unloads a movie clip, which makes that movie clip stop taking up space in the Flash movie. Having many objects animating (like the meteors will soon do) can slow down the Flash Player as well. In the code, the keyword "this" represents the meteor movie clip instance, and unloadMovie is a method of the movie clip class that is built in to Flash. If you want to learn more about movie clip methods, you can look up the movie clip class in Flash Help.

30. If you changed the Background Color, make sure to change it back to black. Then, return to the Main Timeline.

31. Save the file, and keep it open for the next exercise.

What Is attachMovie?

In the next exercise, you are going to use a method called attachMovie to create instances of a movie clip while the Flash movie is playing.

Before you can create an instance of a movie clip using attachMovie, you first need to export that movie clip for use with ActionScript. To do that, right-click (Windows) or CTRL-click (Mac) the movie clip in the Library and choose Linkage, then in the Linkage Properties dialog box (shown in the following illustration), check the Export For ActionScript box.

The attachMovie method accepts three parameters. The first parameter, by default, is the name of the movie clip in the Library. This is also known as the Identifier Name. If you change the Identifier value in the Linkage Properties dialog box, the Identifier Name is that value. If you do not change it, you can simply glance at your Library to get the identifier name, which makes life a lot easier. Trust me. Because this value is a String data type, you need to pass it in using quotes.

The second value is the instance name of the instance you are creating, which is also a string, so it also needs to be in quotes.

The third value is the depth of the movie clip. Depth refers to an object's stacking order, just like layers. Usually when you use attachMovie, you want the object you create to be in front of the other objects. You can do this using the getNextHighestDepth method, which returns the next highest available depth. The code that follows demonstrates the attachMovie method in action.

```
_root.attachMovie("mcMeteor", "meteor_mc", _root.getNextHighestDepth());
```

In this code, attachMovie is being called by _root, or the Main Timeline. This means the instance created using attachMovie will be placed inside the Main Timeline. The first parameter passed in is "mcMeteor", which represents the name of a symbol in the Library. The second parameter is "meteor_mc", which is the instance name of the movie clip being created. The last parameter, _root.getNextHighestDepth, gets the next highest available depth position from the Main Timeline (_root). When the attachMovie method runs, it returns a movie clip.

Another way to use attachMovie is as the value of a variable. This is demonstrated in the code that follows, where the value of the variable meteor is equal to _root.attachMovie(. . .).

```
var meteor:MovieClip;
meteor  = _root.attachMovie("mcMeteor", "meteor_mc",
          _root.getNextHighestDepth());
```

The attachMovie method also has an optional fourth parameter, which is something called the init object. The init object is actually a lot less complicated than it sounds. It is simply an object from which the movie clip created using attachMovie receives its default properties. For example, the following code demonstrates the init object (meteorInit) being connected to an instance of mcMeteor using the init object parameter.

```
var meteorInit:Object = new Object();
meteorInit._x = 50;
_root.attachMovie("mcMeteor", "meteor_mc",
                _root.getNextHighestDepth(),meteorInit);
```

When the meteor instance is created, it will automatically be placed at an X position of 50, because it is connected to the init object, meteorInit. This technique not only works with properties but also works with event handlers. The following code makes the traced statement—"explode!"—show up in the Output window when the meteor instance is clicked.

```
var meteorInit:Object = new Object();
meteorInit.onRelease = function():Void
{
    trace("explode!");
}
_root.attachMovie("mcMeteor", "meteor_mc",
                _root.getNextHighestDepth(),meteorInit);
```

Because the init object, meteorInit, is passed in the attachMovie method, meteor_mc.onRelease is the same as meteorInit.onRelease. This means that when you click the movie clip being created (meteor_mc in this case), which initiates the onRelease event, the meteorInit.onRelease event handler will execute because meteor_mc adopts all the event handler code from meteorInit. Both are equal to a function that traces "explode!"

Just as an attached movie adopts the built-in properties and event handlers of its init object, it also adopts custom properties and methods. For example, the following code connects a custom method, initializeMeteor, to the meteor instance created with attachMovie, and then runs that method (new code is bold).

```
var meteorInit:Object = new Object();
meteorInit.initializeMeteor = function():Void
{
    trace("initialize meteor");
}
```

Creating Enemies: A Meteor Shooting Game

```
_root.attachMovie("mcMeteor", "meteor_mc",
_root.getNextHighestDepth(),meteorInit);
meteor_mc.initializeMeteor();
```

EXERCISE 4-5: Using ActionScript to Generate Enemies

In this exercise you will use the attachMovie method to dynamically create and randomly place instances of the mcMeteor movie clip.

1. Make sure you are working in the file from the last exercise.

2. In the Library, right-click (Windows) or CTRL-click (Mac) the mcMeteor movie clip and choose Linkage. In the Linkage Properties dialog box, check the Export For ActionScript box and click OK. Remember that you don't need to type anything in this window for the identifier name, or else you will have to remember it later.

3. Above the BG layer, create a new layer called **container**. This layer will hold an empty movie clip that you will use to hold all the meteors in the game.

4. Choose Insert | New Symbol to create a new symbol. Name the symbol **mcContainer**, choose Movie Clip for the Type, and click OK.

5. Return to the Main Timeline, and in the container layer, drag an instance of mcContainer on the Stage. You won't see anything because this movie clip is empty. Before you deselect it, set its X and Y positions to 0 and give it an instance name of **container_mc**, as shown here.

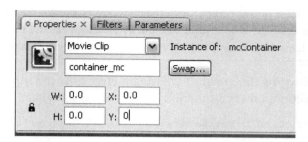

6. Select the first keyframe of the actions layer and open the Actions panel.

7. In the DECLARE VARIABLES AND CREATE OBJECTS section, create a variable called meteorInit with a data type of Object and set it equal to a new instance of the Object class.

```
var meteorInit:Object = new Object();
```

8. Below the code you wrote in the last step, create a custom method for meteorInit called initializeMeteor.

```
meteorInit.initializeMeteor = function():Void
{

}
```

9. Inside the initializeMeteor method, set the X position of this to be a random position between 0 and the width of the Stage. The new code is shown in bold.

```
meteorInit.initializeMeteor = function():Void
{
    this._x = Math.random()* Stage.width;
}
```

10. Below the code you wrote in the last step, set the Y position of this equal to a random number between 0 and the height of the Stage.

```
meteorInit.initializeMeteor = function():Void
{
    this._x = Math.random()* Stage.width;
    this._y = Math.random() * Stage.height;
}
```

NOTE The keyword "this," as used in Steps 9 and 10, will represent an instance of the mcMeteor movie clip. This is because the "this" keyword, in both instances, is inside the initializeMeteor method, which is attached to the meteorInit Object. Any time the this keyword is used inside a method or an event handler attached to an object, the this keyword refers to that object. Once the meteorInit Object is connected to an instance of mcMeteor using the attachMovie method, that instance can use the initializeMeteor method. When it does, the this keyword will then represent that instance of mcMeteor.

11. Now it's time to start creating meteors. At the top of the Define Functions section, create a function called createMeteors.

```
function createMeteors():Void
{

}
```

12. Inside the createMeteors function, create a variable that will represent the temporary instance name of the meteors created in the game. Call the variable meteor and give it a data type of Movie Clip.

```
function createMeteors():Void
{
    var meteor:MovieClip;
}
```

13. Below the code you wrote in the last step, set the meteor variable equal to a movie clip instance created by using container_mc.attachMovie. Remember the first parameter is the name of the movie clip in the Library (unless you changed the value in the Linkage Properties dialog box), the second is the instance name (here you can just use "meteor"), the third is the depth (the highest depth available inside container_mc), and the fourth is the init object (meteorInit).

```
function createMeteors():Void
{
    var meteor:MovieClip;
    meteor = container_mc.attachMovie("mcMeteor", "meteor",
container_mc.getNextHighestDepth(), meteorInit);
}
```

14. Next, use the meteor variable to run the initializeMeteor method.

```
function createMeteors():Void
{
    var meteor:MovieClip;
    meteor = container_mc.attachMovie("mcMeteor", "meteor",
container_mc.getNextHighestDepth(), meteorInit);
    meteor.initializeMeteor();
}
```

15. Scroll down a few lines to find the startGame function you defined earlier. At the bottom of the startGame function, run the createMeteors function. The startGame function should match the code that follows (new code in bold).

```
function startGame():Void
{
    Mouse.hide();
    cursor_mc.startDrag(true);
    cursor_mc._visible = true;
    createMeteors();
}
```

16. Test the movie a few times to see the meteor appear in a random position each time. Sweet!

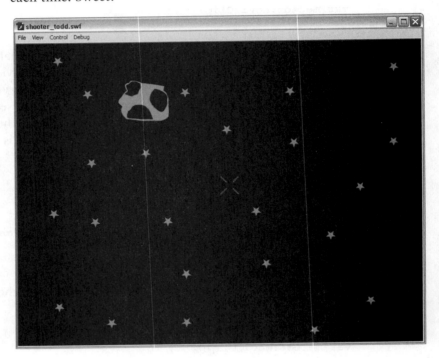

17. Save the file, and keep it open for the next exercise.

Understanding the setInterval Function

The setInterval function runs a function every certain number of milliseconds. You can use this function for animation, or just to run a function every once in a while for any reason. You will use setInterval to run the createMeteors function at random times.

The setInterval function receives three parameters. First comes the object attached to the interval function. If the function that will be running is defined on the Main Timeline, you can pass in _root. If the function that will be running is attached to a movie clip, you pass in the movie clip's instance name. The second parameter is the name of the interval function in the form of a String, so it is in quotes. The third parameter is the interval, or how many milliseconds will pass between each time that the interval function runs. The code that follows runs a function called "createMeteors" that is on the Main Timeline (_root) every second (or every 1000 milliseconds).

```
setInterval(_root, "createMeteors", 1000);
```

If you want the setInterval function to stop running at a certain point, you can use the clearInterval function. In order to use the clearInterval function, the setInterval function must be assigned to a variable with a Number data type. That variable then needs to be passed into the clearInterval function in order to stop the setInterval function. The following code demonstrates the setInterval function being assigned to a variable called meteorInterval. The interval is then cleared immediately using the clearInterval function.

```
var meteorInterval:Number;
meteorInterval = setInterval(_root, "createMeteors", 1000);
clearInterval(meteorInterval);
```

If you want to make the interval rate change each time setInterval runs the interval function, you can clear the interval inside that function and give the interval a new value. This is demonstrated in the following code.

```
var meteorInterval:Number;

function createMeteors():Void
{
    var randomInterval:Number = Math.random() * 1000;
    clearInterval(meteorInterval);
    meteorInterval = setInterval(_root, "createMeteors", randomInterval);
}

meteorInterval = setInterval(_root, "createMeteors", 1000);
```

In this code, the createMeteors function will run after 1000 milliseconds (or once every second). When the createMeteors function runs, the interval is cleared and reset with a new random time between 0 and 1000 milliseconds, which is held in the randomInterval variable.

In the following exercise, you will apply all of these concepts by using the setInterval function to create meteors at random intervals.

EXERCISE 4-6: Using the setInterval Function to Generate Enemies

Now you'll get some practice using the setInterval function to create some enemies.

1. Make sure you are working in the same file from the last exercise.

2. Select the first keyframe of the actions layer (in Scene 1, or the Main Timeline) and open the Actions panel by choosing Window | Actions.

3. In the Actions panel, at the top of the DECLARE VARIABLES AND
CREATE OBJECTS section, create a new variable called meteorInterval
with a data type of Number. You will use this variable to hold the interval
you create using setInterval.

```
var meteorInterval:Number;
```

4. Now you'll use the setInterval function to start creating meteors. At the
bottom of the startGame function, delete the line of code that runs the
createMeteors function. Replace it with code that sets the meteorInterval
variable equal to a setInterval function that runs the createMeteors function
every second (or 1000 milliseconds).

```
function startGame():Void
{
    Mouse.hide();
    cursor_mc.startDrag(true);
    cursor_mc._visible = true;
    meteorInterval = setInterval(_root, "createMeteors", 1000);
}
```

5. Test the movie. Notice the meteors being created every second. Cool!

6. The next step is to randomize the interval each time the createMeteors
function runs. At the bottom of the createMeteors function, use the
clearInterval function to clear the meteorInterval variable.

```
function createMeteors():Void
{
    var meteor:MovieClip;
    meteor = container_mc.attachMovie("mcMeteor", "meteor",
container_mc.getNextHighestDepth(), meteorInit);
    meteor.initializeMeteor();
    clearInterval(meteorInterval);
}
```

7. On the next line of code, give a new value to the meteorInterval variable.
The value should be the same as in Step 4, but with a random number
between 100 and 1000 in place of 1000.

```
function createMeteors():Void
{
    var meteor:MovieClip;
    meteor = container_mc.attachMovie("mcMeteor", "meteor",
            container_mc.getNextHighestDepth(), meteorInit);
    meteor.initializeMeteor();
    clearInterval(meteorInterval);
```

```
meteorInterval = setInterval(_root, "createMeteors",
               Math.random() * 900 + 100);
}
```

8. Test the movie. Notice that the meteors appear at random times. Sweet! Feel free to change the random range you created in the last step.

9. Now, you'll set each meteor to be a random size. At the top of the meteorInit.initializeMeteor method, set the _xscale property of this equal to a random number between 50 and 100, and set the _yscale property of this equal to its _xscale property.

```
meteorInit.initializeMeteor = function():Void
{
    this._xscale = Math.random() * 50 + 50;
    this._yscale = this._xscale;
    this._x = Math.random()* Stage.width;
    this._y = Math.random()* Stage.height;
}
```

10. Test the movie. Notice the random sizes of the meteors. If you like, you can adjust the code you wrote in the last step to produce different random sizes, as shown here.

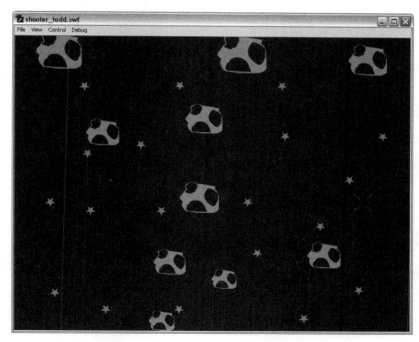

11. Save the file, and keep it open for the next exercise.

EXERCISE 4-7: Moving Enemies

In this exercise, you will make the enemy meteors appear to move closer by scaling them up.

1. Make sure you are working in the same file from the last exercise.

2. Select the first keyframe of the actions layer on the Main Timeline and open the Actions panel.

3. Below the meteorInit.initializeMeteor method, create the skeleton of an event handler for meteorInit.onEnterFrame. Code in this block will be adopted by each meteor instance and will animate the meteor's movement.

```
meteorInit.onEnterFrame = function():Void
{

}
```

4. Inside the event handler you just defined, add 1 to the _xscale property of this, and set its _yscale property equal to its _xscale property.

```
meteorInit.onEnterFrame = function():Void
{
    this._xscale ++;
    this._yscale = this._xscale;
}
```

5. Test the movie, and watch the meteors grow. Nice! Next, you will give each meteor a unique, random growth rate.

6. At the top of the meteorInit.initializeMeteor method, create a new property of this called growthRate. Set the value equal to a random number between 0 and 3.

```
meteorInit.initializeMeteor = function():Void
{
    this.growthRate = Math.random() * 3;
    this._xscale = Math.random() * 50 + 50;
    this._yscale = this._xscale;
    this._x = Math.random()* Stage.width;
    this._y = Math.random()* Stage.height;
}
```

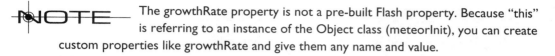

NOTE The growthRate property is not a pre-built Flash property. Because "this" is referring to an instance of the Object class (meteorInit), you can create custom properties like growthRate and give them any name and value.

7. Now, you'll have the meteors grow by their individual growthRate property values instead of 1 each frame. Return to the meteorInit.onEnterFrame event handler. At the top of the code, modify the first line to make the _xscale property increase by the meteor's growth rate instead of 1 each frame.

```
meteorInit.onEnterFrame = function():Void
{
    this._xscale += this.growthRate;
    this._yscale = this._xscale;
}
```

8. Test the movie. Watch each meteor grow at a random speed. You can modify the code you wrote in Step 6 to change the range of random numbers for the growth rate.

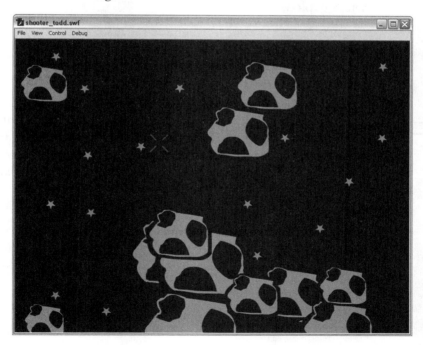

9. Save the file, and keep it open for the next exercise.

EXERCISE 4-8: Destroying Enemies

In this exercise, you will write the code that will make the enemy meteors explode when you click on them.

1. Make sure you are working in the same file from the last exercise.

2. Select the first keyframe of the actions layer and open the Actions panel.

3. At the bottom of the DECLARE VARIABLES AND CREATE OBJECTS section of code, create the skeleton of an onRelease event handler for the meteorInit object.

```
meteorInit.onRelease = function():Void
{

}
```

4. Inside the event handler you just created, type the code that makes the meteor explode when you click it.

```
meteorInit.onRelease = function():Void
{
    this.gotoAndPlay("explode");
}
```

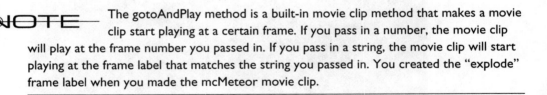

NOTE The gotoAndPlay method is a built-in movie clip method that makes a movie clip start playing at a certain frame. If you pass in a number, the movie clip will play at the frame number you passed in. If you pass in a string, the movie clip will start playing at the frame label that matches the string you passed in. You created the "explode" frame label when you made the mcMeteor movie clip.

5. Test the movie, and click some meteors to watch them explode. Notice that the meteors seem to explode and then reappear. They end up filling the whole screen and ruining the game, as shown in the following screen. What's wrong?

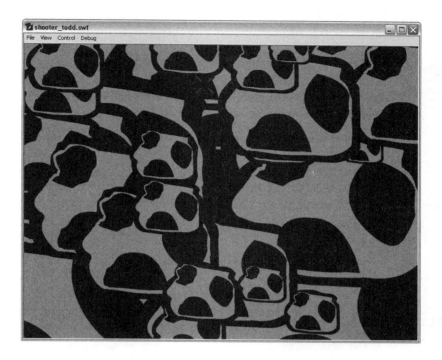

The meteors are not disappearing because they are not unloading. Though you used the unloadMovie method when you created the meteors to make the meteors unload, the code is not working. The problem is that the meteors all have the same instance name, "meteor", as defined in the createMeteor function. Unless movie clips have unique instance names, unexpected problems like this can occur.

6. To solve this problem, you need to create unique instance names for each meteor. Start by creating a variable to hold a number, which you'll add on to the end of each meteor's instance name later. At the top of the DECLARE VARIABLES AND CREATE OBJECTS section of your code, create a variable called meteorNum. Give it a data type of Number and an initial value of 0.

```
var meteorNum:Number = 0;
```

7. Next, you'll add the meteorNum variable at the end of the instance names of the meteors. In the createMeteors function, find the area of code where you set the instance name of the meteors in the line of code where you used attachMovie. After "meteor" and before the comma, use concatenation to add meteorNum onto the end of the instance name string.

```
function createMeteors():Void
{
    var meteor:MovieClip;
    meteor = container_mc.attachMovie("mcMeteor", "meteor" + meteorNum,
            container_mc.getNextHighestDepth(), meteorInit);
    meteor.initializeMeteor();
    clearInterval(meteorInterval);
    meteorInterval = setInterval(_root, "createMeteors",
            Math.random() * 900 + 100);
}
```

> **NOTE** Concatenation refers to connecting strings together. Unlike what the plus operator (+) does in math, with strings the plus operator concatenates values. In this example, the first meteor created will be named "meteor0".

8. Next, you'll simply have to add to the meteorNum variable each time this function runs. At the bottom of the createMeteors function, increment the value of meteorNum by 1.

```
function createMeteors():Void
{
    var meteor:MovieClip;
    meteor = container_mc.attachMovie("mcMeteor", "meteor" + meteorNum,
container_mc.getNextHighestDepth(), meteorInit);
    meteor.initializeMeteor();
    clearInterval(meteorInterval);
    meteorInterval = setInterval(_root, "createMeteors",
            Math.random() * 900 + 100);
    meteorNum ++;
}
```

9. Now, each meteor will have a unique instance name. The first meteor created will be "meteor0". Then, because the meteorNum value increments by one, the next time a meteor is created it will be "meteor1", then "meteor2" . . . you get the point. Test the movie and click on some meteors to watch them explode. Cool!

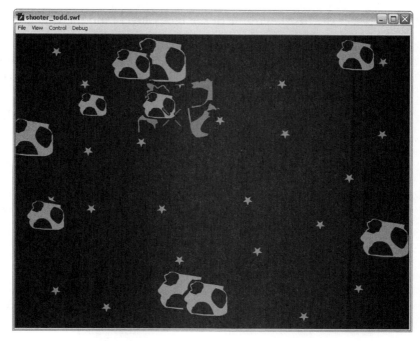

10. Save the file, and keep it open for the next exercise.

EXERCISE 4-9: Creating the Energy Movie Clips

Now you'll begin creating the movie clips that will display the player's energy.

1. Make sure you are working with the file from the last exercise.

2. Choose Insert | New Symbol to create a new, blank symbol.

3. Name the symbol **mcEnergy**, choose Movie Clip for the Type, and click OK.

4. Inside the mcEnergy movie clip, create two new layers named **bar** and **block**. From top to bottom, the layers should be named actions, bar, and block.

5. Select the first keyframe of the actions layer and open the Actions panel. In the Actions panel, write a stop action to stop the movie clip from playing.

```
stop();
```

6. Lock the actions and bar layers.

7. In the block layer, draw a white rectangle with the following properties: 790 pixels wide, 610 pixels high, X position 0, Y position 0. One way to do this is to draw a rectangle of any size, and set all of the properties in the Property Inspector. This rectangle will be used to make the screen flash when the player gets hit by a meteor, or when a meteor scales past a certain point.

8. Select the first keyframe of the block layer, and then click it again and drag to move the keyframe to frame 2.

9. Now, you'll create a simple shape tween animation of the block fading out. Select frame 5 of the block layer and press F6 on your keyboard to create a keyframe.

10. On frame 5, select the block on the Stage. In the Color panel, drag the block's Alpha property down to 0, as shown here.

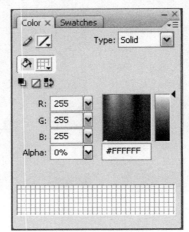

11. To create the shape tween for the block, click in the Timeline between frame 1 and frame 5 of the block layer. Then, in the Property Inspector, set the Tween drop-down menu to Shape. Scrub the Playhead (click and drag the vertical red bar at the top of the Timeline) to preview the shape tween.

12. Extend the Timeline of the bar layer to frame 5 by selecting frame 5 in the bar layer and pressing F5 on your keyboard.

13. On frame 1 of the bar layer, use the Text tool to create a Static text field and type **Energy**. Use a light color (with 100% alpha) for the font and place the text at an X position of 20 and a Y position of 525. I chose 48 pixels for my font size because fonts are generally a little more difficult to read on the Wii.

14. To the right of the text field you just created, create a background for your energy bar. I chose to create a black rectangle with a white stroke.

15. Next, create the energy bar by creating a rectangle roughly the same size as the one you just created with a different fill color than the background and no stroke. Select the energy bar and press F8 on your keyboard to convert it to a movie clip. Name the movie clip **mcBar**, make sure to select Movie Clip for the Type, choose top-left registration, and click OK.

16. Select the instance of mcBar on the Stage and type **bar_mc** in the Instance Name field in the Property Inspector. Then, place the bar_mc movie clip over the energy bar background you created in Step 14, as shown here.

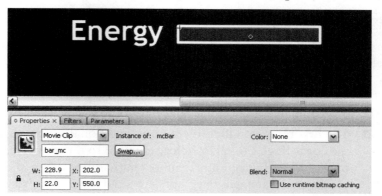

17. Return to the Main Timeline, and create a new layer above the container layer. Name the new layer **energy**.

18. In the energy layer, drag an instance of mcEnergy to the Stage. Place the movie clip at X and Y positions of 0 and name the instance **energy_mc**.

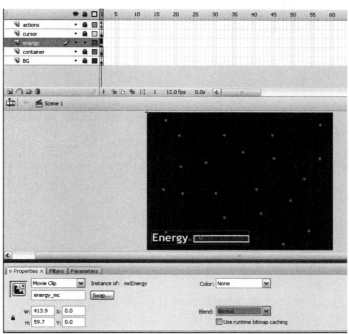

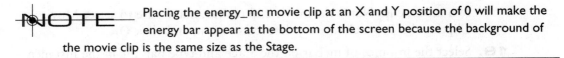

NOTE Placing the energy_mc movie clip at an X and Y position of 0 will make the energy bar appear at the bottom of the screen because the background of the movie clip is the same size as the Stage.

19. Save the file, and keep it open for the next exercise.

EXERCISE 4-10: Losing Energy

In this exercise, I'll show you how to make the energy bar go down when the player gets hit by a meteor.

1. Make sure you are working in the same file from the last exercise.

2. Select the first keyframe of the actions layer and open the Actions panel.

3. The first thing you'll do is create a conditional statement to check if the meteor is large enough (or close enough) to hit the player. At the bottom of the meteorInit.onEnterFrame event handler, create the skeleton of a conditional statement that checks to see if the meteor has reached an _xscale value of 150 or greater.

```
meteorInit.onEnterFrame = function():Void
{
    this._xscale += this.growthRate;
    this._yscale = this._xscale;

    if(this._xscale >= 150)
    {

    }
}
```

TIP You can adjust this amount if you prefer the meteor to be smaller or larger when it damages the player.

4. The first thing to do is move the meteor back a little. Inside the conditional statement you just created, decrease the _xscale and _yscale properties of the meteor by 50.

```
meteorInit.onEnterFrame = function():Void
{
    this._xscale += this.growthRate;
    this._yscale = this._xscale;

    if(this._xscale >= 150)
    {
        this._xscale -= 50;
```

```
        this._yscale -= 50;
    }
}
```

You can adjust this amount if you would like to have the meteors scale back to a different size.

5. Test the movie, and watch the meteors fly back when they get too big. Awesome!

6. Next, make the energy_mc movie clip play to indicate that the player has been damaged.

```
meteorInit.onEnterFrame = function():Void
{
    this._xscale += this.growthRate;
    this._yscale = this._xscale;

    if(this._xscale >= 150)
    {
        this._xscale -= 50;
        this._yscale -= 50;
        energy_mc.play();
    }
}
```

7. Test the movie, and watch the screen flash when the meteors get too close. Cool!

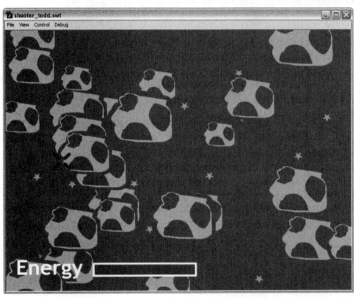

8. Last, make the energy bar go down when the player gets hit. Below the code you wrote in the last step, subtract 10 from the energy bar's _xscale property. Remember that the bar's instance name is bar_mc, and it is inside of energy_mc.

```
meteorInit.onEnterFrame = function():Void
{
    this._xscale += this.growthRate;
    this._yscale = this._xscale;

    if(this._xscale >= 150)
    {
        this._xscale -= 50;
        this._yscale -= 50;
        energy_mc.play();
        energy_mc.bar_mc._xscale -= 10;
    }
}
}
```

NOTE Because the bar movie clip has top-left registration, the left edge of the movie clip will stay in the same place when the movie clip scales down. Therefore, decreasing the _xscale property of the energy bar will give the effect that the energy is draining. If you want the meteors to drain more or less energy when they hit, you can increase or decrease the scale amount. Essentially, that number represents the percentage of energy taken away when the player gets hit.

9. Test the movie. Notice that the energy bar goes down as the meteors hit the player, as shown in the following illustration. Nice! Also notice that the bar scales backward after the energy is all the way down. Not so nice! You'll fix that in the next exercise when I cover losing the game.

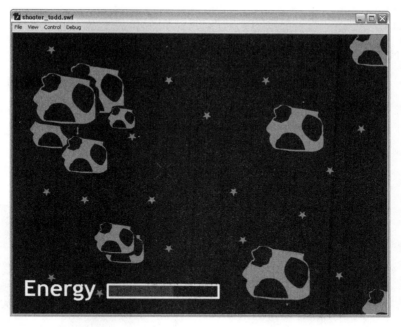

10. Save the file, and keep it open for the next exercise.

EXERCISE 4-11: Losing the Game

In this exercise, you will write the code that checks if the game has been lost.

1. Make sure you are working in the same file from the last exercise.

2. In the Timeline, select the cursor layer and click the Insert button to create a new layer. Name the new layer **end**.

3. On the end layer, draw a black rectangle with no stroke.

4. Select the rectangle, and in the Property Inspector, set the rectangle's X and Y positions to 0, and set the width and height of the rectangle to match the stage.

TIP You can also set the position and size of the rectangle in the Align panel. To do this, make sure to have the To Stage option selected in the Align panel, and then click the Match Width, Match Height, Align Left, and Align Top buttons.

5. In the Toolbar, select the Text tool. You can also use the keyboard shortcut, T.

6. On the end layer, click and drag to draw a text field on the Stage.

7. In the Property Inspector, set the type of the text field to be Dynamic Text, give the text field an instance name of **end_txt**, select white for the font color, and set the text field to be multiline. See the following illustration for a reference.

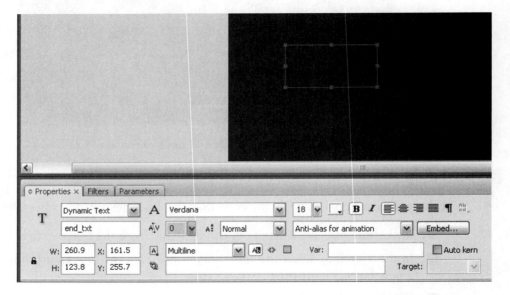

8. With the rectangle and the text field selected, press F8 on your keyboard to convert the rectangle to a symbol.

9. In the Convert To Symbol dialog box, select Movie Clip for the Type, type **mcEnd** for the Symbol Name, and choose top-left registration.

10. On the stage, select the instance of mcEnd you just created, and in the Property Inspector give it an instance name of **end_mc**.

11. Select the first keyframe of the actions layer and open the Actions panel.

12. In the Actions panel, find the startGame function. The code for the startGame function should match this code:

```
function startGame():Void
{
    Mouse.hide();
    cursor_mc.startDrag(true);
    cursor_mc._visible = true;
    meteorInterval = setInterval(_root, "createMeteors", 1000);
}
```

13. At the bottom of the startGame function, write the code that hides the end_mc movie clip. This way, you won't see that movie clip when you start playing the game. Remember, to hide an object using ActionScript, set its _visible property value to false.

```
function startGame():Void
{
    Mouse.hide();
    cursor_mc.startDrag(true);
    cursor_mc._visible = true;
    meteorInterval = setInterval(_root, "createMeteors", 1000);
    end_mc._visible = false;
}
```

14. Next, find the definition for the meteorInit.onEnterFrame event handler. The code in the meteorInit.onEnterFrame event handler should match this code:

```
meteorInit.onEnterFrame = function():Void
{
    this._xscale += this.growthRate;
    this._yscale = this._xscale;

    if(this._xscale >= 150)
    {
        this._xscale -= 50;
        this._yscale -= 50;
        energy_mc.play();
        energy_mc.bar_mc._xscale -= 10;
    }
}
```

15. At the bottom of the conditional (if) statement within the meteorInit.onEnterFrame event handler, create another conditional statement that checks to see if the player's energy is less than or equal to 0.

```
meteorInit.onEnterFrame = function():Void
{
    this._xscale += this.growthRate;
    this._yscale = this._xscale;

    if(this._xscale >= 150)
    {
        this._xscale -= 50;
        this._yscale -= 50;
        energy_mc.play();
        energy_mc.bar_mc._xscale -= 10;
        if(energy_mc.bar_mc._xscale <= 0)
        {

        }
    }
}
```

16. Within the conditional statement you just wrote, write the code that shows the end_mc movie clip.

```
meteorInit.onEnterFrame = function():Void
{
    this._xscale += this.growthRate;
    this._yscale = this._xscale;

    if(this._xscale >= 150)
    {
        this._xscale -= 50;
        this._yscale -= 50;
        energy_mc.play();
        energy_mc.bar_mc._xscale -= 10;
        if(energy_mc.bar_mc._xscale <= 0)
        {
            end_mc._visible = true;
        }
    }
}
```

17. Below the line of code you just wrote, write the code to modify the text inside of the end_mc movie clip to say "You lose.\nClick to play again." Remember, the text field instance name inside of the end_mc movie clip is end_txt, and the text field property to modify text is called "text."

```
meteorInit.onEnterFrame = function():Void
{
    this._xscale += this.growthRate;
    this._yscale = this._xscale;

    if(this._xscale >= 150)
    {
        this._xscale -= 50;
        this._yscale -= 50;
        energy_mc.play();
        energy_mc.bar_mc._xscale -= 10;
        if(energy_mc.bar_mc._xscale <= 0)
        {
            end_mc._visible = true;
            end_mc.end_txt.text = "You lose.\nClick to play again.";
        }
    }
}
```

NOTE When you use ActionScript to place the code "\n" inside a Dynamic text field, Flash creates a new line. So for the code you just typed, the first line would say "You lose." The "\n" code then creates a new line (so you won't actually see "\n" on the screen), and the second line in the text field would say "Click to play again."

18. Below the last line of code you wrote, write the code to show the mouse.

```
meteorInit.onEnterFrame = function():Void
{
    this._xscale += this.growthRate;
    this._yscale = this._xscale;

    if(this._xscale >= 150)
    {
        this._xscale -= 50;
        this._yscale -= 50;
```

```
        energy_mc.play();
        energy_mc.bar_mc._xscale -= 10;
        if(energy_mc.bar_mc._xscale <= 0)
        {
            end_mc._visible = true;
            end_mc.end_txt.text = "You lose.\nClick to play again.";
            Mouse.show();
        }
    }
}
```

19. Test the movie, and allow the meteors to destroy you . . . or get large enough to make your energy go down. Notice the "You lose" message. Sweet! You'll add the interactivity to be able to play again in the next exercise.

20. Save the file, and keep it open for the next exercise.

EXERCISE 4-12: Playing Again

For this exercise, you'll add the interactivity to be able to play the game again once the game ends. In order to play the game again, you need to reset all the variables and objects in the game.

1. Make sure you are working in the file from the last exercise.

2. Make sure you are in the Main Timeline. Then, select the first keyframe of the actions layer and open the Actions panel.

3. In the Actions panel, find the meteorInit.onEnterFrame event handler. The code in the meteorInit.onEnterFrame event handler should look similar to the code that follows:

```
meteorInit.onEnterFrame = function():Void
{
    this._xscale += this.growthRate;
    this._yscale = this._xscale;

    if(this._xscale >= 150)
    {
        this._xscale -= 50;
        this._yscale -= 50;
        energy_mc.play();
        energy_mc.bar_mc._xscale -= 10;
        if(energy_mc.bar_mc._xscale <= 0)
        {
```

```
        end_mc._visible = true;
        end_mc.end_txt.text = "You lose.\nClick to play again.";
        Mouse.show();
    }
  }
}
```

4. In the meteorInit.onEnterFrame event handler, find the code for Mouse.show();. Below that line, write the following code: **end_mc.onPress = startGame**. This will make the startGame function run to restart the game when you click the end_mc movie clip.

```
meteorInit.onEnterFrame = function():Void
{
    this._xscale += this.growthRate;
    this._yscale = this._xscale;

    if(this._xscale >= 150)
    {
        this._xscale -= 50;
        this._yscale -= 50;
        energy_mc.play();
        energy_mc.bar_mc._xscale -= 10;
        if(energy_mc.bar_mc._xscale <= 0)
        {
            end_mc._visible = true;
            end_mc.end_txt.text = "You lose.\nClick to play again.";
            Mouse.show();
            end_mc.onPress = startGame;
        }
    }
}
```

5. On the next line, write the code to clear the meteorInterval using clearInterval. This will make sure Flash isn't continuing to create meteors after the game has ended.

```
meteorInit.onEnterFrame = function():Void
{
    this._xscale += this.growthRate;
    this._yscale = this._xscale;

    if(this._xscale >= 150)
    {
```

```
        this._xscale -= 50;
        this._yscale -= 50;
        energy_mc.play();
        energy_mc.bar_mc._xscale -= 10;
        if(energy_mc.bar_mc._xscale <= 0)
        {
            end_mc._visible = true;
            end_mc.end_txt.text = "You lose.\nClick to play again.";
            Mouse.show();
            end_mc.onPress = startGame;
            clearInterval(meteorInterval);
        }
    }
}
```

6. Test the movie, and lose the game. Then, click the screen to play again. Notice the screen is still filled with meteors, and your energy is below 0, so the game keeps displaying the lose game screen, shown here. You'll fix these problems next.

7. Find the startGame function near the bottom of your code. The startGame function should look similar to the code that follows:

```
function startGame():Void
{
    Mouse.hide();
    cursor_mc.startDrag(true);
    cursor_mc._visible = true;
    meteorInterval = setInterval(_root, "createMeteors", 1000);
    end_mc._visible = false;
}
```

8. The next step is to get rid of all the meteors on the Stage. Because they're all stored inside the container_mc movie clip, unloading the container_mc movie clip will automatically get rid of all the meteors. At the top of the startGame function, write the code to unload the container_mc movie clip. To unload a movie clip, use the unloadMovie method.

```
function startGame():Void
{
    container_mc.unloadMovie();
    Mouse.hide();
    cursor_mc.startDrag(true);
    cursor_mc._visible = true;
    meteorInterval = setInterval(_root, "createMeteors", 1000);
    end_mc._visible = false;
}
```

9. On the next line of code, reset the energy bar's _xscale property to 100.

```
function startGame():Void
{
    container_mc.unloadMovie();
    energy_mc.bar_mc._xscale = 100;
    Mouse.hide();
    cursor_mc.startDrag(true);
    cursor_mc._visible = true;
    meteorInterval = setInterval(_root, "createMeteors", 1000);
    end_mc._visible = false;
}
```

10. Test the movie, and lose the game. Then, click to play again and notice the game resets just as you'd expect it to. Nice!

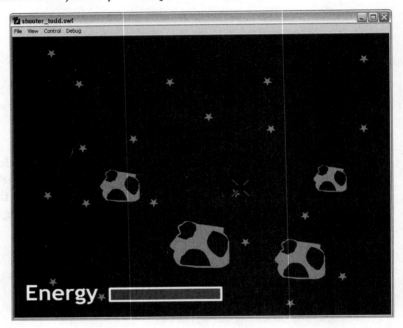

11. Save your file, and keep it open for the next exercise.

EXERCISE 4-13: Winning the Game

Now that you've looked at losing the game and playing again, I'll cover winning the game. For this game, you will specify a certain number of meteors that need to be destroyed before the player's energy runs out. Destroy enough meteors and the player wins.

1. Make sure you are working in the same file from the last exercise.

2. Select the energy layer and click the Insert Layer button to create a new layer above the energy layer. Name the new layer **score**.

3. Select the score layer, and choose the Text tool in the Toolbar, or use the keyboard shortcut T.

4. Hide the end layer by clicking the Show/Hide Layer button on the end layer, as shown here.

5. At the bottom right of the Stage, click to create a text field. In the Property Inspector, make sure the type is set to Static Text. In the text field, type **score**.

6. Press ESC on your keyboard to deselect the text field you just created.

7. In the Property Inspector, change the Text Field type to Dynamic Text.

8. On the right side of the last text field you created, click and drag to draw a dynamic text field on the Stage. This text field will display the player's score.

9. In the Property Inspector, shown next, give the Dynamic text field you just created an instance name of **score_txt**.

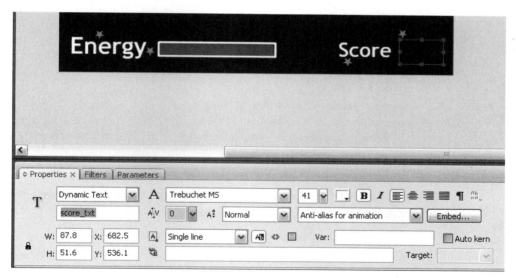

10. Select the first keyframe of the actions layer and open the Actions panel.

11. In the Actions panel, find the DECLARE VARIABLES AND CREATE OBJECTS section. Near the top of that section, below all the other variables you created, create a variable called score, with a data type of Number.

```
// --------DECLARE VARIABLES AND CREATE OBJECTS----------------
var meteorNum:Number = 0;
var meteorInterval:Number;
var meteorInit:Object = new Object();
var score:Number;
```

12. On the next line, create another variable called pointsToWin with a number data type, and a value of 10. This will represent the number of points needed to win the game.

```
var meteorNum:Number = 0;
var meteorInterval:Number;
var meteorInit:Object = new Object();
var score:Number;
var pointsToWin:Number = 10;
```

13. Near the bottom of your code, find the startGame function. Your startGame function should look similar to this code:

```
function startGame():Void
{
    container_mc.unloadMovie();
    energy_mc.bar_mc._xscale = 100;
    Mouse.hide();
    cursor_mc.startDrag(true);
    cursor_mc._visible = true;
    meteorInterval = setInterval(_root, "createMeteors", 1000);
    end_mc._visible = false;
}
```

14. At the top of the startGame function, set the value of the score variable you created to 0.

```
function startGame():Void
{
    score = 0;
    container_mc.unloadMovie();
    energy_mc.bar_mc._xscale = 100;
    Mouse.hide();
    cursor_mc.startDrag(true);
    cursor_mc._visible = true;
```

```
    meteorInterval = setInterval(_root, "createMeteors", 1000);
    end_mc._visible = false;
}
```

15. On the next line, set the value in the score_txt text field equal to the value of the score variable. Remember, you can set the value of text in a Dynamic text field using the text property.

```
function startGame():Void
{
    score = 0;
    score_txt.text = score;
    container_mc.unloadMovie();
    energy_mc.bar_mc._xscale = 100;
    Mouse.hide();
    cursor_mc.startDrag(true);
    cursor_mc._visible = true;
    meteorInterval = setInterval(_root, "createMeteors", 1000);
    end_mc._visible = false;
}
```

16. Now, you'll add to the score variable every time you destroy a meteor. In the DECLARE VARIABLES AND CREATE OBJECTS section of your code, find the meteorInit.onRelease event handler. The code in the meteorInit.onRelease event handler should match this code:

```
meteorInit.onRelease = function():Void
{
    this.gotoAndPlay("explode");
}
```

17. At the bottom of the meteorInit.onRelease event handler, increment the score variable by 1, using the ++ operator.

```
meteorInit.onRelease = function():Void
{
    this.gotoAndPlay("explode");
    score ++;
}
```

18. Just like in the startGame function, place the value of the score in the score_txt text field.

```
meteorInit.onRelease = function():Void
{
    this.gotoAndPlay("explode");
```

```
        score ++;
        score_txt.text = score;
    }
```

19. Next, write a conditional statement to check if the player has gotten enough points to win the game. On the next line of code, create a conditional statement that checks if the value of the score variable is greater than or equal to the pointsToWin variable you defined earlier.

```
meteorInit.onRelease = function():Void
{
    this.gotoAndPlay("explode");
    score ++;
    score_txt.text = score;
    if(score >= pointsToWin)
    {

    }
}
```

20. Now you'll write the code that will run if the player has enough points to win the game. Inside the conditional statement you just created, type the code to show the end_mc movie clip.

```
meteorInit.onRelease = function():Void
{
    this.gotoAndPlay("explode");
    score ++;
    score_txt.text = score;
    if(score >= pointsToWin)
    {
        end_mc._visible = true;
    }
}
```

21. On the next line, set the text in the end_mc.end_txt text field to "You win!\nClick to play again."

```
meteorInit.onRelease = function():Void
{
    this.gotoAndPlay("explode");
    score ++;
    score_txt.text = score;
    if(score >= pointsToWin)
    {
```

```
        end_mc._visible = true;
        end_mc.end_txt.text = "You win!\nClick to play again.";
    }
}
```

22. On the next line, write the code to run the startGame function if you click the end_mc movie clip.

```
meteorInit.onRelease = function():Void
{
    this.gotoAndPlay("explode");
    score ++;
    score_txt.text = score;
    if(score >= pointsToWin)
    {
        end_mc._visible = true;
        end_mc.end_txt.text = "You win!\nClick to play again.";
        end_mc.onPress = startGame;
    }
}
```

23. Just as in the case of losing the game, you also want to show the mouse here. On the next line of code, write the code to show the mouse.

```
meteorInit.onRelease = function():Void
{
    this.gotoAndPlay("explode");
    score ++;
    score_txt.text = score;
    if(score >= pointsToWin)
    {
        end_mc._visible = true;
        end_mc.end_txt.text = "You win!\nClick to play again.";
        end_mc.onPress = startGame;
        Mouse.show();
    }
}
```

24. The last thing you need to do for this function is to make sure to clear the meteorInterval using clearInterval. That way, you make sure Flash isn't creating meteors behind the scenes while the end screen is up. On the next line, write the code to clear the meteorInterval.

```
meteorInit.onRelease = function():Void
{
```

```
        this.gotoAndPlay("explode");
        score ++;
        score_txt.text = score;
        if(score >= pointsToWin)
        {
            end_mc._visible = true;
            end_mc.end_txt.text = "You win!\nClick to play again.";
            end_mc.onPress = startGame;
            Mouse.show();
            clearInterval(meteorInterval);
        }
    }
}
```

25. Test the movie. This time, win the game by destroying enough meteors before your energy runs out. Notice the "You win!" message. Click the message to play again. Congratulations, you've completed another game!

26. Save the file. You can upload it to the Web and play it on your Wii in the same way you uploaded and tested your other games.

CHAPTER 5

Utilizing the Wii Remote: A Hammer Game

SO far, we've looked at creating fairly simple games. This foundation is necessary to create games with advanced interactivity. However, though the games we've created are playable on the Wii, we have yet to truly take advantage of the Wii remote. In the remaining chapters, we will look at creating games creatively, using the Wii remote more as it is used in commercial Wii games.

TAKING ADVANTAGE OF THE WII REMOTE

I just mentioned that we would start taking a look at using the Wii remote more as it is used in commercial games. What does that mean exactly? One of the reasons the Wii is so popular and exciting and fun for people of all ages is that playing games on the Wii requires you to move in realistic ways; ways that simulate real life. In other words, playing a bowling game, for example, on the Wii is much more like bowling in real life than playing the same game on a traditional gaming console. This is because bowling on the Wii actually requires you to move as if you are indeed bowling. Of course, you may already know this. It might even be the reason you decided to get a Wii in the first place.

So how do you mimic that same interactivity in Flash? Though you can't tap into the Wii remote's motion sensors, you can do a lot to mimic them. For example, you'll build a hammer and nail game in this chapter. In the game, you'll have a hammer move up and down to pound in a nail when you move the Wii remote up and down. That way, the Wii remote acts as a pseudo-hammer while you're playing the game. You'll create the interactivity for the game using invisible buttons and simple mouse interactivity.

EXERCISE 5-1: Viewing the Flash File

Before you start writing the code to create the game, take a look at how the .FLA file is set up. I'll also talk briefly about adding photos to a Flash application.

1. In the exercise files, locate hammer.fla.

2. Open the file in Flash and save it as **hammer_{your name}.fla**.

3. Notice there are five layers: actions, hammer, wood, nail, and BG.

4. Hide and unhide the layers to view the content on each layer. Notice that the layers contain some photos. Also notice the instance name of the hammer movie clip is hammer_mc, and the instance name of the nail is nail_mc.

Utilizing the Wii Remote: A Hammer Game

NOTE You can import JPEG, GIF, or PNG files into Flash using File | Import | Import To Stage or File | Import | Import To Library. Once you import a bitmap graphic, that graphic is stored in your Library. To place the bitmap on the Stage, click and drag it from the Library, just like any other Library item. You can place a bitmap inside a movie clip or graphic symbol and animate it using motion tweens just as you would animate a movie clip or graphic symbol.

5. Notice in the Library there are four bitmap graphics (photos) and two movie clips.

6. Double-click the mcHammer movie clip symbol icon in the Library to enter its Timeline. If you expect to see an image of an early '90s hip-hop star, you may be disappointed. On the Stage inside the mcHammer movie clip, you'll see a bitmap graphic of a hammer. When you select the graphic, you will see a gray outline (as shown next), which is an indicator in Flash that you have a bitmap selected.

7. View the nail movie clip in the Library by double-clicking the movie clip symbol for mcNail. Notice that this movie clip also contains a bitmap graphic.

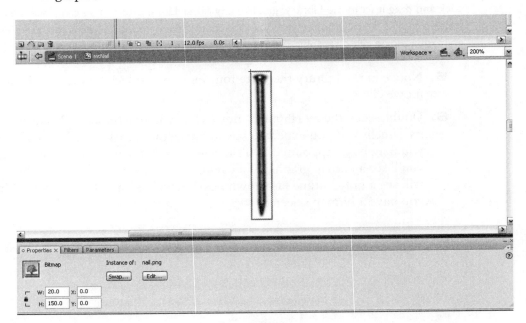

8. Click Scene 1 in the Timeline to return to the Main Timeline.

9. Keep the file open for the next exercise.

Understanding Invisible Buttons

Invisible buttons are simply regular buttons with no up state. Sometimes, invisible buttons have over or down states, but typically invisible buttons only have a hit state. Invisible buttons are a handy tool in creating Wii games in Flash, because they allow you to add interactivity without adding any graphics.

You can create invisible buttons in Flash in a few ways. One way, which is the most common, is to draw the hit area of your button first. Then, you can convert it to a button symbol, and simply drag the Up state keyframe of the button to the Hit state keyframe. On the Stage, an invisible button has a semitransparent cyan color. The following illustration shows an invisible button on the stage.

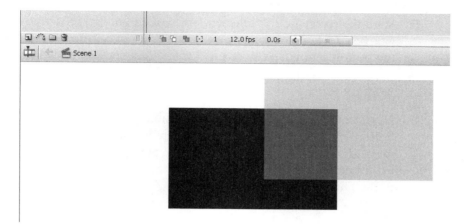

EXERCISE 5-2: Creating Invisible Buttons

In this exercise, you'll create invisible buttons for your game.

1. Make sure you are working in the same file from the last exercise.

2. In the Main Timeline, select the hammer layer and click the Insert Layer button to create a new layer.

3. Name the new layer buttons.

4. On the buttons layer, draw a black rectangle with no stroke.

5. With the rectangle selected, type the following values in the Property Inspector: X:0, Y:0, W:790, H:305.

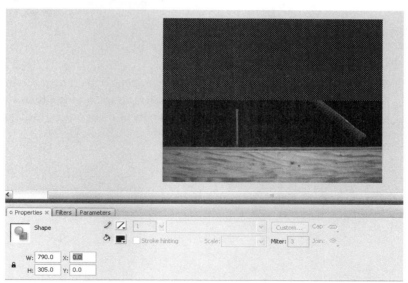

6. With the rectangle still selected, press F8 on your keyboard to open the Convert To Symbol dialog box. There, choose Button for the type, name the button **btnInvis**, choose top left for Registration, and click OK.

7. In the Library, double-click the btnInvis symbol's Button Symbol icon to enter its Timeline.

8. Now, you'll make this button an invisible button. Inside the btnInvis button, make sure no frames are selected by clicking in the Pasteboard (gray area away from the shape on the Stage). Then, click and drag the keyframe on frame 1 (the frame with the word "up" above the frame) to the Hit frame, as shown here.

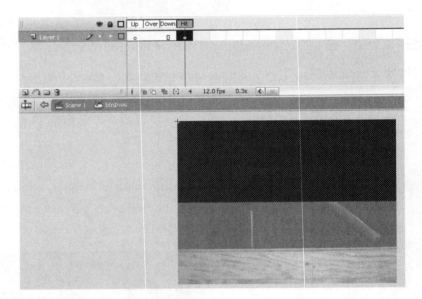

9. At the bottom of the Timeline, click Scene 1 to return to the Main Timeline. It may be difficult to tell in the following illustration, but the button on the Stage is now a transparent cyan color, indicating it's an invisible button. Nice!

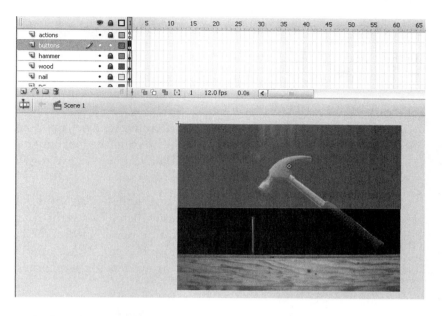

10. With the Selection tool selected, press and hold ALT (Windows) or OPTION (Mac) on your keyboard and click and drag the button on the Stage to create a copy.

11. Make sure the copied button is selected. In the Align panel, check the To Stage button. Then click the Align Left Edge button to align the left edge of the button to the left edge of the Stage, and click the Align Bottom Edge button to align the bottom edge of the button to the bottom of the Stage.

12. Select the top button, and in the Property Inspector name the button **top_btn**. Select the bottom button and in the Property Inspector name the button **bottom_btn**.

13. Save the file, and keep it open for the next exercise.

EXERCISE 5-3: Using Invisible Buttons

In this exercise, you'll add interactivity to the invisible buttons you created to make the hammer swing up and down and pound the nail into the wood.

1. Make sure you are working in the same file from the last exercise.

2. In the Library, double-click the mcHammer movie clip to enter its Timeline. If you are having trouble selecting the mcHammer movie clip, you can lock the buttons layer so that you won't have to worry about accidentally selecting one of the buttons.

3. Inside the mcHammer movie clip, notice the registration point is near the bottom right of the hammer, as shown here. This is the rotation point for this movie clip. Because the registration point is there, the hammer will rotate around that point. If the rotation point of the hammer were at the top left, the hammer would rotate around its top-left corner.

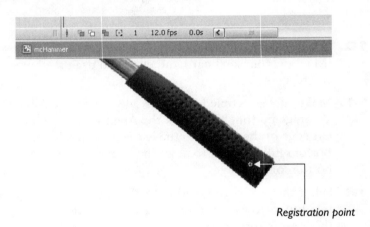

Registration point

4. At the bottom of the Timeline, click the Scene 1 button to return to the Main Timeline.

5. In the Main Timeline, select the first keyframe of the actions layer and open the Actions panel.

6. In the DECLARE VARIABLES AND CREATE OBJECTS section of code, create a variable called bashAmt, with a data type of Number and a value of 15. This variable will represent how much the nail will move down when hit by the hammer. Your code should match the code that follows (new code is bold):

```
// DECLARE VARIABLES AND CREATE OBJECTS

var bashAmt:Number = 15;
```

7. On the next line, create a variable called rotateAmt, with a data type of Number and a default value of –15. This variable will represent the amount the hammer rotates when it swings. The value is negative because the hammer will swing by rotating counterclockwise. If the value were positive, the hammer would rotate clockwise.

```
// DECLARE VARIABLES AND CREATE OBJECTS

var bashAmt:Number = 15;
var rotateAmt:Number = -15;
```

8. In the DEFINE EVENT HANDLERS section of code, create the skeleton of an onRollOver event handler for the bottom_btn button.

```
// DEFINE EVENT HANDLERS

bottom_btn.onRollOver = function():Void
{

}
```

9. Inside the event handler you just created, write the code that rotates the hammer by setting its rotation equal to the rotateAmt variable's value.

```
bottom_btn.onRollOver = function():Void
{
    hammer_mc._rotation = rotateAmt;
}
```

10. On the next line, move the nail down by the amount held in the bashAmt variable.

```
bottom_btn.onRollOver = function():Void
{
    hammer_mc._rotation = rotateAmt;
    nail_mc._y += bashAmt;
}
```

11. On the next line, update the rotateAmt variable by decreasing its value by bashAmt divided by 7. This will make the hammer rotate a little more each time it hits the nail.

```
bottom_btn.onRollOver = function():Void
{
    hammer_mc._rotation = rotateAmt;
    nail_mc._y += bashAmt;
    rotateAmt -= bashAmt / 7;
}
```

NOTE You may be wondering where the number 7 came from. This number actually came from a trial and error process when I initially created the game. At the end of this exercise, you can change this number to modify the change in rotation amount for the hammer if you'd like to see what a different value would look like.

12. Below the bottom_btn.onRollOver event handler, define the skeleton of an onRollOver event handler for the top_btn button.

```
top_btn.onRollOver = function():Void
{

}
```

13. Inside the top_btn.onRollOver event handler you just created, reset the value of the hammer's rotation to zero. This will make the hammer move up when the mouse (or Wii remote) rolls over the top button.

```
top_btn.onRollOver = function():Void
{
    hammer_mc._rotation = 0;
}
```

14. Test the movie, and move your mouse up and down to swing the hammer. Sweet! Well, almost sweet. Notice that the nail goes through the wood and the hammer keeps rotating, which looks a little fake. You'll fix that in the next exercise.

15. Save the file, and keep it open for the next exercise.

EXERCISE 5-4: Winning the Game

In this exercise, you'll stop the nail from going too far into the wood and disable the interactivity of the hammer once the game is over.

1. Make sure you are working in the same file from the last exercise.

2. Hide the buttons layer, and unlock the nail layer if it's locked.

3. On the nail layer, using the Selection tool, move the nail down until it looks as if it is all the way in the wood, as shown next. Then, note the Y position of the nail in the Property Inspector. You'll use this value later.

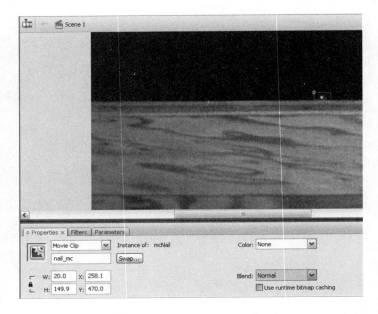

4. Select the first keyframe of the actions layer and open the Actions panel.

5. In your code, at the bottom of the DECLARE VARIABLES AND CREATE OBJECTS section, create a new variable called nailIn, with a data type of Number and a value of 470. This value will represent the value of the nail when it is fully hammered in, and is the same value you got when you moved the nail earlier in this exercise.

```
var bashAmt:Number = 15;
var rotateAmt:Number = -15;
var nailIn:Number = 470;
```

6. At the bottom of the bottom_btn.onRollOver event handler, create the skeleton of a conditional statement that checks to see if the Y position of the nail is greater than or equal to the value of the nailIn variable.

```
bottom_btn.onRollOver = function():Void
{
    hammer_mc._rotation = rotateAmt;
```

```
nail_mc._y += bashAmt;
rotateAmt -= bashAmt / 7;
if(nail_mc._y >= nailIn)
{

}
}
```

7. Inside the conditional statement you just created, set the nail's Y position equal to the nailIn variable's value. This will stop the nail from moving too far down.

```
bottom_btn.onRollOver = function():Void
{
    hammer_mc._rotation = rotateAmt;
    nail_mc._y += bashAmt;
    rotateAmt -= bashAmt / 7;
    if(nail_mc._y >= nailIn)
    {
        nail_mc._y = nailIn;
    }
}
```

8. On the next line of code, disable the interactivity for the bottom_btn button using the button's enabled property.

```
bottom_btn.onRollOver = function():Void
{
    hammer_mc._rotation = rotateAmt;
    nail_mc._y += bashAmt;
    rotateAmt -= bashAmt / 7;
    if(nail_mc._y >= nailIn)
    {
        nail_mc._y = nailIn;
        bottom_btn.enabled = false;
    }
}
```

9. Test the movie, and pound that nail into the wood. Notice the nail stays where it belongs and the hammer stops rotating after you hammer the nail all the way in. Cool! All that you have left to do now is to make a way to play the game multiple times.

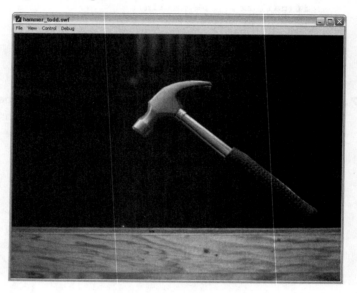

10. Save the file, and keep it open for the next exercise.

EXERCISE 5-5: Playing the Game Again

Now that the game works, you'll make the game playable multiple times.

1. Make sure you are working in the same file from the last exercise.

2. Select the first keyframe of the actions layer and open the Actions panel.

3. At the bottom of the DEFINE VARIABLES AND CREATE OBJECTS section of your code, create a new variable called nailOut, with a data type of Number and a value of the nail's current Y position.

```
var bashAmt:Number = 15;
var rotateAmt:Number = -15;
var nailIn:Number = 470;
var nailOut:Number = nail_mc._y;
```

4. At the bottom of the DEFINE EVENT HANDLERS section of your code, create the skeleton of an onPress event handler for the top_btn button.

```
top_btn.onPress = function():Void
{

}
```

5. Inside the event handler you just created, reset the value of the rotateAmt variable to be –15.

```
top_btn.onPress = function():Void
{
    rotateAmt = -15;
}
```

6. On the next line, re-enable the bottom_btn button using its enabled property.

```
top_btn.onPress = function():Void
{
    rotateAmt = -15;
    bottom_btn.enabled = true;
}
```

7. On the next line, reset the nail's Y position to the value held inside the nailOut variable.

```
top_btn.onPress = function():Void
{
    rotateAmt = -15;
    bottom_btn.enabled = true;
    nail_mc._y = nailOut;
}
```

8. Test the movie, and pound! Once the game is finished, click the top of the screen to start the game over again. Nice!

Another Game Complete!

Congratulations, you just finished another game! Though the game was fairly simple to create, it takes much more advantage of the Wii remote than the other games you've created. Once you upload this game to a web server and play it on your Wii, the Wii remote will act as a hammer as you play the game. In other words, swinging the hammer in the game will actually be pretty close to swinging a hammer in real life.

Now that you're familiar with using the Wii remote in a similar way to how it is used in commercial Wii games, we'll start building games with more complex interactivity.

CHAPTER 6

Applying Advanced Logic and Interactivity: A Paper Rock Scissors Game

NOW

that you have a solid foundation for building games, we'll create something a little more complex. In this chapter, you'll create a paper rock scissors game. In order to create the game, you'll use the same invisible button and interactivity techniques you're already familiar with, as well as some advanced conditional logic that may be new for you.

If you'd like to view the finished game at any time, the name of the file is prs_final.fla.

STARTING A GAME

When you create this game, you're going to start with a pre-built Flash file. Normally when you create a game, you won't start with a Flash file, unless you work with someone else who does that work for you. Usually, you plan out how your game is going to work, with a general idea of the code you will write. Based on how your game works, you'll have an idea of how to set up your Flash file.

For example, in this game we know that our game is going to need paper, rock, and scissors graphics, so it makes sense to create the graphics and convert them into movie clips because we're going to be reusing them. Also, after planning the game, we know that the player hand and enemy hand are going to be using the same graphics, just with one facing the other direction. If we plan our game effectively, we can find a way to use the same hand movie clip for both hands, saving time and making the game play better on the Wii.

EXERCISE 6-1: Viewing the Flash File

Before you start writing the code to create the game, take a look at how the .FLA file is set up.

1. In the exercise files, locate prs.fla.

2. Open the file in Flash and save it as **prs_{your name}.fla**.

3. Notice there are five layers (as shown in the following illustration): actions, end, choices, buttons, and hands.

4. Hide and unhide the layers to view the content on each layer. Lock and unlock the layers, and select the content on each layer to become familiar with the instance names of objects used in this file. In particular, note the instance names of the invisible buttons, the buttons at the bottom of the screen, the end movie clip, and the two hand movie clips.

5. Notice the symbols in the Library. Double-click the Bitmaps folder to expand it and reveal the bitmap images used in this file, shown here.

Folders are a great way to organize your Library. To create a folder, click the New Folder button at the bottom of the Library. Then, you can click and drag objects in your Library to the folder to place those objects in that folder.

6. In the Library, double-click the mcAll movie clip to enter its Timeline. This movie clip is used for both the player hand and the enemy hand. For the enemy hand, the movie clip is in its normal state, and for the player hand, the movie clip is flipped horizontally. Using the same movie clip for the player and the enemy will optimize the performance of this game by saving Flash from having to work with an extra movie clip.

7. Inside the mcAll movie clip, note the layers, the content in the layers, and the frame labels.

8. Scrub the Playhead to view the content at each frame label. Notice the art on the Stage matches the frame label names. You'll use the frame labels later to navigate to different parts of this movie clip.

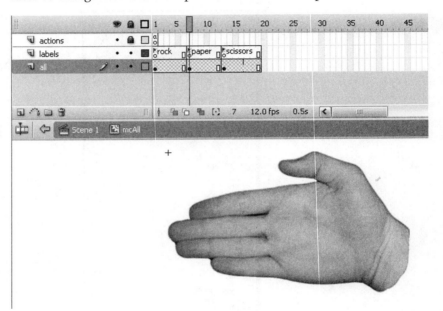

9. Keep the file open for the next exercise.

BEGINNING THE GAME CODE

Now that you've taken a look at the game's .FLA file, you can start writing the basic logic for your game. Whenever you create games, it's good to start out with a detailed idea of how you want the game to work. From there, you can make a general plan of how you're going to write your code, or at least the order in which you're going to write the code. What I like to do is write the basic logic of the game first and then add the extra elements of the game once everything is working properly. You'll start writing the basic logic of your game in the next exercise by creating a way to choose paper, rock, or scissors.

EXERCISE 6-2: Choosing Paper, Rock, or Scissors

In this exercise, I'll talk about attaching dynamic properties to movie clips, and connect the player's choice to whichever button the player clicks.

1. Make sure you are working in the same file from the last exercise.

2. Select the first keyframe of the actions layer in the Main Timeline and open the Actions panel.

3. In the DECLARE VARIABLES AND CREATE OBJECTS section, create a variable called playerChoice. Give the variable a data type of String. Your code should match the code that follows (new code is bold).

```
// DECLARE VARIABLES AND CREATE OBJECTS

var playerChoice:String;
```

4. Below the code you just wrote, create a dynamic property called choice for paper_mc. Set the value of the property to be "paper".

```
var playerChoice:String;

paper_mc.choice = "paper";
```

NOTE A dynamic property simply means a made-up property. Because choice is not a built-in movie clip property, Flash creates a new property on paper_mc called choice. Again, because choice isn't built in to Flash, the value of the property can be any type of data. The reason for using this technique here is to connect each button at the bottom of the screen to a particular choice. For example, when the player clicks the paper_mc movie clip, the player's choice is "paper". You'll take a look at using dynamic properties later on in this exercise.

5. Repeat Step 4 for the rock_mc movie clip and the scissors_mc movie clip. When you are finished, your code should match the code that follows.

```
var playerChoice:String;

paper_mc.choice = "paper";
rock_mc.choice = "rock";
scissors_mc.choice = "scissors";
```

6. In the DEFINE FUNCTIONS section of code, create the skeleton of a function called initializeGame.

```
// DEFINE FUNCTIONS

function initializeGame():Void
{

}
```

7. Inside the initializeGame function, give the playerChoice variable an initial value of "".

```
function initializeGame():Void
{
    playerChoice = "";
}
```

8. On the next line, hide the end_mc movie clip using its _visible property.

```
function initializeGame():Void
{
    playerChoice = "";
    end_mc._visible = false;
}
```

9. In the RUN IMMEDIATELY section, run the initializeGame function.

```
// RUN IMMEDIATELY

initializeGame();
```

10. In the DEFINE EVENT HANDLERS section, create the skeleton of an onRelease event handler that applies to the rock_mc, paper_mc, and scissors_mc movie clips.

```
// DEFINE EVENT HANDLERS

rock_mc.onRelease = paper_mc.onRelease =
scissors_mc.onRelease = function():Void
{

}
```

NOTE Notice in the preceding code that each event handler has the same value. This tells Flash that when the rock_mc movie clip is clicked, do the same thing as when the paper_mc movie clip is clicked, which does the same thing as when the scissors_mc movie clip is clicked, which runs a function. This can be a very effective way of defining event handlers for buttons that all do the same thing. Here, it is effective because whenever one of the buttons is clicked, you want the player's choice to be the choice associated with that particular button.

11. Inside the event handler you just created, set the playerChoice variable equal to the choice associated with whichever button was clicked.

```
rock_mc.onRelease = paper_mc.onRelease = scissors_mc.onRelease = function():Void
{
    playerChoice = this.choice;
}
```

NOTE Remember when I talked about what the keyword *this* means? When inside an event handler, *this* refers to the object the event handler is for, or the object attached to the event. Here, there are three different objects with attached events: rock_mc, paper_mc, and scissors_mc. How do you know which movie clip *this* is referring to? Because this event handler is connected to multiple objects, *this* refers to the object that triggered the event. For example, if rock_mc is clicked, *this* refers to rock_mc. If paper_mc is clicked, *this* refers to paper_mc. Taking this a step further, if scissors_mc is clicked, this.choice is scissors_mc.choice, which is "scissors". Writing code in this condensed way saves time, reduces lines of code, and even makes code easier to change if you ever need to.

12. On the next line, run a function called hideButtons. You'll define this function in a later step, and the function will simply hide all the buttons at the bottom of the screen.

```
rock_mc.onRelease = paper_mc.onRelease = scissors_mc.onRelease = function():Void
{
    playerChoice = this.choice;
    hideButtons();
}
```

13. At the bottom of the DEFINE FUNCTIONS section, below the initializeGame function, create the skeleton of the hideButtons function.

```
function hideButtons():Void
{

}
```

14. Inside the hideButtons function that you just created, write the code to hide the rock_mc movie clip by setting its _visible property to false.

```
function hideButtons():Void
{
    rock_mc._visible = false;
}
```

15. Repeat Step 14 for the paper_mc and scissors_mc movie clips.

```
function hideButtons():Void
{
    rock_mc._visible = false;
    paper_mc._visible = false;
    scissors_mc._visible = false;
}
```

16. Test the movie, and click one of the buttons at the bottom of the screen to make all the buttons disappear, as shown in the following illustration. In the next exercise, you'll add the interactivity to display the player's choice after moving the mouse or Wii remote up and down enough times.

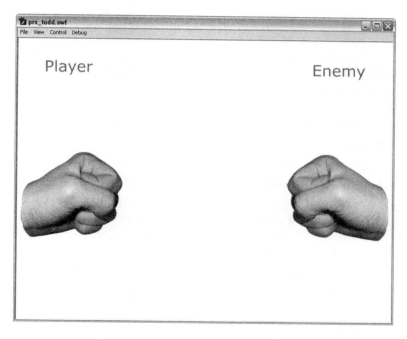

17. Save the file, and keep it open for the next exercise.

ADDING MORE FEATURES

Once you have created the basic logic of your game and it works correctly, it's time to start adding some more features. Usually in my games I do a lot of early testing, trying to see if there are any errors in my code or any problems I may have overlooked when planning the game. Whether you're developing an application in Flash or using any other platform or language, it's always important to test the application often, making sure you're not including anything in your code that could potentially become a problem in the future.

EXERCISE 6-3: Showing the Player's Choice

In this exercise, you'll add the interactivity that allows the player to move the mouse (or Wii remote) up and down to move the player's hand and display the player's choice.

1. Make sure you are working in the file from the last exercise.

2. Select the first keyframe of the actions layer (in the Main Timeline) and open the Actions panel by pressing F9 (Windows) or OPTION-F9 (Mac).

3. In the DECLARE VARIABLES AND CREATE OBJECTS section, below the playerChoice variable you created, create a new variable called downPosition, with a data type of Number and a value of the player_mc movie clip's current Y position. This variable will hold the position of the hand when it moves down.

```
var playerChoice:String;
var downPosition:Number = player_mc._y;

paper_mc.choice = "paper";
rock_mc.choice = "rock";
scissors_mc.choice = "scissors";
```

4. On the next line, create a variable called upPosition, with a data type of Number and a value of the player_mc movie clip's Y position minus 100. This variable will represent the position of the hand when it moves up, which will be 100 pixels above where it is currently.

```
var playerChoice:String;
var downPosition:Number = player_mc._y;
var upPosition:Number = player_mc._y - 100;

paper_mc.choice = "paper";
rock_mc.choice = "rock";
scissors_mc.choice = "scissors";
```

5. On the next line, create a variable called shootCount, with a data type of Number. This value will represent the number of times the player has moved the mouse up and down after making a choice.

```
var playerChoice:String;
var downPosition:Number = player_mc._y;
var upPosition:Number = player_mc._y - 100;
var shootCount:Number;

paper_mc.choice = "paper";
rock_mc.choice = "rock";
scissors_mc.choice = "scissors";
```

6. Find the initializeGame function in the DEFINE FUNCTIONS section in your code. At the bottom of the initializeGame function, give the shootCount an initial value of zero. This will reset this variable each time you start a game.

```
function initializeGame():Void
{
    playerChoice = "";
    end_mc._visible = false;
    shootCount = 0;
}
```

7. Below the code you just wrote, write the code to disable the top_btn button and the bottom_btn button by setting their enabled properties to false. You want to disable these buttons until the player makes a choice. That way, the hands won't move up and down before the player chooses paper, rock, or scissors.

```
function initializeGame():Void
{
    playerChoice = "";
    end_mc._visible = false;
    shootCount = 0;

    top_btn.enabled = false;
    bottom_btn.enabled = false;
}
```

8. In the DEFINE EVENT HANDLERS section, find the rock_mc.onRelease event handler.

9. At the bottom of the rock_mc.onRelease event handler, enable the top_btn button by setting its enabled property to true. This will enable the interactivity for the top_btn button. You don't want to enable the bottom_btn button just yet; you'll do that once you roll over the top_btn button. I'll talk more about why you'll enable the button there later.

```
rock_mc.onRelease = paper_mc.onRelease =
scissors_mc.onRelease = function():Void
{
    playerChoice = this.choice;
    hideButtons();
    top_btn.enabled = true;
}
```

10. Below the event handler for rock_mc.onRelease, create the skeleton of an event handler for top_btn.onRollOver.

```
top_btn.onRollOver = function():Void
{

}
```

11. Inside the top_btn.onRollOver event handler, enable the bottom_btn button by setting its enabled property to true.

```
top_btn.onRollOver = function():Void
{
    bottom_btn.enabled = true;
}
```

12. Next, you'll move the player_mc movie clip up once the top_btn button is rolled over. To do that, set the _y property of the player_mc movie clip equal to the upPosition variable.

```
top_btn.onRollOver = function():Void
{
    bottom_btn.enabled = true;
    player_mc._y = upPosition;
}
```

13. Below the top_btn.onRollOver event handler, create the skeleton for a bottom_btn.onRollOver event hander. This will define what happens when you roll over the bottom button after you have made a choice of paper, rock, or scissors and have rolled over the top_btn button. Your code should match this code:

```
bottom_btn.onRollOver = function():Void
{

}
```

14. Inside the bottom_btn.onRollOver event handler, write the code to move the player_mc movie clip back to the down position by setting its _y property equal to the downPosition variable.

```
bottom_btn.onRollOver = function():Void
{
    player_mc._y = downPosition;
}
```

15. Test the movie, and click one of the bottom buttons to select paper, rock, or scissors. Then, move your mouse up and down to make the player's hand move up and down, as shown next. Sweet! The next step is showing the player's choice after the hand moves down enough times.

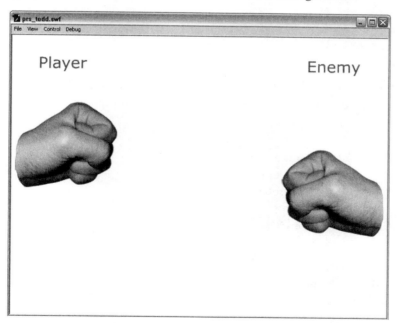

16. Right below the last line of code you wrote, increment the shootCount variable by 1 using the ++ operator. This will add 1 to the value of the shootCount variable each time the hand moves down.

```
bottom_btn.onRollOver = function():Void
{
    player_mc._y = downPosition;
    shootCount ++;
}
```

17. On the next line, create the skeleton of a conditional statement that checks to see if the shootCount variable is greater than or equal to 3. This will define what happens if the hand has moved down three or more times. If your way of playing this game requires the hand to move down four times (example: "rock, paper, scissors, shoot!"), then you can change this number to 4 instead.

```
bottom_btn.onRollOver = function():Void
{
    player_mc._y = downPosition;
    shootCount ++;
    if(shootCount >= 3)
    {

    }
}
```

18. Inside the conditional statement you just created, run a function called endGame. You'll define this function in the next step.

```
bottom_btn.onRollOver = function():Void
{
    player_mc._y = downPosition;
    shootCount ++;
    if(shootCount >= 3)
    {
        endGame();
    }
}
```

19. At the bottom of the DEFINE FUNCTIONS section, create the skeleton of a function called endGame.

```
function endGame():Void
{

}
```

20. Inside the endGame function, write the code that makes the player_mc movie clip go to the appropriate frame by using the gotoAndStop method and passing in the playerChoice variable.

```
function endGame():Void
{
    player_mc.gotoAndStop(playerChoice);
}
```

21. On the next two lines, disable the top_btn button and the bottom_btn button by setting their enabled properties to false. That way, once you see the player's choice, the player_mc movie clip will stop moving when you move the mouse up and down. If you omitted this code, and chose paper, for example, you could move your mouse up and down to see a nice karate chop. Karate chops are great, but not exactly ideal for this game.

```
function endGame():Void
{
    player_mc.gotoAndStop(playerChoice);
    top_btn.enabled = false;
    bottom_btn.enabled = false;
}
```

22. Test the movie, and choose paper, rock, or scissors at the bottom of the screen. Then move the mouse up and down three times to make the hand display the choice you made; I chose paper, as shown here.

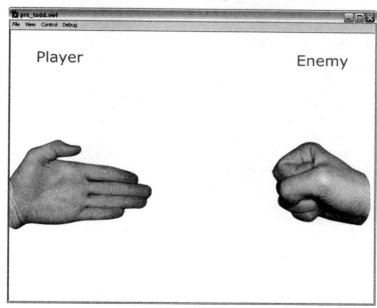

23. Save the file, and keep it open for the next exercise.

EXERCISE 6-4: Creating Enemy Artificial Intelligence

In this exercise, you'll create some basic enemy artificial intelligence by making the enemy choose paper, rock, or scissors.

1. Make sure you are working in the same file from the last exercise.

2. Select the first keyframe of the actions layer and open the Actions panel by pressing F9 (Windows) or OPTION-F9 (Mac).

3. Below the other variables you created in the DECLARE VARIABLES AND CREATE OBJECTS section of code, create another variable called choices with a data type of Array. Set the value of choices to be an array that contains "paper", "rock", and "scissors". This array holds all the choices the enemy could make.

```
var playerChoice:String;
var downPosition:Number = player_mc._y;
var upPosition:Number = player_mc._y - 100;
var shootCount:Number;
var choices:Array = ["paper", "rock", "scissors"];

paper_mc.choice = "paper";
rock_mc.choice = "rock";
scissors_mc.choice = "scissors";
```

4. On the next line, create a variable called enemyChoice with a data type of String.

```
var playerChoice:String;
var downPosition:Number = player_mc._y;
var upPosition:Number = player_mc._y - 100;
var shootCount:Number;
var choices:Array = ["paper", "rock", "scissors"];
var enemyChoice:String;

paper_mc.choice = "paper";
rock_mc.choice = "rock";
scissors_mc.choice = "scissors";
```

5. In the DEFINE FUNCTIONS section, find the initializeGame function.

6. At the top of the initializeGame function, set the value of enemyChoice to a random index of the choices array. This will reset the value of the enemyChoice variable to be a random value each time you play the game.

```
function initializeGame():Void
{
    enemyChoice = choices[Math.floor(Math.random() * choices.length)];
    playerChoice = "";
    end_mc._visible = false;
    shootCount = 0;


    top_btn.enabled = false;
    bottom_btn.enabled = false;
}
```

NOTE The code you just wrote may seem pretty complex, so let's talk about how it works. To capture an index of an array, you type the name of the array (which in this case is choices), and square brackets (the open square bracket here is right after choices and the closed square bracket is right before the semicolon). The value inside the brackets represents the index number you are referring to inside the array. Here, you're using Math.floor() to round down a random number (the opening parenthesis is right after floor, and the closing parenthesis is right before the closing square bracket). The random number is created by multiplying Math.random() (which generates a random number between 0 and up to, but not including, 1), by the length of the choices array (choices.length), which is 3. Therefore, the random number will be between 0 and up to, but not including, 3, and will be rounded down using Math.floor(), so it will be 0, 1, or 2. If the random number is 0, choices[0] will be selected, which will set the value of enemyChoice to "paper", the first index of the choices array.

7. Now, you'll move the enemy hand with the player hand. In the DEFINE EVENT HANDLERS section of code, find the top_btn.onRollOver event handler.

8. At the bottom of the top_btn.onRollOver event handler, make the enemy_mc movie clip move up to the same position as the player_mc movie clip by setting its _y property equal to the upPosition variable.

```
top_btn.onRollOver = function():Void
{
```

```
        bottom_btn.enabled = true;
        player_mc._y = upPosition;
        enemy_mc._y = upPosition;
    }
```

9. In the same section of code, find the bottom_btn.onRollOver event handler.

10. At the top of the bottom_btn.onRollOver event handler, set the _y property of the enemy_mc movie clip equal to the downPosition variable. This will make the enemy_mc move down along with the player_mc movie clip.

```
bottom_btn.onRollOver = function():Void
{
    enemy_mc._y = downPosition;
    player_mc._y = downPosition;
    shootCount ++;
    if(shootCount >= 3)
    {
        endGame();
    }
}
```

11. In the DEFINE FUNCTIONS section of code, locate the endGame function.

12. At the top of the endGame function, make the enemy_mc go to the frame that corresponds with the enemyChoice variable by using the gotoAndStop method and passing in the enemyChoice variable.

```
function endGame():Void
{
    enemy_mc.gotoAndStop(enemyChoice);
    player_mc.gotoAndStop(playerChoice);
    top_btn.enabled = false;
    bottom_btn.enabled = false;
}
```

13. Test the movie, make a choice, and move the mouse up and down until you see the player's choice and the enemy's choice, as shown next. Now you have another working game. Sweet!

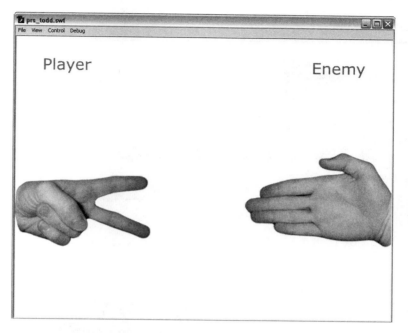

14. Save the file, and keep it open for the next exercise.

EXERCISE 6-5: Winning the Game

Now that your basic game is set up, you'll write the logic that makes Flash determine who the winner is.

1. Make sure you are working in the same file from the last exercise.

2. In the Library, double-click the symbol icon for mcEnd to enter its Timeline.

3. Inside the mcEnd movie clip, note the instance name of the text field on the Stage is end_txt, as shown in Figure 6-1.

4. At the bottom of the Timeline, click the Scene 1 button to return to the Main Timeline.

5. On the Main Timeline, select the first keyframe of the actions layer and open the Actions panel by pressing F9 (Windows) or OPTION-F9 (Mac).

6. In the DEFINE FUNCTIONS section, find the endGame function.

FIGURE 6-1

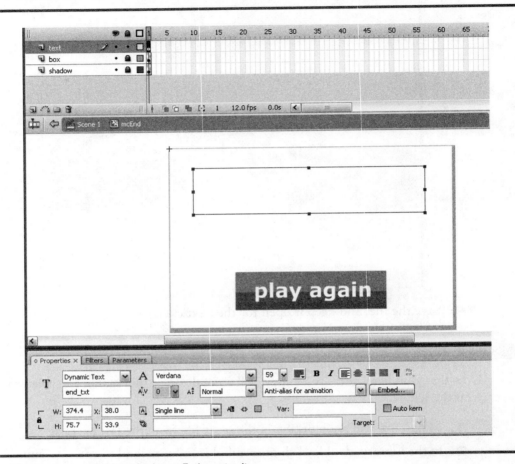

Viewing the text field inside the mcEnd movie clip

7. At the top of the endGame function, create a variable called win1, with a data type of Boolean and a value of playerChoice == "rock" && enemyChoice == "scissors". This represents one possible winning scenario: the player's choice being rock and the enemy's choice being scissors. If that is the case, the value of this variable will be true.

```
function endGame():Void
{
    var win1:Boolean = playerChoice ==
"rock" && enemyChoice == "scissors";
```

```
enemy_mc.gotoAndStop(enemyChoice);
player_mc.gotoAndStop(playerChoice);
top_btn.enabled = false;
bottom_btn.enabled = false;
}
```

8. On the next line, repeat Step 7, with the following changes: change win1
to win2, change "rock" to "paper", and change "scissors" to "rock". This
represents the second winning scenario, when the player's choice is paper
and the enemy's choice is rock.

```
function endGame():Void
{
    var win1:Boolean = playerChoice ==
    "rock" && enemyChoice == "scissors";
    var win2:Boolean = playerChoice ==
    "paper" && enemyChoice == "rock";

    enemy_mc.gotoAndStop(enemyChoice);
    player_mc.gotoAndStop(playerChoice);
    top_btn.enabled = false;
    bottom_btn.enabled = false;
}
```

9. On the next line, repeat Step 7, with win3 in place of win1, "scissors"
instead of "rock", and "paper" instead of "scissors". This represents the
third winning scenario.

```
function endGame():Void
{
    var win1:Boolean = playerChoice ==
    "rock" && enemyChoice == "scissors";
    var win2:Boolean = playerChoice ==
    "paper" && enemyChoice == "rock";
    var win3:Boolean = playerChoice ==
    "scissors" && enemyChoice == "paper";

    enemy_mc.gotoAndStop(enemyChoice);
    player_mc.gotoAndStop(playerChoice);
    top_btn.enabled = false;
    bottom_btn.enabled = false;
}
```

NOTE — Remember that two equal signs (==) mean "is equal to," which is different than one equal sign (=), which is used to assign values. This is a common error when working with conditional statements. Also remember that two ampersands (&&) mean "and" in ActionScript.

10. Next, you'll show the end_mc movie clip. At the bottom of the endGame function, show the end_mc movie clip by setting its _visible property to true.

```
function endGame():Void
{
    var win1:Boolean = playerChoice ==
    "rock" && enemyChoice == "scissors";
    var win2:Boolean = playerChoice ==
    "paper" && enemyChoice == "rock";
    var win3:Boolean = playerChoice ==
    "scissors" && enemyChoice == "paper";

    enemy_mc.gotoAndStop(enemyChoice);
    player_mc.gotoAndStop(playerChoice);
    top_btn.enabled = false;
    bottom_btn.enabled = false;

    end_mc._visible = true;
}
```

11. Next, you'll create some conditional statements to check all the possible ending scenarios for the game. First, you'll check for a tie. Below the last line of code you wrote, create the skeleton of a conditional statement that checks to see if the values of the playerChoice and enemyChoice variables are the same.

```
function endGame():Void
{
    var win1:Boolean = playerChoice ==
    "rock" && enemyChoice == "scissors";
    var win2:Boolean = playerChoice ==
    "paper" && enemyChoice == "rock";
    var win3:Boolean = playerChoice ==
    "scissors" && enemyChoice == "paper";

    enemy_mc.gotoAndStop(enemyChoice);
    player_mc.gotoAndStop(playerChoice);
```

```
     top_btn.enabled = false;
     bottom_btn.enabled = false;

     end_mc._visible = true;

     if(playerChoice == enemyChoice)
     {


     }
}
```

12. Inside the conditional statement you just created, set the text field (end_txt) inside end_mc to display the text "Tie!" using the text field's text property.

```
function endGame():Void
{
     var win1:Boolean = playerChoice ==
     "rock" && enemyChoice == "scissors";
     var win2:Boolean = playerChoice ==
     "paper" && enemyChoice == "rock";
     var win3:Boolean = playerChoice ==
     "scissors" && enemyChoice == "paper";

     enemy_mc.gotoAndStop(enemyChoice);
     player_mc.gotoAndStop(playerChoice);
     top_btn.enabled = false;
     bottom_btn.enabled = false;

     end_mc._visible = true;

     if(playerChoice == enemyChoice)
     {
          end_mc.end_txt.text = "Tie!";
}
}
```

13. Below the conditional statement you just created, create an else if conditional statement that checks to see if the player won. To do this, you can use the || (or) operator to check whether win1, win2, or win3 is true.

```
function endGame():Void
{
```

```
var win1:Boolean = playerChoice ==
"rock" && enemyChoice == "scissors";
var win2:Boolean = playerChoice ==
"paper" && enemyChoice == "rock";
var win3:Boolean = playerChoice ==
"scissors" && enemyChoice == "paper";

enemy_mc.gotoAndStop(enemyChoice);
player_mc.gotoAndStop(playerChoice);
top_btn.enabled = false;
bottom_btn.enabled = false;

end_mc._visible = true;

if(playerChoice == enemyChoice)
{
    end_mc.end_txt.text = "Tie!";
}
else if(win1 || win2 || win3)
{

}
}
```

NOTE The code you just wrote will evaluate whether the value of win1 OR win2 OR win3 is true. The values of those variables are based on the player and enemy choices, as defined at the top of this function. If any one of those values is true, it means the player won, and the code in the curly braces will run.

14. Inside the conditional statement you just created, set the value of the text field inside end_mc to be "You win!"

```
function endGame():Void
{
    var win1:Boolean = playerChoice ==
    "rock" && enemyChoice == "scissors";
    var win2:Boolean = playerChoice ==
    "paper" && enemyChoice == "rock";
    var win3:Boolean = playerChoice ==
    "scissors" && enemyChoice == "paper";
```

```
enemy_mc.gotoAndStop(enemyChoice);
player_mc.gotoAndStop(playerChoice);
top_btn.enabled = false;
bottom_btn.enabled = false;

end_mc._visible = true;

if(playerChoice == enemyChoice)
{
    end_mc.end_txt.text = "Tie!";
}
else if(win1 || win2 || win3)
{
    end_mc.end_txt.text = "You win!";
}
}
```

15. Below the else if statement you just created, create the skeleton of an else statement. The code in this else statement will run if the player lost, or if none of the other conditions were true.

```
function endGame():Void
{
    var win1:Boolean = playerChoice ==
    "rock" && enemyChoice == "scissors";
    var win2:Boolean = playerChoice ==
    "paper" && enemyChoice == "rock";
    var win3:Boolean = playerChoice ==
    "scissors" && enemyChoice == "paper";

    enemy_mc.gotoAndStop(enemyChoice);
    player_mc.gotoAndStop(playerChoice);
    top_btn.enabled = false;
    bottom_btn.enabled = false;

    end_mc._visible = true;

    if(playerChoice == enemyChoice)
    {
        end_mc.end_txt.text = "Tie!";
    }
```

```
    else if(win1 || win2 || win3)
    {
        end_mc.end_txt.text = "You win!";
    }
else
{

}
}
```

16. Inside the else statement you just created, set the text field inside end_mc to display "You lose!"

```
function endGame():Void
{
    var win1:Boolean = playerChoice ==
    "rock" && enemyChoice == "scissors";
    var win2:Boolean = playerChoice ==
    "paper" && enemyChoice == "rock";
    var win3:Boolean = playerChoice ==
    "scissors" && enemyChoice == "paper";

    enemy_mc.gotoAndStop(enemyChoice);
    player_mc.gotoAndStop(playerChoice);
    top_btn.enabled = false;
    bottom_btn.enabled = false;

    end_mc._visible = true;

    if(playerChoice == enemyChoice)
    {
        end_mc.end_txt.text = "Tie!";
    }
    else if(win1 || win2 || win3)
    {
        end_mc.end_txt.text = "You win!";
    }
    else
        {
```

Applying Advanced Logic and Interactivity: A Paper Rock Scissors Game

```
            end_mc.end_txt.text = "You lose!";
        }
    }
```

17. Test the movie, and play the game to see the win, lose, or tie message, shown here. Nice!

18. Save the file, and keep it open for the next exercise.

EXERCISE 6-6: Playing the Game Multiple Times

What game is complete if you can't play it over and over again? In this exercise, you'll make the game re-playable.

1. Make sure you are working in the same file from the last exercise.

2. Select the first keyframe of the actions layer and open the Actions panel by pressing F9 (Windows) or OPTION-F9 (Mac).

3. In the DEFINE FUNCTIONS section, locate the endGame function.

4. Near the middle of the endGame function, find the line of code that sets the end_mc movie clip's _visible property to true.

5. Below that line of code, write the code to run the initializeGame function when you click the end_mc movie clip.

```
function endGame():Void
{
    var win1:Boolean = playerChoice ==
    "rock" && enemyChoice == "scissors";
    var win2:Boolean = playerChoice ==
    "paper" && enemyChoice == "rock";
    var win3:Boolean = playerChoice ==
    "scissors" && enemyChoice == "paper";

    enemy_mc.gotoAndStop(enemyChoice);
    player_mc.gotoAndStop(playerChoice);
    top_btn.enabled = false;
    bottom_btn.enabled = false;

    end_mc._visible = true;
    end_mc.onRelease = initializeGame;

    if(playerChoice == enemyChoice)
    {
        end_mc.end_txt.text = "Tie!";
    }
    else if(win1 || win2 || win3)
    {
        end_mc.end_txt.text = "You win!";
    }
    else
    {
        end_mc.end_txt.text = "You lose!";
    }
}
```

6. Test the movie, and play through the game. Then, click the end_mc movie clip to play the game again. Notice the buttons don't appear on the Stage, and the hands do not display fists. You'll fix that in the next few steps.

Applying Advanced Logic and Interactivity: A Paper Rock Scissors Game

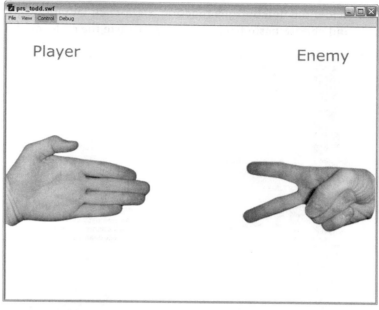

7. First, you'll copy and modify the hideButtons function to make a function that shows buttons. In the DEFINE FUNCTIONS section, locate the hideButtons function.

8. Select the entire hideButtons function and right-click or CTRL-click (Mac) the selected code and choose Copy from the menu that appears to copy the code, as shown here.

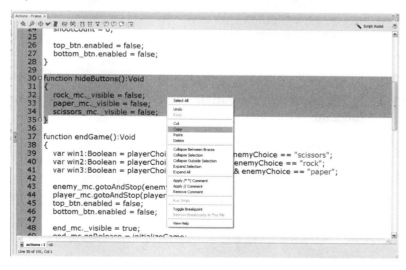

9. Below the hideButtons function, right-click (Windows) or CTRL-click (Mac) and choose paste from the menu to paste the code, as shown next.

10. In the pasted code, change the name of the function to showButtons, and set the _visible property of each button to true instead of false.

```
function showButtons():Void
{
    rock_mc._visible = true;
    paper_mc._visible = true;
    scissors_mc._visible = true;
}
```

11. In the same section of code, find the initializeGame function.

12. At the bottom of the initializeGame function, run the showButtons function.

```
function initializeGame():Void
{
```

```
enemyChoice = choices[Math.floor(Math.random() *
choices.length)];
playerChoice = "";
end_mc._visible = false;
shootCount = 0;

top_btn.enabled = false;
bottom_btn.enabled = false;

showButtons();
}
```

13. On the next two lines, make the player_mc and enemy_mc movie clips go to frame 1 and stop, by using the gotoAndStop method and passing in a value of 1. This will make the player and enemy hands display their default graphics; the same graphics as when you start the game initially.

```
function initializeGame():Void
{
    enemyChoice = choices[Math.floor(Math.random() *
    choices.length)];
    playerChoice = "";
    end_mc._visible = false;
    shootCount = 0;

    top_btn.enabled = false;
    bottom_btn.enabled = false;

    showButtons();
    player_mc.gotoAndStop(1);
    enemy_mc.gotoAndStop(1);
}
```

14. Test the movie, and play through the game—again and again. Congratulations, you've finished another game!

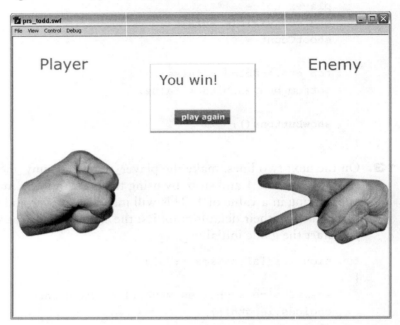

15. Save the file. You can now upload it to the Web just like your other games and try it out on a Wii.

CHAPTER 7

Adding Circular Motion Detection: A Clock Game

IN this chapter, you'll take everything you've done with interactivity and build on it by creating a clock game. In the clock game, your goal is to match the time on a big clock to the time on a smaller clock. The game will allow you to rotate the clock hands by moving the Wii remote or mouse in a circular motion. Depending on whether you are moving the mouse clockwise or counterclockwise, the hands on the clock will either move forward or backward.

If you'd like to view the finished game at any time, the name of the file is clock_final.fla.

CREATING THE INTERACTIVITY FOR THE CLOCK

Controlling the movement of the hands on the clock will require much more complex interactivity than what you've done up to this point. So far, you've made games that use the Wii remote similar to a mouse, and games that mimic commercial Wii games in that you can move the mouse or Wii remote up and down to simulate something in real life.

Making the clock hands rotate clockwise or counterclockwise is going to take a different approach and will come with a few challenges. Before you create a game, it's always best to think of the challenges you might face, and at least one possible solution. First, Flash does not have a built-in rotation detector, so you'll have to find a way to simulate that. Second, even if you build a rotation detector, how will Flash know which direction the player is rotating the Wii remote or mouse?

Here's the solution I came up with, and it's likely not the only one: divide the Stage into four sections, and place four invisible buttons on the Stage—one in each corner (see Figure 7-1).

You can then control the button interactivity using the onRollOver event that you've been working with already. This time, however, it will be a little different. When you roll over a button, for example, the direction that the clock rotates will be calculated based on not only the button you rolled over, but also the last button you rolled over. You could start by giving each button a number (see Figure 7-2). Then, if you roll over button 1, for example, and the next button you roll over is button 2, it's safe to assume you want the clock to rotate clockwise. If, on the other hand, you roll over button 2 and then button 1, you more than likely want to rotate the clock counterclockwise.

FIGURE 7-1

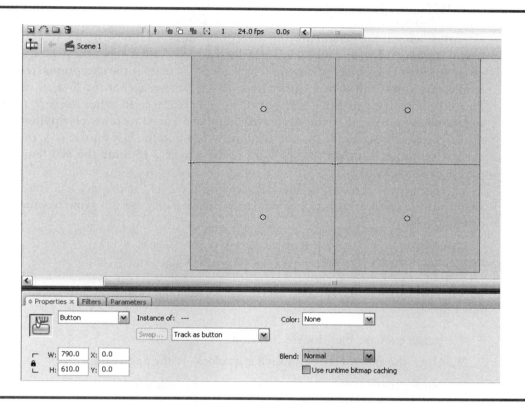

Four invisible buttons on the Stage—one at each corner

FIGURE 7-2

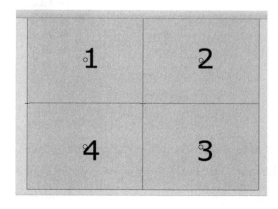

Numbered buttons

So then, can you say that if the current button rolled over is greater than the last button, you are rotating clockwise and vice versa? Not exactly, but it's a start. Consider this: what if the person playing the game rotates the mouse or Wii remote over button 1, then 2, 3, 4, and then 1 again? Clearly, 1 is less than 4, but the person is definitely rotating clockwise. What you'll have to do is create some exceptions. (For example, the game will detect clockwise rotation in two scenarios: first, if the last button number is 4 and the current button number is 1; second, when the current button number is greater than the last button number.) The same principle applies to rotating counterclockwise. If the current button is 4 and the last button is 1, or if the current button is less than the last button, the player is rotating the Wii remote or mouse counterclockwise.

There's a quick look at the interactivity you'll create for the clock. It may seem pretty intense, and it is, but once you create it, you can use the same technique in other games.

EXERCISE 7-1: Viewing the Flash File

Before you start writing the code to create the game, take a look at how the .FLA file is set up.

1. In the exercise files, locate clock.fla.

2. Open the file in Flash and save it as **clock_{your name}.fla**.

3. Notice there are six layers (as shown in the following illustration): actions, end, buttons, target, clock, and BG.

4. Show and hide the layers to see the content in each layer.

5. Notice that the end layer contains one movie clip, end_mc.

6. Notice that the buttons layer contains four buttons: tl_btn, tr_btn, br_btn, and bl_btn.

Adding Circular Motion Detection: A Clock Game

7. Notice the target layer contains a dynamic text field, target_txt, a movie clip, target_mc, and a static text field that says "Target time".

8. Notice the clock layer contains one movie clip, clock_mc.

9. Double-click the mcClock movie clip symbol in the Library to enter its Timeline.

10. Inside the mcClock movie clip, notice there are two movie clips: hour_mc and minute_mc, representing the hour and minute hands.

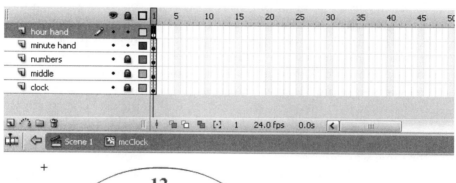

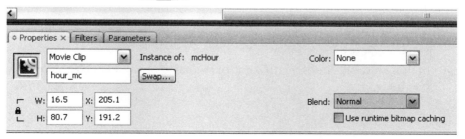

11. At the bottom of the Timeline, click the Scene 1 button to return to the Main Timeline.

12. Keep the file open for the next exercise.

PREPARING TO WRITE ACTIONSCRIPT CODE

Now that we've taken a look at how the Flash file is set up, we can begin writing the code to make this file into a game. The first step is to set up some of the variables and functions you are going to use.

When you are going through this process for your own games, how do you know what variables to create? You can start by identifying what data will need to be stored in variables. For example, in this game, we're going to have to capture whether the user is rotating the Wii remote clockwise or counterclockwise. To do that, we first need to store all the buttons in an array, which means we'll have to create an array variable. From there, we'll need to keep track of the last button the user rolled over (stored in another variable) and the button the user is currently over (stored in yet another variable). To find the variables you need for your game, you can look at how your game will work and think about what data you'll have to keep track of in the same way.

You'll also have to define functions when you create your own games. How do you know which code should go in a function? First, you should check what mouse interactivity is going to be in your game. In this game, there are going to be four roll-over buttons, so we'll need functions (or event handler functions) to react to when the buttons are rolled over. From there, think about tasks your game will be repeating often. In this game, we're going to rotate the clock hands multiple times, so it's good to put the code that rotates the hand in a function. If you can't think of any other places to create functions, look for places in your code where you are typing the same thing multiple times with slight variation. Those blocks of code can typically be placed in one function that reacts slightly differently based on parameters that are passed in. For example, in our code, we're going to have a function to rotate the hands of a clock. Instead of creating a function for each clock or for each hand, we can create one function that takes a parameter for the clock and rotates the hands of that clock.

EXERCISE 7-2: Setting Up the Flash File

In this exercise, you'll set up some of the basic variables and functions you'll be using for this game.

1. Make sure you are working in the same file from the last exercise.

2. Select the first keyframe of the actions layer and open the Actions panel by pressing F9 (Windows) or OPTION-F9 (Mac).

3. In the DECLARE VARIABLES AND CREATE OBJECTS section, create a variable called rotateAmt, with a data type of Number and a value of 30. This will represent the amount of rotation to apply to the minute hand when it rotates. Your code should match the code that follows (new code is bold):

```
// DECLARE VARIABLES AND CREATE OBJECTS

var rotateAmt:Number = 30;
```

NOTE The number 30 is not some random number, but rather a calculation of 360 divided by 12. Why 360 divided by 12? One goal for this game is to make the minute hand move only five minutes at a time. The number 12 comes from 60 (the number of minutes in an hour) divided by 5 (the amount of minutes to move). 360 comes from a full circle having 360 degrees. 360 divided by 12 represents the rotation amount that will show five minutes on the clock.

4. On the next line, create another variable called buttons, with a data type of Array and a value of [tl_btn, tr_btn, br_btn, bl_btn]. This array will hold all the buttons, and you'll use it to create loops that run a block of code on all the buttons.

```
// DECLARE VARIABLES AND CREATE OBJECTS

var rotateAmt:Number = 30;
var buttons:Array = [tl_btn, tr_btn, br_btn, bl_btn];
```

5. Below the code you just wrote, create a variable called currentButtonNum, with a data type of Number. This will represent the number connected to the current button being rolled over.

```
// DECLARE VARIABLES AND CREATE OBJECTS

var rotateAmt:Number = 30;
var buttons:Array = [tl_btn, tr_btn, br_btn, bl_btn];

var currentButtonNum:Number;
```

6. On the next line, create a variable called lastButtonNum, with a data type of Number. This will represent the previous button that was rolled over.

```
var rotateAmt:Number = 30;
var buttons:Array = [tl_btn, tr_btn, br_btn, bl_btn];

var currentButtonNum:Number;
var lastButtonNum:Number;
```

7. On the next line, create a variable called cw1, with a data type of Boolean. This variable will represent the first scenario for the player rotating clockwise, which I'll talk about in more detail in the next exercise.

```
var rotateAmt:Number = 30;
var buttons:Array = [tl_btn, tr_btn, br_btn, bl_btn];

var currentButtonNum:Number;
var lastButtonNum:Number;
var cw1:Boolean;
```

8. On the next three lines, create three more variables: cw2, ccw1, and ccw2. All the variables should have a Boolean data type. These variables will represent the other scenarios for rotating the mouse or Wii remote clockwise and counterclockwise, which I'll also talk about in more detail in the next exercise.

```
var rotateAmt:Number = 30;
var buttons:Array = [tl_btn, tr_btn, br_btn, bl_btn];

var currentButtonNum:Number;
var lastButtonNum:Number;
var cw1:Boolean;
var cw2:Boolean;
var ccw1:Boolean;
var ccw2:Boolean;
```

9. In the DEFINE FUNCTIONS section, create the skeleton of a function called initializeGame.

```
// DEFINE FUNCTIONS

function initializeGame():Void
```

```
{

}
```

10. In the initializeGame function, set the _rotation property of the hour hand
(clock_mc.hour_mc) to 0. This will reset the rotation of the hour hand each
time you play the game.

```
function initializeGame():Void
{
    clock_mc.hour_mc._rotation = 0;
}
```

11. On the next line, set the _rotation property of the minute hand
(clock_mc.minute_mc) to 0 to reset the rotation of the minute
hand each time you play the game.

```
function initializeGame():Void
{
    clock_mc.hour_mc._rotation = 0;
    clock_mc.minute_mc._rotation = 0;
}
```

12. On the next line, run a function called enableAll, and pass in a value of
true. You'll define the enableAll function later in this exercise.

```
function initializeGame():Void
{
    clock_mc.hour_mc._rotation = 0;
    clock_mc.minute_mc._rotation = 0;
    enableAll(true);
}
```

13. On the next line, set the _visible property of the end_mc movie clip to false.
This will hide the end_mc movie clip when the game starts.

```
function initializeGame():Void
{
    clock_mc.hour_mc._rotation = 0;
    clock_mc.minute_mc._rotation = 0;
    enableAll(true);
    end_mc._visible = false;
}
```

14. Below the initializeGame function, create the skeleton of a function called enableAll. The function should receive one parameter, isEnabled, which should have a data type of Boolean. This function will enable or disable all the buttons, depending on the value passed in.

```
function enableAll(isEnabled:Boolean):Void
{

}
```

15. Inside the enableAll function, create the skeleton of a "for" loop that loops for the length of the buttons array.

```
function enableAll(isEnabled:Boolean):Void
{
    for(var i:Number = 0; i < buttons.length; i++)
    {

    }
}
```

16. Inside the loop you just created, set the enabled property of buttons[i] to the value passed into the function as isEnabled.

```
function enableAll(isEnabled:Boolean):Void
{
    for(var i:Number = 0; i < buttons.length; i++)
    {
        buttons[i].enabled = isEnabled;
    }
}
```

NOTE The enableAll function allows you to pass in the isEnabled parameter, which has either a true or false value. Since the "for" loop is inside the enableAll function, the true or false value that's passed in via the isEnabled parameter is applied to all the buttons in the buttons array. For example, consider what would happen if you ran the enableAll function and passed in false, as in the following code:

```
enableAll(false);
```

Flash would set the enabled property for each button in the buttons array to false. The buttons in the buttons array would not react to mouse clicks, rollovers, etc.

17. On the next line of code, set the onRollOver event for buttons[i] to run a function called buttonOver. You'll define the buttonOver function later in this exercise.

```
function enableAll(isEnabled:Boolean):Void
{
    for(var i:Number = 0; i < buttons.length; i++)
    {
        buttons[i].enabled = isEnabled;
        buttons[i].onRollOver = buttonOver;
    }
}
```

 Up to this point, you've been referencing functions by typing the function name and parentheses (example: myFunction()). Here, don't use parentheses because you aren't actually running the buttonOver function. Rather, you're connecting it to the onRollOver event of each button in the buttons array. This way, the buttonOver function will run each time you roll over a button. This is simply a more readable alternative to typing out the entire function definition using " = function():Void {}" etc. right here.

18. On the next line, create a dynamic property on buttons[i] called num, with a value of i. This property connects each button with a number. Then, the top-left button will have a num value of 0, the top right a num value of 1, the bottom right a num value of 2, and the bottom left a num value of 3. With the buttons connected to numbers, you can more easily add the rotation interactivity.

```
function enableAll(isEnabled:Boolean):Void
{
    for(var i:Number = 0; i < buttons.length; i++)
    {
        buttons[i].enabled = isEnabled;
        buttons[i].onRollOver = buttonOver;
        buttons[i].num = i;
    }
}
```

TIP Here's a quick recap of what this loop is doing so far:

1. Setting the enabled property of each button equal to the value passed in via the isEnabled parameter.
2. Setting the onRollOver event of each button to trigger the buttonOver function.
3. Setting the dynamic property, num, of each button equal to the button's index in the buttons array.

19. In the DEFINE EVENT HANDLERS section, create the skeleton of a function called buttonOver.

```
// DEFINE EVENT HANDLERS

function buttonOver():Void
{

}
```

20. In the RUN IMMEDIATELY section, run the initializeGame function.

```
// RUN IMMEDIATELY

initializeGame();
```

21. Save the file, and keep it open for the next exercise.

EXERCISE 7-3: Moving the Clock Hands

In this exercise, you'll add the interactivity to the buttons to make the clock hands rotate when you move your mouse in a circular motion.

1. Make sure you are working in the same file from the last exercise.

2. Select the first keyframe of the actions layer and open the Actions panel by pressing F9 (Windows) or OPTION-F9 (Mac).

3. In the DEFINE EVENT HANDLERS section, locate the buttonOver event handler function.

4. In the buttonOver function, set the value of the currentButtonNum variable to the num property of whichever button was clicked on. The num property was set initially in the enableAll function.

```
function buttonOver():Void
{
    currentButtonNum = this.num;
}
```

NOTE Remember that because the "this" keyword is being used in an event handler (because it was connected to the onRollOver event for each button in the loop you wrote earlier), "this" represents the current button being rolled over. Also note that "this.num" represents the value of the dynamic property "num" for that particular button, which is the index number of that button in the buttons array.

5. On the next line, create the skeleton of a conditional statement that checks to see if the lastButtonNum variable is undefined.

```
function buttonOver():Void
{
    currentButtonNum = this.num;
    if(lastButtonNum == undefined)
    {

    }
}
```

TIP The lastButtonNum variable will be undefined until the value is set inside the if statement. Later on in this function, you'll check the value of lastButtonNum against the values of other variables. If lastButtonNum is undefined, you could potentially get an error. This if statement prevents that error.

6. Inside the conditional statement you just created, set the value of the lastButtonNum variable equal to the num property of the button that was clicked. The lastButtonNum variable will hold the previous button that was rolled over. In this case, if the lastButtonNum variable is undefined (which it will be until you set a value for it), the value will be whatever button is rolled over.

```
function buttonOver():Void
{
    currentButtonNum = this.num;
    if(lastButtonNum == undefined)
    {
        lastButtonNum = this.num;
    }
}
```

7. Below the conditional statement you just created, set the value of cw1 to currentButtonNum == 0 && lastButtonNum == 3. This is one of the scenarios for the rotation of the mouse or Wii remote being clockwise, where the current button number is 0 and the last button number is 3. If that is the case, the value of cw1 will be true.

```
function buttonOver():Void
{
    currentButtonNum = this.num;
    if(lastButtonNum == undefined)
    {
        lastButtonNum = this.num;
    }
    cw1 = currentButtonNum == 0 && lastButtonNum == 3;
}
```

8. On the next line, set the value of the cw2 variable to currentButtonNum == lastButtonNum + 1. This is the second scenario for clockwise rotation, where the currentButtonNum variable is equal to the lastButtonNum variable plus 1. In other words, if the last button rolled over was 1, and the current button is 2, the mouse or Wii remote is rotating clockwise. If that is the case, the value of cw2 will be true.

```
function buttonOver():Void
{
    currentButtonNum = this.num;
    if(lastButtonNum == undefined)
    {
        lastButtonNum = this.num;
    }
    cw1 = currentButtonNum == 0 && lastButtonNum == 3;
    cw2 = currentButtonNum == lastButtonNum + 1;
}
```

9. Now, you'll set the values of the ccw1 and ccw2 variables in the same way that you set the cw1 and cw2 variables, with the values changed to indicate counterclockwise rotation. On the next line, set the value of the ccw1 variable to currentButtonNum == 3 && lastButtonNum == 0.

```
function buttonOver():Void
{
    currentButtonNum = this.num;
    if(lastButtonNum == undefined)
    {
        lastButtonNum = this.num;
    }
```

```
        cw1 = currentButtonNum == 0 && lastButtonNum == 3;
        cw2 = currentButtonNum == lastButtonNum + 1;
        ccw1 = currentButtonNum == 3 && lastButtonNum == 0;
    }
```

10. On the next line, set the value of the ccw2 variable to currentButtonNum == lastButtonNum – 1.

```
function buttonOver():Void
{
    currentButtonNum = this.num;
    if(lastButtonNum == undefined)
    {
        lastButtonNum = this.num;
    }
    cw1 = currentButtonNum == 0 && lastButtonNum == 3;
    cw2 = currentButtonNum == lastButtonNum + 1;
    ccw1 = currentButtonNum == 3 && lastButtonNum == 0;
    ccw2 = currentButtonNum == lastButtonNum - 1;
}
```

11. Below the last code you wrote, create the skeleton of a conditional statement that checks to see if the value of cw1 or the value of cw2 is true. This conditional statement will run the code in curly braces if the person playing the game is rotating the mouse or Wii remote clockwise.

```
function buttonOver():Void
{
    currentButtonNum = this.num;
    if(lastButtonNum == undefined)
    {
        lastButtonNum = this.num;
    }
    cw1 = currentButtonNum == 0 && lastButtonNum == 3;
    cw2 = currentButtonNum == lastButtonNum + 1;
    ccw1 = currentButtonNum == 3 && lastButtonNum == 0;
    ccw2 = currentButtonNum == lastButtonNum - 1;

    if(cw1 || cw2)
    {

    }
}
```

12. Inside the conditional statement you just created, run a function called updateClock, passing in clock_mc and rotateAmt (the variable you defined earlier representing the rotation amount for the minute hand). The updateClock function, which you'll define later in this exercise, will move the hands on the clock.

```
function buttonOver():Void
{
    currentButtonNum = this.num;
    if(lastButtonNum == undefined)
    {
        lastButtonNum = this.num;
    }
    cw1 = currentButtonNum == 0 && lastButtonNum == 3;
    cw2 = currentButtonNum == lastButtonNum + 1;
    ccw1 = currentButtonNum == 3 && lastButtonNum == 0;
    ccw2 = currentButtonNum == lastButtonNum - 1;

    if(cw1 || cw2)
    {
        updateClock(clock_mc, rotateAmt);
    }
}
```

13. Below the conditional statement you just created, create the skeleton of an else if statement that checks if the ccw1 variable is true or the ccw2 variable is true. This conditional statement will run the code in curly braces if the person playing the game is rotating the mouse or Wii remote counterclockwise.

```
function buttonOver():Void
{
    currentButtonNum = this.num;
    if(lastButtonNum == undefined)
    {
        lastButtonNum = this.num;
    }
    cw1 = currentButtonNum == 0 && lastButtonNum == 3;
    cw2 = currentButtonNum == lastButtonNum + 1;
    ccw1 = currentButtonNum == 3 && lastButtonNum == 0;
    ccw2 = currentButtonNum == lastButtonNum - 1;

    if(cw1 || cw2)
```

```
    {
        updateClock(clock_mc, rotateAmt);
    }
    else if(ccw1 || ccw2)
    {

    }
}
```

14. In the conditional statement you just created, run the updateClock function, passing in clock_mc and –rotateAmt (the amount is negative because the rotation value will be negative when the clock moves counterclockwise).

```
function buttonOver():Void
{
    currentButtonNum = this.num;
    if(lastButtonNum == undefined)
    {
        lastButtonNum = this.num;
    }
    cw1 = currentButtonNum == 0 && lastButtonNum == 3;
    cw2 = currentButtonNum == lastButtonNum + 1;
    ccw1 = currentButtonNum == 3 && lastButtonNum == 0;
    ccw2 = currentButtonNum == lastButtonNum - 1;

    if(cw1 || cw2)
    {
        updateClock(clock_mc, rotateAmt);
    }
    else if(ccw1 || ccw2)
    {
        updateClock(clock_mc, -rotateAmt);
    }
}
```

15. At the very bottom of the buttonOver function, set the value of lastButtonNum to the num value of the button that was rolled over. That way the lastButtonNum value will be stored when you roll over the next button.

```
function buttonOver():Void
{
```

```
        currentButtonNum = this.num;
        if(lastButtonNum == undefined)
        {
            lastButtonNum = this.num;
        }
        cw1 = currentButtonNum == 0 && lastButtonNum == 3;
        cw2 = currentButtonNum == lastButtonNum + 1;
        ccw1 = currentButtonNum == 3 && lastButtonNum == 0;
        ccw2 = currentButtonNum == lastButtonNum - 1;

        if(cw1 || cw2)
        {
            updateClock(clock_mc, rotateAmt);
        }
        else if(ccw1 || ccw2)
        {
            updateClock(clock_mc, -rotateAmt);
        }
        lastButtonNum = this.num;
    }
```

NOTE You may be wondering why I set the currentButtonNum equal to this.num at the beginning of this function and set lastButtonNum equal to this.num at the end of this function. This can potentially be confusing. Basically, you use the currentButtonNum variable to capture the index number of the button being rolled over, and use that information throughout the function to rotate the clock. Once the information is captured and used, you place the index number of the button rolled over in the lastButtonNum variable. In this way, you capture the information about the last button that was rolled over (which, until you roll over another button, is the same as the current button) and store it until you roll over another button, so when you roll over the next button you have the information about the last button.

---

16. At the bottom of the DEFINE FUNCTIONS section, create the skeleton of a function called updateClock, which receives two parameters: one called clock with a MovieClip data type, and another called updateValue with a Number data type. I'll discuss the updateValue parameter later in this exercise.

```
function updateClock(clock:MovieClip,
updateValue:Number):Void
```

```
{

}
```

17. Inside the updateClock function, add the updateValue to the _rotation value of the minute_mc movie clip inside the clock movie clip. This will rotate the clock's minute hand clockwise if the value of the updateValue parameter is positive, and counterclockwise if the value is negative.

```
function updateClock(clock:MovieClip,
updateValue:Number):Void
{
    clock.minute_mc._rotation += updateValue;
}
```

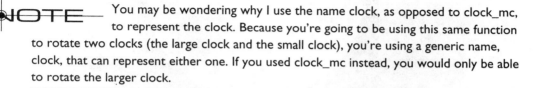

NOTE You may be wondering why I use the name clock, as opposed to clock_mc, to represent the clock. Because you're going to be using this same function to rotate two clocks (the large clock and the small clock), you're using a generic name, clock, that can represent either one. If you used clock_mc instead, you would only be able to rotate the larger clock.

18. On the next line, add the updateValue divided by 12 to the _rotation property of the hour hand (hour_mc) inside the clock movie clip. This will rotate the hour hand by 1/12 the rate that the minute hand rotates, which will make the clock on the screen move like a real clock. In other words, each time the minute hand makes a full rotation (12 five-minute steps), the hour hand takes a single one-hour step.

```
function updateClock(clock:MovieClip,
updateValue:Number):Void
{
    clock.minute_mc._rotation += updateValue;
    clock.hour_mc._rotation += updateValue / 12;
}
```

19. Test the movie (see Figure 7-3), and move the mouse in a clockwise circle to watch the clock hands rotate clockwise. Then, move the mouse in a counterclockwise circle to watch the clock hands move counterclockwise. Awesome!

FIGURE 7-3

The clock hands move just the way they're supposed to.

CAUTION Sometimes, you will have errors in your code that will show messages in the Output window that tell you exactly where the problem is. Other times, the error messages will be difficult to understand, or the movie will not work as it should and you won't see any error messages at all. If that's the case when you test the movie, go back through this exercise and compare your code to the code in the book, paying the most attention to the smallest details (typos—including capitalization, parentheses, square brackets, curly braces, semicolons, colons, etc.).

20. Save the file, and keep it open for the next exercise.

EXERCISE 7-4: Creating a Target Time

In this exercise, you'll add the interactivity to the target_txt text field and the target_mc movie clip so that both display the time the player needs to set the clock_mc movie clip.

1. Make sure you are working in the same file from the last exercise.

2. Select the first keyframe of the actions layer and open the Actions panel by pressing F9 (Windows) or OPTION-F9 (Mac).

3. In the DECLARE VARIABLES AND CREATE OBJECTS section, below the other variables you created, create a new variable called targetMinutes, with a Number data type. This number will represent the number the minute hand will be set to on the small (or target) clock.

```
var rotateAmt:Number = 30;
var buttons:Array = [tl_btn, tr_btn, br_btn, bl_btn];

var currentButtonNum:Number;
var lastButtonNum:Number;
var cw1:Boolean;
var cw2:Boolean;
var ccw1:Boolean;
var ccw2:Boolean;
var targetMinutes:Number;
```

4. On the next line, create another variable called targetHour, also with a data type of Number. This variable will represent where the hour hand should be on the target clock.

```
var rotateAmt:Number = 30;
var buttons:Array = [tl_btn, tr_btn, br_btn, bl_btn];

var currentButtonNum:Number;
var lastButtonNum:Number;
var cw1:Boolean;
var cw2:Boolean;
var ccw1:Boolean;
var ccw2:Boolean;
var targetMinutes:Number;
var targetHour:Number;
```

5. On the next line, create a variable called targetMinuteRotation, with a data type of Number. This variable will represent the number that holds the target minutes converted to a rotation amount, which will later be expressed in degrees.

```
var rotateAmt:Number = 30;
var buttons:Array = [tl_btn, tr_btn, br_btn, bl_btn];

var currentButtonNum:Number;
var lastButtonNum:Number;
var cw1:Boolean;
var cw2:Boolean;
var ccw1:Boolean;
var ccw2:Boolean;
var targetMinutes:Number;
var targetHour:Number;
var targetMinuteRotation:Number;
```

6. On the next line, create another variable called targetHourRotation, also with a data type of Number. This variable will hold the rotation value that will rotate the minute hand enough to wind the hour hand to the correct hour.

```
var rotateAmt:Number = 30;
var buttons:Array = [tl_btn, tr_btn, br_btn, bl_btn];

var currentButtonNum:Number;
var lastButtonNum:Number;
var cw1:Boolean;
var cw2:Boolean;
var ccw1:Boolean;
var ccw2:Boolean;
var targetMinutes:Number;
var targetHour:Number;
var targetMinuteRotation:Number;
var targetHourRotation:Number;
```

7. On the next line, create a variable called fullTargetRotation, with a data type of Number. This variable will represent the full amount of rotation to rotate both the minute and hour hands to the correct positions, and will be the sum of targetMinuteRotation and targetHourRotation.

```
var rotateAmt:Number = 30;
var buttons:Array = [tl_btn, tr_btn, br_btn, bl_btn];

var currentButtonNum:Number;
var lastButtonNum:Number;
var cw1:Boolean;
var cw2:Boolean;
var ccw1:Boolean;
var ccw2:Boolean;
var targetMinutes:Number;
var targetHour:Number;
var targetMinuteRotation:Number;
var targetHourRotation:Number;
var fullTargetRotation:Number;
```

UNDERSTANDING THE ROTATION VARIABLES

I mentioned that fullTargetRotation will be the sum of targetMinuteRotation and targetHourRotation. Then why not set the value now? This is because the values of targetMinuteRotation and targetHourRotation must be set first. If you set the value now, fullTargetRotation would be equal to the sum of two numbers that have no values, which not only could cause an error, but simply won't work properly. You'll define all the values in the initializeGame function.

Here's a quick recap of the variables you've created so far in this exercise:

)   **targetMinutes**   Where the minute hand will be located on the target clock

)   **targetHour**   Where the hour hand will be located on the target clock

)   **targetMinuteRotation**   How many degrees the minute hand on the target clock needs to rotate to reach targetMinutes

)   **targetHourRotation**   How many degrees the minute hand on the target clock needs to rotate so that the target clock's hour hand reaches targetHour

)   **fullTargetRotation**   The total amount of rotation needed to move both the hour and minute hands to their correct positions

8. In the DEFINE FUNCTIONS section of code, find the initializeGame function.

9. At the top of the initializeGame function, set the value of targetHour to be a random integer between 1 and 12.

```
function initializeGame():Void
{
    targetHour = Math.round(Math.random() * 11 + 1);

    clock_mc.hour_mc._rotation = 0;
    clock_mc.minute_mc._rotation = 0;
    enableAll(true);
    end_mc._visible = false;
}
```

NOTE In the preceding code, Math.random() * 11 gives a random number between 0 and 11, but not including 11. Adding 1 then makes the random range between 1 and 12, but not including 12. Using Math.round to round the number gives a random integer between 1 and 12, including 12.

10. On the next line, give the value of targetMinutes a random number that is a multiple of 5 between 0 and 55. This will keep the minute hand at five-minute intervals. But how do you get multiples of 5? One way is to get a random number between 0 and 11 and multiply that number by 5.

```
function initializeGame():Void
{
    targetHour = Math.round(Math.random() * 11 + 1);
    targetMinutes = Math.round(Math.random() * 11) * 5;

    clock_mc.hour_mc._rotation = 0;
    clock_mc.minute_mc._rotation = 0;
    enableAll(true);
    end_mc._visible = false;
}
```

11. Below the code you just wrote, set the value of targetHourRotation to targetHour * 360. This will make the minute hand rotate in full circles (hence 360, for the number of degrees in a circle) for each hour, making the hour hand rotate appropriately.

```
function initializeGame():Void
{
    targetHour = Math.round(Math.random() * 11 + 1);
    targetMinutes = Math.round(Math.random() * 11) * 5;

    targetHourRotation = targetHour * 360;

    clock_mc.hour_mc._rotation = 0;
    clock_mc.minute_mc._rotation = 0;
    enableAll(true);
    end_mc._visible = false;
}
```

12. On the next line, set the value of targetMinuteRotation to targetMinutes/5 *
rotateAmt. This will convert the number of minutes to a value between 0
and 11 (by dividing the value by 5), and multiply that value by the rotation
amount, which will convert a number of minutes to a rotation value and
make the minute hand rotate to the appropriate minute.

```
function initializeGame():Void
{
    targetHour = Math.round(Math.random() * 11 + 1);
    targetMinutes = Math.round(Math.random() * 11) * 5;

    targetHourRotation = targetHour * 360;
    targetMinuteRotation = targetMinutes/5 * rotateAmt;

    clock_mc.hour_mc._rotation = 0;
    clock_mc.minute_mc._rotation = 0;
    enableAll(true);
    end_mc._visible = false;
}
```

13. On the next line, set the value of fullTargetRotation to the sum of
targetHourRotation and targetMinuteRotation. This will give the full
rotation amount for the minute hand to wind the target clock into the
exact position when you pass this value into the updateClock function.

```
function initializeGame():Void
{
    targetHour = Math.round(Math.random() * 11 + 1);
```

```
        targetMinutes = Math.round(Math.random() * 11) * 5;

        targetHourRotation = targetHour * 360;
        targetMinuteRotation = targetMinutes/5 * rotateAmt;
        fullTargetRotation = targetHourRotation +
        targetMinuteRotation;

        clock_mc.hour_mc._rotation = 0;
        clock_mc.minute_mc._rotation = 0;
        enableAll(true);
        end_mc._visible = false;
    }
```

14. Below the code you just wrote, set the rotation of the hour and minute hands (hour_mc and minute_mc) for the target clock to 0. This will reset the rotation of the clock each time you play the game, which is necessary because the updateClock function will update the rotation of the clock relative to the clock's current position. In other words, all the variables

UNDERSTANDING HOW THE CODE WORKS

Assume that the target clock is currently at 12 o'clock.

Assume that the targetMinute is 30.

Assume, also, that targetHour has randomly come up with a value of 2, so the full target time would be 2 hours and 30 minutes, or 2:30.

Let's say targetHourRotation is equal to a value of 720 (360 * 2 with the number 2 being the value of targetHour).

Let's also say that targetMinuteRotation has a value of 180 (like the previous example with the minute hand).

This code will add those two values together for a sum of 900 (720 + 180).

Flash will then apply a value of 900 to the _rotation value of minute_ mc. This will rotate the minute hand 900 degrees. If the minute hand is pointing at 12 o'clock, it will make two full revolutions (360 degrees * 2 = 720) plus 180 degrees, which will leave the minute hand pointing at 6 (30 minutes past the hour).

Flash will then apply a rotation value of 75, or 900 divided by 12, to the hour hand, because the hour hand rotated 1/12 of the distance of the minute hand. Rotating the hour hand at a value 75 will place it halfway between the 2 and the 3, making the clock accurately represent 2:30.

you've just defined will rotate the clock perfectly, but only if the initial rotation values of the clock hands are 0.

```
function initializeGame():Void
{
    targetHour = Math.round(Math.random() * 11 + 1);
    targetMinutes = Math.round(Math.random() * 11) * 5;

    targetHourRotation = targetHour * 360;
    targetMinuteRotation = targetMinutes/5 * rotateAmt;
    fullTargetRotation = targetHourRotation +
    targetMinuteRotation;

    target_mc.hour_mc._rotation = 0;
    target_mc.minute_mc._rotation = 0;

    clock_mc.hour_mc._rotation = 0;
    clock_mc.minute_mc._rotation = 0;
    enableAll(true);
    end_mc._visible = false;
}
```

15. Below the code you just wrote, run the updateClock function, passing in target_mc (the smaller target clock on the right side of the Stage) for the clock parameter and fullTargetRotation for the updateValue. This will make the target clock hands rotate to match the randomly chosen time.

```
function initializeGame():Void
{
    targetHour = Math.round(Math.random() * 11 + 1);
    targetMinutes = Math.round(Math.random() * 11) * 5;

    targetHourRotation = targetHour * 360;
    targetMinuteRotation = targetMinutes/5 * rotateAmt;
    fullTargetRotation = targetHourRotation +
    targetMinuteRotation;

    target_mc.hour_mc._rotation = 0;
    target_mc.minute_mc._rotation = 0;

    updateClock(target_mc, fullTargetRotation);
```

```
clock_mc.hour_mc._rotation = 0;
clock_mc.minute_mc._rotation = 0;
enableAll(true);
end_mc._visible = false;
}
```

16. Test the movie, and look at the clock on the right side of the screen to see it show a random time, as shown here. You can test the movie multiple times to see the clock at other random times. Nice!

17. Next, you'll set a value for the target_txt text field so that you can see the target value as a numbered time. One problem you'll run into for this is that if the minute value is 0 or 5, Flash will not display those values as two digits (example: if the time is 8:05, your clock will display 8:05, but Flash will display 8:5). To work around this, below the last code you wrote, create the skeleton of a conditional statement that checks if the targetMinutes value is less than 10.

```
function initializeGame():Void
{
    targetHour = Math.round(Math.random() * 11 + 1);
    targetMinutes = Math.round(Math.random() * 11) * 5;

    targetHourRotation = targetHour * 360;
    targetMinuteRotation = targetMinutes/5 * rotateAmt;
    fullTargetRotation = targetHourRotation +
    targetMinuteRotation;

    target_mc.hour_mc._rotation = 0;
    target_mc.minute_mc._rotation = 0;

    updateClock(target_mc, fullTargetRotation);

    if(targetMinutes < 10)
    {

    }

    clock_mc.hour_mc._rotation = 0;
    clock_mc.minute_mc._rotation = 0;
    enableAll(true);
    end_mc._visible = false;
}
```

18. Inside the conditional statement you just created, set the text property of the target_txt text field to display the time using the targetHour and targetMinutes variables. Make sure to add a 0 before the targetMinutes variable, or else the time will display improperly.

```
function initializeGame():Void
{
    targetHour = Math.round(Math.random() * 11 + 1);
    targetMinutes = Math.round(Math.random() * 11) * 5;

    targetHourRotation = targetHour * 360;
    targetMinuteRotation = targetMinutes/5 * rotateAmt;
    fullTargetRotation = targetHourRotation +
    targetMinuteRotation;
```

```
        target_mc.hour_mc._rotation = 0;
        target_mc.minute_mc._rotation = 0;

        updateClock(target_mc, fullTargetRotation);

        if(targetMinutes < 10)
        {
            target_txt.text = targetHour + ":0" +
            targetMinutes;
        }

        clock_mc.hour_mc._rotation = 0;
        clock_mc.minute_mc._rotation = 0;
        enableAll(true);
        end_mc._visible = false;
    }
```

NOTE This code will make the target_txt text field display the target time. First, the text field will display the targetHour variable's value (random value between 1 and 12), then the text field will display a colon (:) and a 0, then the value of the targetMinutes variable, which in this case will be 0 or 5 (because this conditional statement will only be true if targetMinutes is less than 10). So, if the targetHour variable had a value of 10, and the targetMinutes variable had a value of 5, the text field would display 10, then a colon and 0, and then 5, which would look like 10:05.

19. Below the conditional statement you created, create the skeleton of an else statement. The code inside this statement will run if the targetMinutes variable has a value of 10 or more.

```
function initializeGame():Void
{
    targetHour = Math.round(Math.random() * 11 + 1);
    targetMinutes = Math.round(Math.random() * 11) * 5;

    targetHourRotation = targetHour * 360;
    targetMinuteRotation = targetMinutes/5 * rotateAmt;
    fullTargetRotation = targetHourRotation +
    targetMinuteRotation;

    target_mc.hour_mc._rotation = 0;
    target_mc.minute_mc._rotation = 0;

    updateClock(target_mc, fullTargetRotation);
```

```
    if(targetMinutes < 10)
    {
        target_txt.text = targetHour + ":0" +
        targetMinutes;
    }
    else
    {

    }

    clock_mc.hour_mc._rotation = 0;
    clock_mc.minute_mc._rotation = 0;
    enableAll(true);
    end_mc._visible = false;
}
```

20. Inside the else statement you just created, set the target_txt text field to display the time as you did before, but without adding the 0.

```
function initializeGame():Void
{
    targetHour = Math.round(Math.random() * 11 + 1);
    targetMinutes = Math.round(Math.random() * 11) * 5;

    targetHourRotation = targetHour * 360;
    targetMinuteRotation = targetMinutes/5 * rotateAmt;
    fullTargetRotation = targetHourRotation +
    targetMinuteRotation;

    target_mc.hour_mc._rotation = 0;
    target_mc.minute_mc._rotation = 0;

    updateClock(target_mc, fullTargetRotation);

    if(targetMinutes < 10)
    {
        target_txt.text = targetHour + ":0" +
        targetMinutes;
    }
    else
    {
        target_txt.text = targetHour + ":" +
        targetMinutes;
```

```
        }

        clock_mc.hour_mc._rotation = 0;
        clock_mc.minute_mc._rotation = 0;
        enableAll(true);
        end_mc._visible = false;
    }
```

21. Test the movie, and notice the target time in the text field matches the time on the clock below it, as shown in the following illustration. Sweet!

22. Save the file, and keep it open for the next exercise.

EXERCISE 7-5: Winning the Game

In this exercise, you'll take a look at winning the game when the main clock's hands match the target clock's hands.

1. Make sure you are working in the same file from the last exercise.

2. Select the first keyframe of the actions layer and open the Actions panel by pressing F9 (Windows) or OPTION-F9 (Mac).

3. In the DECLARE VARIABLES AND CREATE OBJECTS section, below all the other variables you created, create two new variables: startTime and endTime. Both variables should have a Number data type.

```
var rotateAmt:Number = 30;
var buttons:Array = [tl_btn, tr_btn, br_btn, bl_btn];

var currentButtonNum:Number;
var lastButtonNum:Number;
var cw1:Boolean;
var cw2:Boolean;
var ccw1:Boolean;
var ccw2:Boolean;
var targetMinutes:Number;
var targetHour:Number;
var targetMinuteRotation:Number;
var targetHourRotation:Number;
var fullTargetRotation:Number;

var startTime:Number;
var endTime:Number;
```

4. In the DEFINE FUNCTIONS section, find the initializeGame function.

5. At the top of the initializeGame function, set the startTime equal to getTimer(). The getTimer function captures the amount of time (in milliseconds) that the Flash movie has been playing.

```
function initializeGame():Void
{
    startTime = getTimer();

    targetHour = Math.round(Math.random() * 11 + 1);
    targetMinutes = Math.round(Math.random() * 11) * 5;

    targetHourRotation = targetHour * 360;
    targetMinuteRotation = targetMinutes/5 * rotateAmt;
    fullTargetRotation = targetHourRotation +
    targetMinuteRotation;

    target_mc.hour_mc._rotation = 0;
```

```
    target_mc.minute_mc._rotation = 0;

    updateClock(target_mc, fullTargetRotation);

    if(targetMinutes < 10)
    {
        target_txt.text = targetHour + ":0" +
        targetMinutes;
    }
    else
    {
        target_txt.text = targetHour + ":" +
        targetMinutes;
    }

    clock_mc.hour_mc._rotation = 0;
    clock_mc.minute_mc._rotation = 0;
    enableAll(true);
    end_mc._visible = false;
}
```

6. In the DEFINE FUNCTIONS section, find the enableAll function.

7. At the bottom of the loop inside the enableAll function, add the code that will run a function called checkWin when buttons[i] (or each button) is clicked. You'll define the checkWin function later in this exercise.

```
function enableAll(isEnabled:Boolean):Void
{
    for(var i:Number = 0; i < buttons.length; i++)
    {
        buttons[i].enabled = isEnabled;
        buttons[i].onRollOver = buttonOver;
        buttons[i].num = i;
        buttons[i].onRelease = checkWin;
    }
}
```

8. At the bottom of the DEFINE EVENT HANDLERS section, create the skeleton of an event handler function called checkWin.

```
function checkWin():Void
{

}
```

9. Inside the checkWin function you just created, create the skeleton of a conditional statement that checks to see if the main clock's hour hand and the target clock's hour hand have the same value for _rotation.

```
function checkWin():Void
{
    if(clock_mc.hour_mc._rotation ==
    target_mc.hour_mc._rotation)
    {

    }
}
```

NOTE Notice you are only checking to see if the hour hands match. Why not the minute hands as well? This is because the hour hands move along with the minute hands. For example, in order to display the time 7:30, the clock would have the minute hand at 6 (30 minutes) and the hour hand would not be exactly at 7, but rather halfway between 7 and 8. In other words, the minute hand is not unique for a particular time, but the hour hand is because it only makes one rotation for the entire 12 hours that the clock can display. To imagine this, picture a clock without an hour hand. How would you tell the time? You would know how many minutes past an hour, but not know what hour the clock is representing. A clock with no minute hand, however, can be used to know the hour and at least estimate the minutes because the position of the hour hand is unique for each minute.

10. Inside the conditional statement you just created, set the value of endTime to (getTimer() – startTime) / 1000. This will capture the timer's value once the correct time has been reached and subtract the startTime variable's value to show how long it took the player to get clock_mc to display the correct time. Then, divide that value (wrapped in parentheses) by 1000 to make the value in seconds instead of milliseconds (unless you prefer to see the time to be displayed in milliseconds).

```
function checkWin():Void
{
    if(clock_mc.hour_mc._rotation ==
    target_mc.hour_mc._rotation)
    {
        endTime = (getTimer() - startTime) / 1000;
    }
}
```

NOTE   The startTime variable represents the time on the timer (retrieved by the built-in getTimer function) when the player started the game. Subtracting that value from the time when the player ends the game (using the getTimer function when the game is finished) gives you the amount of time it took the player to finish the game.

11. On the next line, set the _visible property of end_mc to true to display the end movie clip.

```
function checkWin():Void
{
    if(clock_mc.hour_mc._rotation ==
    target_mc.hour_mc._rotation)
    {
        endTime = (getTimer() - startTime) / 1000;
        end_mc._visible = true;
    }
}
```

12. On the next line, make the text field (end_txt) inside the end_mc movie clip display the endTime variable's value, followed by a space and "seconds".

```
function checkWin():Void
{
    if(clock_mc.hour_mc._rotation ==
    target_mc.hour_mc._rotation)
    {
        endTime = (getTimer() - startTime) / 1000;
        end_mc._visible = true;
        end_mc.end_txt.text = endTime + " seconds";
    }
}
```

13. Test the movie, match the target time, and click on the Stage to display the end_mc movie clip and see your ending time, as shown here. Cool! One problem, though: the hands keep rotating if you move the mouse after the game is over. You'll fix that in the next exercise.

14. Save the file, and keep it open for the next exercise.

EXERCISE 7-6: Playing the Game Again

Now, you'll add the interactivity to play the game multiple times.

1. Make sure you are working in the same file from the last exercise.

2. Select the first keyframe of the actions layer and open the Actions panel.

3. In the DEFINE EVENT HANDLERS section, find the checkWin event handler function.

4. At the bottom of the conditional statement inside the checkWin function, disable the interactivity for all the buttons by running the enableAll function and passing in a value of false.

```
function checkWin():Void
{
    if(clock_mc.hour_mc._rotation ==
    target_mc.hour_mc._rotation)
    {
        endTime = (getTimer() - startTime) / 1000;
        end_mc._visible = true;
        end_mc.end_txt.text = endTime + " seconds";
        enableAll(false);
    }
}
```

5. On the next line, set the end_mc movie clip to run the initializeGame function when it is clicked.

```
function checkWin():Void
{
    if(clock_mc.hour_mc._rotation ==
    target_mc.hour_mc._rotation)
    {
        endTime = (getTimer() - startTime) / 1000;
        end_mc._visible = true;
        end_mc.end_txt.text = endTime + " seconds";
        enableAll(false);
        end_mc.onRelease = initializeGame;
    }
}
```

NOTE Remember when you started making this game and you set the value of an event to run a function? You're doing the same thing here. Again, you don't place parentheses after the initializeGame function name, because you don't want it to run right now. Rather, you want it to run when the player clicks end_mc, or when end_mc's onRelease event is triggered.

6. Test the movie, and win the game. Click the end_mc movie clip to play again. Great!

7. Save the file, upload it to the Web, and have a blast playing it on your Wii! Congratulations, you made yet another Wii game!

CHAPTER **8**

Detecting Acceleration: A Running Game

IN this chapter, you'll build your most advanced game yet—a running game. This game will implement nearly all that you have learned up to this point, as well as add a few new techniques to your tool belt, like detecting the speed the player is moving the Wii remote and scrolling a background. I'll also talk about how to make the game so that the player has to continually move the mouse or Wii remote up and down in order to keep up their running pace.

EXERCISE 8-1: Previewing the Finished Game

In this exercise, you'll prepare to create this game by looking at the finished game to see what you're creating.

1. In the exercise files, locate and open running_final.fla.

2. Test the movie. Move the mouse up and down to make the runner run. Notice how the background scrolls, with each element moving at a different speed. Also notice the speed indicator and distance information at the bottom of the screen. Once you run far enough, you cross the finish line and the game ends. If you run fast enough, you get a medal, as shown in the following illustration. You can also see the time it took. If you click the end message, you can play the game again.

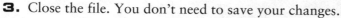

3. Close the file. You don't need to save your changes.

EXERCISE 8-2: Viewing the Flash File

In this exercise, you'll take a look at how the Flash file is set up for this game.

1. In the exercise files, locate and open running.fla.

2. Save the file as **running_{your name}.fla**.

3. In the Timeline, notice there are seven layers, as shown here.

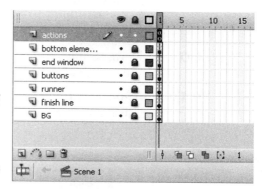

4. Hide, unhide, lock, and unlock the layers and select the art on the Stage of each layer to become familiar with the instance names of the objects on the Stage. The main objects you'll be working with are runner_mc (the runner), bg_mc (the background), and the elements at the bottom of the Stage.

5. In the Library, double-click the Movie Clip symbol icon for mcBG to enter its Timeline.

6. Inside the mcBG movie clip, notice there are five layers.

7. Lock and unlock the layers to view the content on each layer. Notice that most of the layers contain two instances of the same movie clip that are side by side, as shown in the following illustration. Setting up the file in this way will help you scroll the background movie clips while the runner is running.

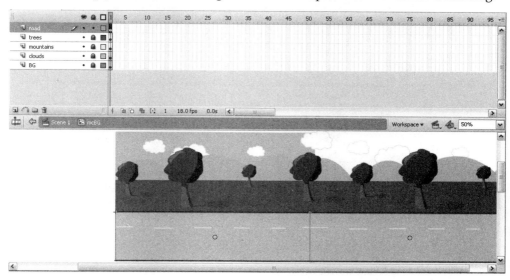

8. In the Library, double-click the Movie Clip symbol icon for the mcRunner movie clip to enter its Timeline.

9. Notice that the mcRunner movie clip has two layers: labels and runner. The labels layer contains two frame labels: run and finished. The runner layer contains three keyframes, each containing a different movie clip. All of the movie clips may look the same because they have the same first keyframe, but they all contain different animations. On frame 1, the runner is an instance of mcRunnerStatic.

10. At the run frame label, the runner is an instance of mcRunning, with an instance name of mcMoving.

11. At the finished frame label (shown here), the runner is an instance of mcFinished with an instance name of moving_mc.

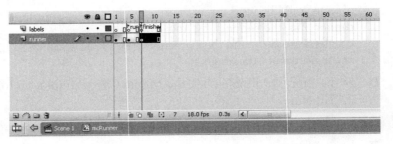

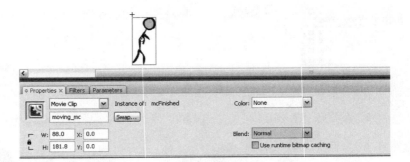

12. Next, take a look at the different runner movie clips. In the Library, double-click the Movie Clip symbol icon for the mcRunnerStatic movie clip to enter its Timeline.

13. Inside the mcRunnerStatic movie clip, notice there is one layer, containing a simple drawing of a runner.

14. In the Library, double-click the Movie Clip symbol icon for the mcRunning movie clip to enter its Timeline.

15. Inside the mcRunning movie clip, notice there are three frames. Scrub the Playhead to preview the animation of the runner running.

16. In the Library, double-click the Movie Clip symbol icon for the mcFinished movie clip to enter its Timeline.

17. Inside the mcFinished movie clip, notice there are three layers: labels, medal, and runner.

18. The labels layer, shown here, contains three frame labels: gold, silver, and bronze, which correspond to the art on the frames in the runner layer. Click and drag the Playhead to view the art on the different frames.

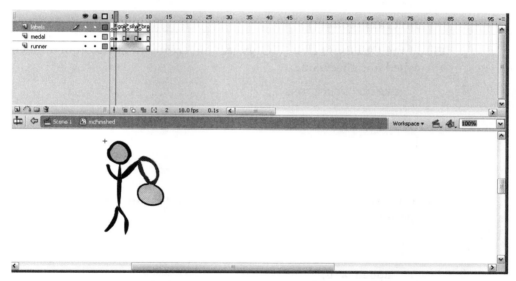

19. At the bottom of the Timeline, click the Scene 1 button to return to the Main Timeline.

20. Keep the file open for the next exercise.

EXERCISE 8-3: Controlling the Runner's Speed

Now, you'll start writing the ActionScript code that controls how fast the runner is running.

1. Make sure you are working in the same file from the last exercise.

2. Select the first keyframe of the actions layer and open the Actions panel by pressing F9 (Windows) or OPTION-F9 (Mac).

3. In the DECLARE VARIABLES AND CREATE OBJECTS section, create a variable called speed with a data type of Number. This number will represent the rate at which the runner is moving, and I'll talk more about this variable throughout the rest of this chapter. Your code should match the code that follows (new code is bold):

```
// DECLARE VARIABLES AND CREATE OBJECTS

var speed:Number;
```

4. In the RUN IMMEDIATELY section of code, run a function called initializeGame. You'll define this function in the next step.

```
// RUN IMMEDIATELY

initializeGame();
```

5. In the DEFINE FUNCTIONS section, create the skeleton of a function called initializeGame.

```
// DEFINE FUNCTIONS

function initializeGame():Void
{

}
```

6. Inside the initializeGame function you just created, set the value of the speed variable to 0.

```
function initializeGame():Void
{
    speed = 0;
}
```

7. On the next line, run a function called enableAll, and pass in true, true. This function will enable all the buttons and animation for this game, and you'll define it in the next step.

```
function initializeGame():Void
{
    speed = 0;
    enableAll(true, true);
}
```

8. On the next line, make the runner_mc movie clip go to its first frame and stop by using the gotoAndStop method and passing in a value of 1.

```
function initializeGame():Void
{
    speed = 0;
    enableAll(true, true);
    runner_mc.gotoAndStop(1);
}
```

NOTE You may be wondering why I use frame numbers sometimes and frame labels at other times. I prefer to use frame labels in just about every case, unless I'm navigating to frame 1. This is because seeing frame 1 in my code tells me that the movie clip (runner_mc in this case) is going to display its initial state.

9. On the next line, set the _visible property of the end_mc movie clip to false. That way, you won't see the end message when you start playing the game.

```
function initializeGame():Void
{
    speed = 0;
    enableAll(true, true);
    runner_mc.gotoAndStop(1);
    end_mc._visible = false;
}
```

10. Below the initializeGame function, create the skeleton of a function called enableAll. The enableAll function should receive two parameters: isEnabled, which has a Boolean data type, and isAnimating, which has a Boolean data type as well.

```
function enableAll(isEnabled:Boolean, isAnimating:Boolean):Void
{

}
```

11. Inside the enableAll function create the skeleton of a conditional statement that checks whether the value of isAnimating is true.

```
function enableAll(isEnabled:Boolean, isAnimating:Boolean):Void
{
```

```
        if(isAnimating)
        {

        }
    }
```

12. Inside the conditional statement you just created, set the value of
_root.onEnterFrame to run a function called run. The run function
will make the runner run, and you'll define it later in this exercise.

```
function enableAll(isEnabled:Boolean, isAnimating:Boolean):Void
{
    if(isAnimating)
    {
        _root.onEnterFrame = run;
    }
}
```

Remember that you aren't running the "run" function here, which is why there are no
parentheses after the function name. You are just telling Flash that the onEnterFrame
event connected to _root will trigger the "run" function. As in the previous chapter, this is a
more readable alternative to defining the entire function here.

13. Below the conditional statement you just wrote, create an else statement's
skeleton.

```
function enableAll(isEnabled:Boolean, isAnimating:Boolean):Void
{
    if(isAnimating)
    {
        _root.onEnterFrame = run;
    }
    else
    {

    }
}
```

14. In the else statement you just created, delete _root.onEnterFrame. This will
stop the run function from executing every frame.

```
function enableAll(isEnabled:Boolean, isAnimating:Boolean):Void
{
    if(isAnimating)
    {
```

```
        _root.onEnterFrame = run;
    }
    else
    {
        delete _root.onEnterFrame;
    }
}
```

15. Below the else statement you created, set the enabled property of top_btn and bottom_btn to the value passed in through the isEnabled parameter.

```
function enableAll(isEnabled:Boolean, isAnimating:Boolean):Void
{
    if(isAnimating)
    {
        _root.onEnterFrame = run;
    }
    else
    {
        delete _root.onEnterFrame;
    }
    top_btn.enabled = isEnabled;
    bottom_btn.enabled = isEnabled;
}
```

16. In the DEFINE EVENT HANDLERS section, create the skeleton of an event handler function for top_btn.onRollOver and bottom_btn.onRollOver.

```
// DEFINE EVENT HANDLERS

top_btn.onRollOver = bottom_btn.onRollOver = function():Void
{

}
```

17. Inside the event handler you just created, create the skeleton of a conditional statement that checks if speed is less than 10.

```
top_btn.onRollOver = bottom_btn.onRollOver = function():Void
{
    if(speed < 10)
    {

    }
}
```

18. Inside the conditional statement you just created, write the code to increment the speed variable by 1 using the ++ operator.

```
top_btn.onRollOver = bottom_btn.onRollOver = function():Void
{
    if(speed < 10)
    {
        speed ++;
    }
}
```

19. Below the top_btn.onRollOver event handler, create the skeleton of an event handler function called run.

```
function run():Void
{

}
```

NOTE   Notice this function is in the DEFINE EVENT HANDLERS section as opposed to being in the DEFINE FUNCTIONS section. Why? Remember, this function is connected to the onEnterFrame event for _root, as you specified earlier. Because it's attached to the onEnterFrame event, it's an event handler. Also remember that event handlers, by definition, are just functions that are attached to events.

20. Inside the run function, execute a function called setSpeed. You'll define the setSpeed function later in this exercise.

```
function run():Void
{
    setSpeed();
}
```

21. On the next line, execute a function called showSpeed. This function, which you'll define later in this exercise, will display the current speed at the bottom of the screen.

```
function run():Void
{
    setSpeed();
    showSpeed();
}
```

22. At the bottom of the DEFINE FUNCTIONS section, create the skeleton of a function called setSpeed.

```
function setSpeed():Void
{

}
```

23. Inside the setSpeed function, create the skeleton of a conditional statement that checks whether speed is greater than zero.

```
function setSpeed():Void
{
    if(speed > 0)
    {

    }
}
```

24. Now, you'll make this function reduce the speed variable every frame. Remember, any code in this function will execute along with the frame rate of the Flash movie (because it's running inside the run function, which is connected to _root.onEnterFrame). Inside the conditional statement you just created, decrease the value of speed by .4. This value is something I got through trial and error, but it works pretty well on the Wii to make running fun and challenging. You can change it if you want, though.

```
function setSpeed():Void
{
    if(speed > 0)
    {
        speed -= .4;
    }
}
```

25. On the next line, use the gotoAndStop method to make the runner_mc go to the run frame and stop. This will make the runner animate so long as the speed value is greater than zero.

```
function setSpeed():Void
{
    if(speed > 0)
    {
        speed -= .4;
        runner_mc.gotoAndStop("run");
    }
}
```

NOTE — This code will make the runner_mc movie clip stop at its "run" frame. At that frame is a movie clip that contains the running animation. When runner_mc gets to the "run" frame, the running animation will play unless you tell it not to using ActionScript. This is because movie clips animate independently of the Timelines they are in.

26. Below the if statement you created, create the skeleton of an else statement.

```
function setSpeed():Void
{
    if(speed > 0)
    {
        speed -= .4;
        runner_mc.gotoAndStop("run");
    }
    else
    {

    }
}
```

27. Inside the else statement you just created, set the speed value to 0. This will make sure the value of the speed variable doesn't go lower than 0.

```
function setSpeed():Void
{
    if(speed > 0)
    {
        speed -= .4;
        runner_mc.gotoAndStop("run");
    }
    else
    {
        speed = 0;
    }
}
```

28. On the next line, make the runner_mc movie clip go to the first frame using the gotoAndStop method. This will stop the runner from running if the speed variable's value is zero.

```
function setSpeed():Void
{
    if(speed > 0)
    {
        speed -= .4;
        runner_mc.gotoAndStop("run");
    }
    else
    {
        speed = 0;
        runner_mc.gotoAndStop(1);
    }
}
```

29. Below the setSpeed function, create the skeleton of a function called showSpeed. This function will display the runner's current speed.

```
function showSpeed():Void
{

}
```

30. Inside the showSpeed function, set the _xscale property of the speed_mc movie clip to speed * 10.

```
function showSpeed():Void
{
    speed_mc._xscale = speed * 10;
}
```

NOTE The _xscale property is a percentage used to scale an object horizontally. A value of 100 is 100% horizontal scale, which is no scale at all. So when the speed variable has a value of 10, the speed_mc movie clip will be at its normal, non-scaled size. As the speed variable approaches 0, the speed_mc movie clip will scale down, until it has an _xscale of 0, which will make the movie clip no longer visible.

31. Test the movie, and move your mouse up and down on the Stage to make the speed go up. The faster you go, the more the speed value increases. Cool!

There's only one problem here: sometimes the speed_mc movie clip scales too far to the left or too far to the right. You'll fix that in the next steps.

32. Below the code you just wrote, create the skeleton of a conditional statement that checks if the _xscale property of the speed_mc movie clip is greater than 100.

```
function showSpeed():Void
{
    speed_mc._xscale = speed * 10;

    if(speed_mc._xscale > 100)
    {

    }
}
```

33. Inside the conditional statement you just created, set the _xscale property of speed_mc equal to 100. This will make sure the speed_mc movie clip doesn't scale too far.

```
function showSpeed():Void
{
    speed_mc._xscale = speed * 10;

    if(speed_mc._xscale > 100)
    {
```

```
        speed_mc._xscale = 100;
    }
}
```

34. Below the conditional statement you just created, repeat Steps 32 and 33, but with the following changes: the conditional statement should check whether the _xscale property of speed_mc is less than 0, and that property should be set to 0 inside the conditional statement. That way, the _xscale property of speed_mc won't go below 0.

```
function showSpeed():Void
{
    speed_mc._xscale = speed * 10;

    if(speed_mc._xscale > 100)
    {
        speed_mc._xscale = 100;
    }
    if(speed_mc._xscale < 0)
    {
        speed_mc._xscale = 0;
    }
}
```

35. Test the movie again, and move the mouse up and down to make the runner run. This time, the speed bar stays in the appropriate boundaries. Great!

36. Save the file, and keep it open for the next exercise.

EXERCISE 8-4: Animating the Background Elements

Now that you can control the runner's speed, how about animating the background elements to make it look like the runner is actually moving, instead of running in place. To do this, you'll use a technique called scrolling, and move each layer in the background at a different speed.

1. Make sure you are working in the same file from the last exercise.

2. Select the first keyframe of the actions layer and open the Actions panel.

3. In the DEFINE EVENT HANDLERS section, locate the run event handler function.

4. At the bottom of the run function, execute a function called moveGraphics. The moveGraphics function will move the background graphics, and you'll define it later in this exercise.

```
function run():Void
{
    setSpeed();
    showSpeed();
    moveGraphics();
}
```

5. At the bottom of the DEFINE FUNCTIONS section, create the skeleton of a function called moveGraphics.

```
function moveGraphics():Void
{

}
```

6. In the moveGraphics function, run a function called scrollMc, passing in the road movie clips (road1_mc and road2_mc) inside of bg_mc, and speed * 5. The scrollMc function, which you'll define later in this exercise, will scroll two movie clips (the first two parameters), at the rate specified in the third parameter.

```
function moveGraphics():Void
{
    scrollMc(bg_mc.road1_mc,bg_mc.road2_mc,speed * 5);
}
```

7. Repeat Step 6 for the trees (trees1_mc and trees2_mc) with a rate of speed * 3, for the mountains (mountains1_mc and mountains2_mc) with a rate of speed * 2, and for the clouds (clouds1_mc and clouds2_mc) with a rate of speed.

```
function moveGraphics():Void
{
    scrollMc(bg_mc.road1_mc,bg_mc.road2_mc,speed * 5);
    scrollMc(bg_mc.trees1_mc,bg_mc.trees2_mc,speed * 3);
    scrollMc(bg_mc.mountains1_mc,bg_mc.mountains2_mc,speed * 2);
    scrollMc(bg_mc.clouds1_mc,bg_mc.clouds2_mc,speed);
}
```

 Remember that all of these movie clips are inside bg_mc, so you have to write the full paths to each one (example: bg_mc.road1_mc).

8. Below the moveGraphics function create the skeleton of a function called scrollMc. Make the function receive three parameters: mc1, with a MovieClip data type; mc2, also a MovieClip data type; and rate, with a Number data type.

```
function scrollMc(mc1:MovieClip, mc2:MovieClip, rate:Number):Void
{

}
```

9. Inside the scrollMc function, move the mc1 movie clip to the left at the rate passed in.

```
function scrollMc(mc1:MovieClip, mc2:MovieClip, rate:Number):Void
{
    mc1._x -= rate;
}
```

10. Next, create a conditional statement that checks if the _x property of the mc1 movie clip is less than or equal to the rate minus mc1._width. This will check if the mc1 movie clip has moved too far to the left.

```
function scrollMc(mc1:MovieClip, mc2:MovieClip, rate:Number):Void
{
    mc1._x -= rate;
    if(mc1._x <= rate - mc1._width)
    {

    }
}
```

11. Inside the conditional statement you just created, reset the _x property of mc1 to 0. This will cause each movie clip passed in as mc1 to move to the left until it moves off the Stage, then go back to its original X position, 0.

```
function scrollMc(mc1:MovieClip, mc2:MovieClip, rate:Number):Void
{
    mc1._x -= rate;
    if(mc1._x <= rate - mc1._width)
    {
        mc1._x = 0;
    }
}
```

12. Test the movie, and move your mouse up and down to watch the background animate. Notice that once a movie clip moves too far to the left, it loops back to its original position. Cool! All you have to do is move the mc2 movie clips along with the mc1 movie clips and you'll have a seamless scrolling background.

13. Below the conditional statement you created, set the position of the mc2 movie clip to be at the right edge of the mc1 movie clip (the right edge would be mc1._x + mc1._width), minus 10 pixels (so the movie clips overlap just a little).

```
function scrollMc(mc1:MovieClip, mc2:MovieClip, rate:Number):Void
{
```

```
mc1._x -= rate;
if(mc1._x <= rate - mc1._width)
{
    mc1._x = 0;
}
mc2._x = mc1._x + mc1._width - 10;
}
```

NOTE Remember that because the movie clips all have top-left registration, a movie clip's _x property holds its left edge position (in the preceding code, that's mc1._x). The right edge of a movie clip can then be found by adding the movie clip's width. Example: mc1._x = left edge; mc1._x + mc1._width = right edge.

14. Test the movie and move your mouse up and down to behold the seamless scrolling background, shown in the following illustration. Sweet!

TIP When you are creating your own scrolling backgrounds, make sure to keep the background art simple around the edges. This will help you create seamless scrolling.

15. Save the file, and keep it open for the next exercise.

EXERCISE 8-5: Converting Pixels to Yards

How many pixels are in a yard? Even though the two units of measurement aren't directly comparable, you'll build a formula in this exercise to connect the two.

1. Make sure you are working in the same file from the last exercise.

2. On the Stage, select the runner_mc movie clip, shown in Figure 8-1. Notice in the Property Inspector that the height of the runner is about 200 pixels. Assume that in real life your runner would be about six feet tall. Now, there are three feet in a yard, which makes the runner two yards tall. If the runner is 200 pixels in height in Flash, and two yards in imaginary life, the number of pixels per yard is 100 (200 pixels divided by two yards). Now, you can use this number in Flash to emulate yards for the run.

FIGURE 8-1

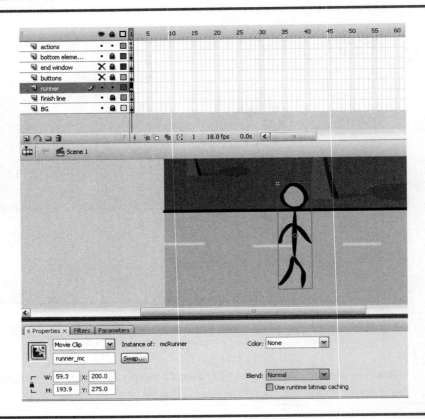

Viewing the runner_mc movie clip

Detecting Acceleration: A Running Game

3. Select the first keyframe of the actions layer and open the Actions panel.

4. In the DECLARE VARIABLES AND CREATE OBJECTS section, create a variable called pixelsPerYard, with a Number data type and a value of 100.

```
var speed:Number;
var pixelsPerYard:Number = 100;
```

5. On the next line, create a variable called totalYards, with a data type of Number and a value of 30. This will represent how many yards the player will have to run before the run is over.

```
var speed:Number;
var pixelsPerYard:Number = 100;
var totalYards:Number = 30;
```

6. On the next three lines, create three more variables with a Number data type: pixelsTraveled, distanceInYards, and yardPercent. The pixelsTraveled variable will represent how many pixels the runner has traveled, distanceInYards will represent that pixel value in yards, and yardPercent will represent the percentage of yards the player has already run.

```
var speed:Number;
var pixelsPerYard:Number = 100;
var totalYards:Number = 30;
var pixelsTraveled:Number;
var distanceInYards:Number;
var yardPercent:Number;
```

7. In the DEFINE FUNCTIONS section, find the initializeGame function.

8. At the top of the initializeGame function, give the pixelsTraveled, distanceInYards, and yardPercent variables initial values of 0.

```
function initializeGame():Void
{
    pixelsTraveled = 0;
    distanceInYards = 0;
    yardPercent = 0;
    speed = 0;
    enableAll(true, true);
    runner_mc.gotoAndStop(1);
    end_mc._visible = false;
}
```

9. Locate the moveGraphics function.

10. At the top of the moveGraphics function, you'll update the pixelsTraveled variable along with updating the graphics on the screen. Specifically, pixelsTraveled will grow at the same rate the road moves (speed * 5). That way, you can be sure that the number of pixelsTraveled is accurate, because the runner moves at the same rate as the ground.

```
function moveGraphics():Void
{
    pixelsTraveled += speed * 5;
    scrollMc(bg_mc.road1_mc,bg_mc.road2_mc,speed * 5);
    scrollMc(bg_mc.trees1_mc,bg_mc.trees2_mc,speed * 3);
    scrollMc(bg_mc.mountains1_mc,bg_mc.mountains2_mc,speed * 2);
    scrollMc(bg_mc.clouds1_mc,bg_mc.clouds2_mc,speed);
}
```

11. Save the file, and keep it open for the next exercise.

EXERCISE 8-6: Going the Distance!

Now that you have a yard system set up, take a look at running the complete distance and showing the progress at the bottom of the screen.

1. Make sure you are working in the same file from the last exercise.

2. In the Library, double-click the Movie Clip symbol icon for the mcDistance movie clip.

3. Inside the mcDistance movie clip (shown in Figure 8-2), notice there is a 100-frame animation. Scrub the Playhead to preview the animation. This will correspond to the percentage of yards the person playing the game has traveled, so you'll use this animation to show the progress of the runner.

4. In the Timeline, click the Scene 1 button to return to the Main Timeline.

FIGURE 8-2

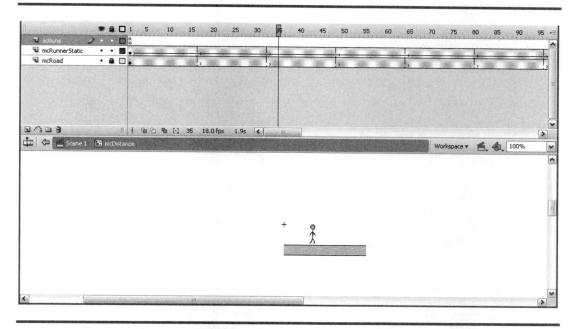

Viewing the animation inside the mcDistance movie clip

5. On the bottom elements layer, select the dynamic text field at the bottom of the Stage to note its instance name in the Property Inspector, distance_txt (see Figure 8-3). You'll use this text field to display the number of yards the player has traveled.

6. Select the first keyframe of the actions layer and open the Actions panel.

7. In the DEFINE EVENT HANDLERS section, locate the run event handler function.

FIGURE 8-3

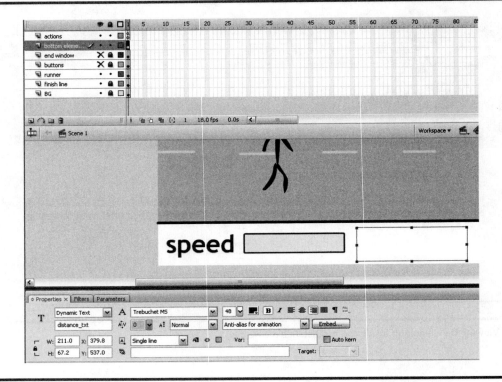

Viewing the distance_txt text field

8. At the bottom of the run function, execute a function called showDistance. The show distance function, which you'll define later in this exercise, will display the distance information at the bottom of the screen.

```
function run():Void
{
    setSpeed();
    showSpeed();
    moveGraphics();
    showDistance();
}
```

9. At the bottom of the DEFINE FUNCTIONS section, create the skeleton of a function called showDistance.

```
function showDistance():Void
{

}
```

10. Inside the showDistance function, set the distanceInYards variable's value to pixelsTraveled divided by pixelsPerYard. This converts the pixel distance into yards (or at least fake yards in this game).

```
function showDistance():Void
{
    distanceInYards = pixelsTraveled / pixelsPerYard;
}
```

11. On the next line, set the value of yardPercent to Math.round(distanceInYards / totalYards * 100). This will get the percentage of yards traveled (distanceInYards / totalYards), multiply it by 100, then round the number so it can represent a frame for the distance_mc movie clip to display.

```
function showDistance():Void
{
    distanceInYards = pixelsTraveled / pixelsPerYard;
    yardPercent = Math.round(distanceInYards / totalYards * 100);
}
```

TIP Remember that the value of totalYards is 30, as specified at the top of your code.

12. On the next line, make the distance_mc movie clip go to the frame number held in the yardPercent variable by using the gotoAndStop method and passing in yardPercent.

```
function showDistance():Void
{
    distanceInYards = pixelsTraveled / pixelsPerYard;
    yardPercent = Math.round(distanceInYards / totalYards * 100);
    distance_mc.gotoAndStop(yardPercent);
}
```

NOTE Notice yardPercent is not in quotes, unlike "run" when you used gotoAndStop to navigate to a frame label to make the runner run. This is because yardPercent is actually a Number. If the value yardPercent were placed in quotes, Flash would look for a frame label called "yardPercent" instead of going to the frame number held in the yardPercent variable.

13. Test the movie, and run. Watch the distance_mc movie clip on the bottom right update as you run, as shown here. Sweet!

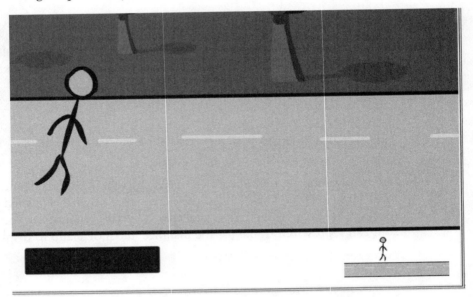

TIP If your movie isn't working properly, chances are the problem is a simple typo. Review the code you wrote for this exercise, comparing it to the code in the book, to fix any errors.

14. Now, you'll make the text field (distance_txt) on the Stage display how many yards you have traveled. On the next line, set the value of the text field to Math.floor(distanceInYards) + " yds". This will take the distanceInYards variable and make it a whole number, using Math.floor() (Math.floor() rounds numbers down . . . to the floor), and adds on a space and yds, to indicate the number is in yards.

```
function showDistance():Void
{
    distanceInYards = pixelsTraveled / pixelsPerYard;
    yardPercent = Math.round(distanceInYards / totalYards * 100);
    distance_mc.gotoAndStop(yardPercent);
    distance_txt.text = Math.floor(distanceInYards) + " yds";
}
```

15. Test the movie, and run again. Watch the text at the bottom of the screen update as you run, as shown here. Nice!

16. Save the file, and keep it open for the next exercise.

EXERCISE 8-7: Ending the Game

In this exercise, I'll show you how to end the game once the player has ran for the full distance. You'll also display the player's ending time.

1. Make sure you are working in the same file from the last exercise.

2. Select the first keyframe of the actions layer and open the Actions panel by pressing F9 (Windows) or OPTION-F9 (Mac).

3. At the bottom of the DECLARE VARIABLES AND CREATE OBJECTS section, create a new variable called finished, with a data type of Boolean. You'll use this variable later on to make sure a particular block of code runs only once, when the game is finished.

```
var speed:Number;
var pixelsPerYard:Number = 100;
var totalYards:Number = 30;
var pixelsTraveled:Number;
var distanceInYards:Number;
var yardPercent:Number;
var finished:Boolean;
```

4. On the next two lines, create two variables: startTime and endTime; both with a data type of Number. These variables will represent the time you started playing the game and the time you finished.

```
var speed:Number;
var pixelsPerYard:Number = 100;
var totalYards:Number = 30;
var pixelsTraveled:Number;
var distanceInYards:Number;
var yardPercent:Number;
var finished:Boolean;
var startTime:Number;
var endTime:Number;
```

5. In the DEFINE FUNCTIONS section, locate the initializeGame function.

6. At the top of the initializeGame function, set the value of finished to false.

```
function initializeGame():Void
{
    finished = false;
    pixelsTraveled = 0;
    distanceInYards = 0;
    yardPercent = 0;
    speed = 0;
    enableAll(true, true);
    runner_mc.gotoAndStop(1);
    end_mc._visible = false;
}
```

7. On the next line, set the value of the startTime variable to getTimer(). Remember, getTimer() gives the amount of time, in milliseconds, that the Flash movie has been playing.

```
function initializeGame():Void
{
    finished = false;
    startTime = getTimer();
    pixelsTraveled = 0;
    distanceInYards = 0;
    yardPercent = 0;
    speed = 0;
    enableAll(true, true);
    runner_mc.gotoAndStop(1);
    end_mc._visible = false;
}
```

8. Locate the showDistance function.

9. At the bottom of the showDistance function, create the skeleton of a conditional statement that checks if the distanceInYards value is greater than or equal to the totalYards value. The code in the curly braces will then run if the player has run the total number of yards or more.

```
function showDistance():Void
{
    distanceInYards = pixelsTraveled / pixelsPerYard;
    yardPercent = Math.round(distanceInYards / totalYards * 100);
    distance_mc.gotoAndStop(yardPercent);
    distance_txt.text = Math.floor(distanceInYards) + " yds";
    if(distanceInYards >= totalYards)
    {

    }
}
```

10. Inside the conditional statement you just created, run a function called finish. You'll define the finish function later in this exercise.

```
function showDistance():Void
{
    distanceInYards = pixelsTraveled / pixelsPerYard;
    yardPercent = Math.round(distanceInYards / totalYards * 100);
    distance_mc.gotoAndStop(yardPercent);
    distance_txt.text = Math.floor(distanceInYards) + " yds";

     if(distanceInYards >= totalYards)
     {
         finish();
     } (is this line supposed to be here?)

}
```

11. At the bottom of the DEFINE FUNCTIONS section, create the skeleton of a function called finish.

```
function finish():Void
{

}
```

12. Inside the finish function, write a conditional statement that checks whether the finished variable is false. One way to do this is using the ! (NOT) operator.

```
function finish():Void
{
    if(!finished)
    {

    }
}
```

 In the preceding code, *!finished* means "if the value of finished is false." If the ! (NOT) operator were omitted, the code would check if the value of finished were true.

13. Inside the conditional statement you just created, set the value of finished to true. This will make sure the code in this statement will run only once after the game is finished.

```
function finish():Void
{
    if(!finished)
    {
        finished = true;
    }
}
```

14. On the next line, set the value of endTime to (getTimer() – startTime) / 1000. Just as in the clock game, this value will calculate the difference between where the timer is now and when the game started, and divide the value by 1000 to convert the milliseconds into seconds.

```
function finish():Void
{
    if(!finished)
    {
        finished = true;
        endTime = (getTimer() - startTime) / 1000;
    }
}
```

NOTE — The value of endTime here works in the same way as it did in the last chapter. Remember that the getTimer function is a built-in Flash function that gives you the number of milliseconds that the Flash movie has been playing. At the beginning of the game, you capture that value and hold it in the startTime variable. At the end of the game, you use the getTimer function to get the number of milliseconds the movie has been playing (which will be more than when the game started) and you subtract the value of the startTime variable. That gives you the amount of time between when the game ended and when the game began.

15. On the next line, run the enableAll function, passing in a value of false for the first parameter to disable the button interactivity and true for the second parameter to keep animating objects on the screen. This way, once the player runs far enough, the player can no longer increase the runner's speed by moving the mouse or Wii remote up and down, so the runner will gradually slow down until the speed value is 0.

```
function finish():Void
{
    if(!finished)
    {
        finished = true;
        endTime = (getTimer() - startTime) / 1000;
        enableAll(false, true);
    }
}
```

16. Below the conditional statement you just created, create another conditional statement that checks if the speed variable's value is less than or equal to 0. In this conditional statement, you'll place all the code that happens at the very end of the game (receiving a medal, seeing the ending time, etc.).

```
function finish():Void
{
    if(!finished)
    {
        finished = true;
        endTime = (getTimer() - startTime) / 1000;
        enableAll(false, true);
    }
    if(speed <= 0)
    {

    }
}
```

17. Inside the conditional statement you just created, set the _visible property of the end_mc movie clip to true. This will show the end_mc movie clip.

```
function finish():Void
{
    if(!finished)
    {
        finished = true;
        endTime = (getTimer() - startTime) / 1000;
        enableAll(false, true);
    }
    if(speed <= 0)
    {
        end_mc._visible = true;
    }
}
```

18. Inside the end_mc movie clip is a text field named time_txt. On the next line, set the text in that text field to display the endTime value, a space, and "seconds".

```
function finish():Void
{
    if(!finished)
    {
        finished = true;
        endTime = (getTimer() - startTime) / 1000;
        enableAll(false, true);
    }
    if(speed <= 0)
    {
        end_mc._visible = true;
        end_mc.time_txt.text = endTime + " seconds";
    }
}
```

19. Test the movie, and run the race. When you get to the end, notice the end movie clip appears with your time, as shown in the following illustration. Cool!

20. Save the file, and keep it open for the next exercise.

TROUBLESHOOTING ERRORS

If the movie is not working properly, check your code for errors. Where do you look? That depends on what the error is. If the message in the Output window is clear and tells you the line of code where the error was, you can look in that line of your code. If the message in the Output window is confusing, or if there are no error messages and your game still doesn't work properly, you can always compare your code to the code in this exercise. Another way to debug (or fix errors in) your code is to start by analyzing the problem. For example, if the game is just not ending, it may be a problem with the code that checks to see if the game has ended. In that case, you would look for an error in the conditional statement that checks if the distanceInYards value is greater than or equal to the totalYards value. You may have a semicolon where it shouldn't be, as shown in the code below.

```
If(distanceInYards >= totalYards);
```

Going through the process of analyzing problems and guessing possible sources can help you greatly in fixing errors in your code.

EXERCISE 8-8: Finishing Touches

Now that you've ended the game, let's give the player a medal according to how fast they ran, as well as animate the finish line. You'll even make the game re-playable.

1. Make sure you are working in the same file from the last exercise.

2. Select the first keyframe of the actions layer and open the Actions panel by pressing F9 (Windows) or OPTION-F9 (Mac).

3. At the bottom of the DECLARE VARIABLES AND CREATE OBJECTS section, create three variables: goldTime, silverTime, and bronzeTime. Give all the variables a Number data type, and values of totalYards / 5 for gold, totalYards / 4 for silver, and totalYards / 3 for bronze. These values represent the amount of time you have to make in order to receive a particular medal. You can adjust these values later if you'd like.

```
var speed:Number;
var pixelsPerYard:Number = 100;
var totalYards:Number = 30;
var pixelsTraveled:Number;
var distanceInYards:Number;
var yardPercent:Number;
var finished:Boolean;
var startTime:Number;
var endTime:Number;
var goldTime:Number = totalYards / 5;
var silverTime:Number = totalYards / 4;
var bronzeTime:Number = totalYards / 3;
```

4. Below the variables you just created, create another variable called flStartX, with a data type of Number and a value of finishLine_mc._x. This variable will hold the initial X position of the finishLine_mc movie clip.

```
var speed:Number;
var pixelsPerYard:Number = 100;
var totalYards:Number = 30;
var pixelsTraveled:Number;
var distanceInYards:Number;
var yardPercent:Number;
var finished:Boolean;
var startTime:Number;
var endTime:Number;
```

```
var goldTime:Number = totalYards / 5;
var silverTime:Number = totalYards / 4;
var bronzeTime:Number = totalYards / 3;
var flStartX:Number = finishLine_mc._x;
```

> **NOTE** The finishLine_mc movie clip is not visible on the Stage, because it's in the Pasteboard (the gray area outside the Stage). Even though finishLine_mc is not on the Stage, you can still use ActionScript to communicate with and control it.

5. On the next line, create another variable called yardsFromPlayer with a data type of Number and a value of (flStartX – runner_mc._x) / pixelsPerYard. This value represents how many yards the finish line is from the runner. First the pixel distance is calculated (the value in parentheses), and then that number is divided by the number of pixels per yard to calculate the yard distance.

```
var speed:Number;
var pixelsPerYard:Number = 100;
var totalYards:Number = 30;
var pixelsTraveled:Number;
var distanceInYards:Number;
var yardPercent:Number;
var finished:Boolean;
var startTime:Number;
var endTime:Number;
var goldTime:Number = totalYards / 5;
var silverTime:Number = totalYards / 4;
var bronzeTime:Number = totalYards / 3;
var flStartX:Number = finishLine_mc._x;
var yardsFromPlayer:Number = (flStartX - runner_mc._x) / pixelsPerYard;
```

6. In the DEFINE FUNCTIONS section, locate the initializeGame function.

7. At the top to the initializeGame function, set the _x property of finishLine_mc to flStartX. This will reset the X position of the finish line each time you play the game.

```
function initializeGame():Void
{
    finishLine_mc._x = flStartX;
    finished = false;
    startTime = getTimer();
```

```
    pixelsTraveled = 0;
    distanceInYards = 0;
    yardPercent = 0;
    speed = 0;
    enableAll(true, true);
    runner_mc.gotoAndStop(1);
    end_mc._visible = false;
}
```

8. In the DEFINE EVENT HANDLERS section, locate the run event handler function.

9. At the bottom of the run function, execute a function called moveFinishLine. You'll define the moveFinishLine function later in this exercise.

```
function run():Void
{
    setSpeed();
    showSpeed();
    moveGraphics();
    showDistance();
    moveFinishLine();
}
```

10. At the bottom of the DEFINE FUNCTIONS section, create the skeleton of a function called moveFinishLine.

```
function moveFinishLine():Void
{

}
```

11. Inside the moveFinishLine function, create a conditional statement that checks if the distanceInYards value is greater than or equal to totalYards – yardsFromPlayer. This conditional statement will check to make sure if it's time to start moving the finish line. It's time to start moving the finish line when there are as many yards to go as there are yards from the finish line to the player.

```
function moveFinishLine():Void
{
    if(distanceInYards >= totalYards - yardsFromPlayer)
    {
```

```
        }
    }
```

12. Inside the conditional statement you just created, move the finishLine_mc
movie clip to the left at the same rate as the road (speed * 5). That way, it
will appear that the finish line is on the road, as opposed to floating above
the road.

```
function moveFinishLine():Void
{
    if(distanceInYards >= totalYards - yardsFromPlayer)
    {
        finishLine_mc._x -= speed * 5;
    }
}
```

13. Test the movie, and run like the wind! When you reach the end, notice the
finish line (shown in the following illustration) animating. Sweet!

14. Locate the finish function.

15. Inside the finish function, find the conditional statement that checks if
speed is less than or equal to zero.

16. At the bottom of that conditional statement, make the runner_mc movie clip go to the finished frame label and stop by using the gotoAndStop method and passing in a value of "finished".

```
function finish():Void
{
    if(!finished)
    {
        finished = true;
        endTime = (getTimer() - startTime) / 1000;
        enableAll(false, true);
    }
    if(speed <= 0)
    {
        end_mc._visible = true;
        end_mc.time_txt.text = endTime + " seconds";
        runner_mc.gotoAndStop("finished");
    }
}
```

17. On the next line, create the skeleton of a conditional statement that checks if the endTime is less than or equal to the goldTime variable's value.

```
function finish():Void
{
    if(!finished)
    {
        finished = true;
        endTime = (getTimer() - startTime) / 1000;
        enableAll(false, true);
    }
    if(speed <= 0)
    {
        end_mc._visible = true;
        end_mc.time_txt.text = endTime + " seconds";
        runner_mc.gotoAndStop("finished");
        if(endTime <= goldTime)
        {

        }
    }
}
```

18. Inside the conditional statement you just created, make the moving_mc movie clip (inside the runner_mc movie clip) go to the "gold" frame label and stop, by using the gotoAndStop method and passing in a value of "gold".

```
function finish():Void
{
    if(!finished)
    {
        finished = true;
        endTime = (getTimer() - startTime) / 1000;
        enableAll(false, true);
    }
    if(speed <= 0)
    {
        end_mc._visible = true;
        end_mc.time_txt.text = endTime + " seconds";
        runner_mc.gotoAndStop("finished");
        if(endTime <= goldTime)
        {
            runner_mc.moving_mc.gotoAndStop("gold");
        }
    }
}
```

19. Below the conditional statement you just created, repeat Step 18 twice, once for silver and once for bronze. Instead of if statements, use else if statements, and make sure the time variables and frame label names are the appropriate names.

```
function finish():Void
{
    if(!finished)
    {
        finished = true;
        endTime = (getTimer() - startTime) / 1000;
        enableAll(false, true);
    }
    if(speed <= 0)
    {
        end_mc._visible = true;
        end_mc.time_txt.text = endTime + " seconds";
```

```
            runner_mc.gotoAndStop("finished");
            if(endTime <= goldTime)
            {
                runner_mc.moving_mc.gotoAndStop("gold");
            }
            else if(endTime <= silverTime)
            {
                runner_mc.moving_mc.gotoAndStop("silver");
            }
            else if(endTime <= bronzeTime)
            {
                runner_mc.moving_mc.gotoAndStop("bronze");
            }
        }
    }
```

20. Below the else if statement that checks the endTime against the bronzeTime, set the end_mc.onRelease value to run the initializeGame function so that you can play the game multiple times.

```
function finish():Void
{
    if(!finished)
    {
        finished = true;
        endTime = (getTimer() - startTime) / 1000;
        enableAll(false, true);
    }
    if(speed <= 0)
    {
        end_mc._visible = true;
        end_mc.time_txt.text = endTime + " seconds";
        runner_mc.gotoAndStop("finished");
        if(endTime <= goldTime)
        {
            runner_mc.moving_mc.gotoAndStop("gold");
        }
        else if(endTime <= silverTime)
        {
            runner_mc.moving_mc.gotoAndStop("silver");
        }
        else if(endTime <= bronzeTime)
```

```
        {
            runner_mc.moving_mc.gotoAndStop("bronze");
        }
        end_mc.onRelease = initializeGame;
    }
}
```

NOTE Make sure not to put opening and closing parentheses after initializeGame, because again you don't want to run the function now. Rather, you want it to run when the onRelease event for end_mc is triggered.

21. Test the movie, play the game, and get the medal . . . or bow your head in shame. Click the end_mc movie clip to play the game again. Yeah!

22. Save the file. You can close it when you're done playing.

So that's it! Now you have the skills to create all kinds of fun Wii games. Have a blast!

Index

exclamation points (!) in conditional
    statements, 71
expanding layer folders, 19
exploding meteors, 133–138, 150–153
Export For ActionScript option, 139, 141
exporting movie clips, 138–139
Eyedropper tool, 8

F

Fetch program, 120
File Transfer Protocol (FTP), 120–122
file types, 2
Fill icon, 14
fills
    color, 4
    shapes, 9
finish function, 289–292, 297–301
finishing touches in running game,
    294–301
FireFTP add-on, 120–122
.FLA files, 2
floor function, 207
flyout items, 4
folders
    creating, 193
    layers, 19
for loops, 75–76
forward slashes (/)
    for comments, 46
    for division, 52
FPS (frames per second), 4, 28
frame-by-frame animations, 32–33
Frame command, 29
frame rate, 4, 28
frames, 28
    blank, 30–31
    converting to keyframes, 135
    deleting, 31

functions in, 56
keyframes. *See* keyframes
labels, 131, 150
moving and copying, 31
regular, 29
selecting, 30–31
frames per second (FPS), 4, 28
Free Transform tool, 6
FTP (File Transfer Protocol), 120–122
function keyword, 55
functions, 53
    creating, 230–231
    custom, 55–59
    event handlers, 67–69
    intervals, 144–147
    methods, 66
    parameters, 59–63
    return values, 63–66
    simple, 53–55
    variables in, 118

G

games
    clock. *See* clock game
    .FLA files, 102–103
    hammer and nail. *See* hammer and
        nail game
    loss determination, 110–114
    meteor shooting. *See* meteor
        shooting game
    mouse and mask interactivity,
        103–105
    paper, rock, scissors. *See* paper, rock,
        scissors game
    plans, 101
    playing, 122–123
    random numbers, 114–120
    running. *See* running game